P9-BUH-437

Barnacle Parp's
CHAIN SAW GUIDE

Barnacle Parp's
CHAIN SAW GUIDE

Walter Hall

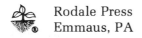 Rodale Press
Emmaus, PA

Library of Congress Cataloging in Publication Data

Hall, Walter.
    Barnacle Parp's chain saw guide.

    Includes index.
    1. Chain saws.   I. Title.
TS850.H294   621.9'3   77-10328
ISBN 0-87857-197-3
ISBN 0-87857-190-6 pbk.

Printed in the United States of America on recycled paper.

2 4 6 8 10 9 7 5 3

Acknowledgements

First, a special thanks to Blake Stretton (Mr. Chain Saw) and Monica McCoy of Stihl Inc., for information, illustrations, material, and patient advice that went far beyond the call of commercial interest. And another thanks to Stihl Inc. for the drawing of the Stihl 041 that appears on the jacket of this book.

The author gratefully acknowledges the illustrations, information, and technical material supplied by the following organizations: Allis Chalmers; Beaird-Poulan Chain Saws; Bell Industries (Nielsen); Clinton Engines; John Deere; The Defiance Company; Didier Manufacturing Company; Dolmar North American; Echo Chain Saws; Granberg Industries; Haddon Tool Company; Homelite Division of Textron; Husqvarna, Inc.; Jonsereds Chain Saws; Lancaster Pump; Massey-Ferguson; McCulloch Corporation; Omark Industries; Oregon Saw Chain; Partner Industries, Inc.; Pioneer Chain Saws; Piqua Engineering, Inc.; Sandvik, Inc.; Skil Corporation; Solo Chain Saws; Taos Equipment Company; V.I.P. Industries; Windsor Machine Company.

The author gratefully acknowledges the special contributions of the following: Air Cooled Engine Service, Iowa City; Jesse Haddon, McHenry, Illinois; Hup Electric Motors, Cedar Rapids, Iowa; Michael Julian, Creede, Colorado; Mitchell Kaufman, Silver Cliff, Colorado; Kirkwood Community College of Iowa; Allan and Cinda Kornblum, West Branch, Iowa; McCabe Equipment Company, Iowa City; Pyramid Services, Iowa City; Greg Redlin, Iowa City; Mary Temple, Denver, Colorado; Freeman "Skeeter" Wilkenson, Silver Cliff, Colorado.

My deepest gratitude to my partner, Nancy Jonas, for managing everything during the writing of this book and for expert preparation of the manuscript. Without this assistance, there would be no book.

Barnacle Parp says
this book is for
Amigo,
Norwegian Wood,
and
Three-Legged Muskrat

Preface

The author wishes to make a few statements before you go any further. The first is that his friends call him "Parp" and he will appreciate your indulgence hereafter.

The second is that this book is an honest endeavor. No one connected in any way with the production of this book has any interest whatsoever in promoting the products of any of the manufacturers or companies mentioned in this book. No one connected with this book has ever requested, received, or been offered any chain saws, gifts, or bribes of any kind. No "test models," no exchanges, trades or deals. What Parp says here, he believes. When he's wrong, he's just plain wrong.

When Parp began this book, there was no general guide to chain saws in existence.

Parp felt the book was needed and so began the research that led to the present volume. And that's the whole story. Now there's just one last necessary statement.

Although a great deal of care, responsible research, and experience have gone into the production of this book, neither the author nor the publisher can assume any responsibility for any accident, injury, or loss that may result from errors or from following the procedures outlined in this book, or from using a chain saw. As the owner's manual for one imported chain saw says,

"Attention! The use of chain saws may be riskful."

Contents

Introduction

WHAT IS A CHAIN SAW?

A chain saw, according to the *American Heritage Dictionary,* is "A power saw with teeth linked in an endless chain." There's nothing like a definition that doesn't tell you what the subject means. In this case, it's because a chain saw, in itself, has no meaning. The only good definition of a machine is a description of its function. The word "function" is defined in the same dictionary as "The natural or proper action for which a person, office, mechanism, or organ is fitted or employed."

So, according to Parp, the only way to define a chain saw is to describe the proper or natural action for which it is fitted. That's what this book is about and we're not going to ignore the implications of the the words "proper" and "natural." Can we describe a "natural" or "proper" action for something as unnatural as a complex piece noisy and foul-smelling machinery? We can try. For now, we can just say that a brief definition of a chain saw is a brief description of what it does. It cuts wood.

WHO NEEDS A CHAIN SAW?

Anyone who cuts wood or uses cut wood.

If you have or are going to have a wood-burning stove or a fireplace, you certainly need a chain saw. It will pay for itself in one week of cutting your own wood, or less. If your wood-burning heater is efficient, you can significantly lower your utility bills and your consumption of the nonrenewable and disappearing energy sources as natural gas, oil, and coal. Several excellent chain saws cost less than two cords of cut wood and practically everyone lives near some source of seasoned logs.

If you have a fireplace, you know that a deep satisfaction comes from sitting by the fire. Another satisfaction, a stranger and older one, comes from simply bringing in that split wood from the porch. Another comes from passing or standing near the woodpile in the backyard. How many of us have stood in a small yard in the middle of the city, at night, staring at a stack of firewood and found ourselves transported far from the buildings and the noise to a place of trees and stars?

The shapes and colors and smells of your own wood supply can fill your mind with a primitive wonder at your ingenuity and your magical ability to keep the wolves away. The experience is deepened immeasurably when you know you went and got the wood and cut it yourself. Anyone can do it, and everyone should. All forms of life crave the wilderness for health, survival, and sanity. There is a wilderness within you that you must preserve.

Whoever you are and wherever you live, you can escape to the peace and strangeness of the wild spirit within you by finding, cutting, chopping, and contemplating your own wood supply, your store against the winter. By doing so you will also help, just a little, to fight the giant fuel conspiracies of governments, conglomerates, and friendly neighborhood utility companies. It really doesn't matter whether you do it with a chain saw or not. A chain saw just makes it easier.

If you build things out of wood, a chain saw will greatly increase the number and kinds of things you can build, the places where you can build them, and the materials you can use. With a chain saw you can easily and quickly learn to make your own lumber. Any kind of lumber. And the lumber you make will likely be more attractive, durable, and natural than anything you'd buy in a lumber yard at a considerable price.

If you are a professional builder or carpenter, you doubtless already use chain saws in your work because they are accurate, portable, dependable, versatile, and loud. If you're a logger, you've always cursed chain saws and always will, but you use them to help supply the wood that provides the rest of us with housing, furniture, toilet paper, and the zillion little senseless frills that our culture thrives upon.

Farming a small or medium-sized farm, or an independent farm of any size, is hard enough without spending Sunday mornings clearing brush, pruning trees, and building fences by hand. A good chain saw speeds these operations, and hundreds of other farm chores.

Then there's another group of people, many of whom are completely unfamiliar with chain saws, who need them as much as anyone. They are the new homesteaders, the back-to-the-landers, the folks who are heading for the woods, the mountains, or the country.

Out there where you're going you'll need firewood every day, and you'll need buildings, fences, tree houses, and all the other things a chain saw can provide. It doesn't matter if you've never seen a chain saw and it doesn't matter whether you've been in the woods for five years or are just getting ready to go. You need a chain saw, and you can take Parp's word for it. It doesn't even matter at all if you're no good with machines and you're scared to death of anything that makes noise, cuts stuff, and might blow up. It won't be long now before your saw is your saw and you have your own way with it. It won't be long before you're the expert who can fell dead trees safely, cut your own firewood, make your own lumber, and keep your own chain saw correctly sharpened and running perfectly.

Finally, if you're a woman who went back to the land with someone who finds it difficult to lace his shoes in the morning, you certainly need a chain saw. After you use it to cut the first decent wood supply since you arrived, you can use it to wake him up and chase him out. And that's the only violence in this book.

HOW DOES A CHAIN SAW AFFECT THE ENVIRONMENT?

Now that's a tough question. Nobody really knows because the answer is all bound up with contemporary forestry methods, the zillion frills, the corporations, and the governments, not to mention thoughtless individuals.

Here's an interesting fact: the total timber harvest for 1900, before the chain saw, was 12.1 billion cubic feet; the total timber harvest for 1973 was 12.3 billion cubic feet, with extensive use of tractors, cranes, and chain saws. Almost the same.

The amount of waste involved is impossible for an outsider to determine because the government and the lumber companies always lump fuel and waste figures together. Apparently they feel that if we use wood to heat a cabin, that's a waste of wood, but if they use living trees to make cigarette cartons, or toothpaste, or plastic, that's efficient.

Weyerhaeuser Lumber Company says that in 1950, 21 percent of each acre of harvested timber went into lumber. Seventy-nine percent, they say, was "fuel and waste." In 1973, 28 percent went for lumber, 10 percent for plywood, 9 percent for particleboard, 32 percent for linerboard (the official name for toilet paper) and 21 percent for fuel for the company's own boiler plants. Apparently there was no waste.

A chain saw is dangerous to the environment if it is used in any way that is not fitting, proper, or natural. If you yourself do not use your chain saw to cut living trees for firewood or for fun, you'll have little effect on the environment. There are millions of unused cords of dead firewood left in the forests every year and that's not likely to change suddenly.

As for the emissions from a chain saw, they are relatively slight. A chain saw sounds and smells awful, but it really puts out far less poison than an automobile and is far more efficient in fuel consumption. If you use fuel in any other way, you use more fuel per work minute than you use with a chain saw.

The Central Institute for Industrial Medicine at Hamburg, West Germany, and the Dolmar chain saw people recently cooperated in extensive tests of the effect of chain saw emissions on operators. These tests were really scientific, elaborate, and tough, Parp says, and too complex to detail here. The results suggested that using a chain saw is considerably less harmful than being around a cigarette smoker.

WHO INVENTED THE CHAIN SAW?

Andreas Stihl, in 1926 or 1927, depending how you look at it. Stihl invented the first two machines that resembled the modern chain saw, and he was the first person to envision the ultimate development of the chain saw. The whole story is considerably more complex and funny, in a way, because it obscures itself. That healthy force known as young capitalism made the refinement of the chain saw possible through incentive, individualism, and competition. That same force, in its uglier and more decadent form as corporate consciousness, also deprived us of the true history of the chain saw's development by obscuring it with dozens of conflicting claims. War, pride, and prejudice added their confusions, too.

The real beginning of the chain saw is tied to the beginning of woodcutting and that, of course, is not within the scope of history. Even the specific idea of using chains moved by machines to tear down trees goes back to at least 1770. From the time of the first fire to the present, people all over the world have tried to find easier, faster, and safer ways of obtaining wood from the forest. All of that is a major part of the history of the chain saw. How, then, can we separate this single invention from all the rest of those efforts? Let's follow the trail of some of the most recent events, pieced together by Parp, and see who really invented the chain saw, and how.

In 1896, the Allis Chalmers Manufacturing Company first used electricity to help power a sawmill. In 1904, Jacob Smith of Des Moines, Iowa, invented a crank-operated, semiportable woodcutting machine. A year later, the Ashland Iron Works in Oregon developed a similar saw that was powered by compressed air. All this was part of the beginning, worldwide effort to mechanize the forest products industry. In Canada, Sweden, Germany, and other countries, inventors and engineers at the turn of the century were making the first Industrial Age attempts to speed lumber production. Most of the inventions and developments were unsuccessful in themselves, and never went into production. Most, in fact, were completely unknown to all but the people who worked with them. None of these inventions was portable, none was intended for use in the forest itself, and not one was a chain saw.

In 1910, R. L. Muir of California invented a saw that cut wood with a moving chain—or sort of a chain. The cutting attachment was a chain of cutting edges that traveled around a steel bar. That part bore a notable resemblance to the modern chain saw, but it was driven by a huge machine mounted on a giant cart. A crane was used to lift and lower the cutting bar. Although intended for mill yard use, this machine pointed the way, or would have if the right people had been looking. Muir's invention, like most of the others, was unsuccessful in industrial terms because it never went into production.

About the same time, a great American named Charles Wolf was gaining national recognition as an inventor and engineer. He was one of the inventors and developers of the submarine. He also built electric tramways and railroads and things of that sort. He installed the first fully electric sawmill for the Blackwell Lumber Company in Coeur d'Alene, Idaho. As a result, he encountered a smaller electric saw built by the Potlatch Lumber Company for their own use. It gave him ideas. Wolf developed a refined model that became the first crew-operated, chain-equipped, woodcutting machine produced and sold in quantity. It was still electric and it was intended primarily for mill use, and not for carting about in the woods.

Somewhat later, a brilliant and meticulous Swedish engineer named von Westfelt became the first person to operate a chain-equipped woodcutting machine in the woods. The chain rode on a giant U-shaped bow guide and was driven by a flexible shaft that was rotated by a separate gasoline engine. Many other engineers experimented with flexible shaft machinery through the years, including the American, Arthur Mall. This was not the answer to bringing the saw and the engine together.

Von Westfelt's chain was a beautiful handmade masterpiece. Each link was shaped by hand and was connected by springs formed through old-world metalsmithing. Von Westfelt worked very hard on his futuristic machine and continually improved it through the years. It was produced in limited quantity and sold in Sweden, Germany, Russia, and other countries. Today, the Swedish chain saws made by Husqvarna, Jonsereds, and Partner are among the world's finest machines.

In 1921, back in the United States, another brilliant inventor named Charles H. Ferguson was designing a new, lightweight, gasoline engine generator. This had no immediate effect on the development of the chain saw, but Ferguson is certainly a major part of chain saw history. Electricity was not yet available in most rural areas. Ferguson's invention was designed to supply the power to light homes in these areas. That's why he called it the "Homelite." Homelite didn't produce any chain saws until 1949, but they sure have from then on.

Andreas Stihl was a young inventor, repairman, and putterer in Stuttgart, Germany, in the 1920s. Those were pleasant years in the old towns near the Black Forest, and most folks lived at a slower pace than the frantic Americans across the ocean. Andreas Stihl earned his modest living in this atmosphere by repairing all sorts of things, as well as by building some innovative but rather mundane machinery for the folks thereabouts.

Andreas Stihl loved nature and he loved the forest so, quite naturally, he frequently loafed in the woods. Why not? His business was not a pressing burden. He loved to rest on the warm grass and listen to the many varieties of birds singing in the trees. None of the birds or small animals seemed frightened of Stihl. He would lie there motionless with his eyes closed as dozens of forest residents scampered and chirped and chattered.

One day Stihl was loafing in the woods and watching a logging crew working near the skid road down the hill. The workers were using hand-powered saws to fell giant trees. Stihl thought about how awful it would be to have to work like that. His heart went out to the loggers.

Time went on and almost every day Stihl loafed in the forest, watching the loggers work. After a while, he began to notice some changes in the way they worked. They were starting to get machines. Unfortunately, the machines didn't work very well and didn't seem to help the poor loggers very much. Their labors still looked unbearably difficult to the young Stihl. He contemplated this every day, under the trees. The subject began to occupy his mind as he strolled back to his little shop, and even while he listened to classical music on his radio, and fixed small appliances for his neighbors.

Although Stihl's mind was in the woods, he was not idle. In 1923, he invented the world's first gasoline-powered washing machine. Parp says he wanted to use gasoline because the tank would run dry and stop the machine automatically. That way, he could put in a load of clothes and a little gasoline, and forget about it as he headed for the woods.

All this time, don't forget, Charles H. Ferguson is in the woods, too, but he's going door to door selling Homelite generators to all the progressive United States country dwellers.

One sunny afternoon in Stuttgart, Stihl was enjoying a beer in his favorite garden when he recognized two of the loggers at the next table. He overheard enough of their conversation to understand that they were in town to buy some materials with which they hoped to repair their newest logging machine. Stihl attempted to introduce himself but the loggers were anxious to return to their work site before their foreman came looking for them.

Back in the woods the next day, Stihl struck up a friendship with some of the loggers. They liked the affable young fellow and enjoyed his amusing questions about cutting trees and using machines. They showed him their brand-new von Westfelt woodcutter, which was not working. Stihl managed to get it running, a little, but he now realized how inefficient and unreliable the thing was. From that day forward, Andreas Stihl never stopped thinking of ways to improve woodcutting methods and make the load a little lighter for his logger friends.

Stihl devoted himself to the study of existing power saws and found that they were not good machines. For one thing, they kept getting bigger and heavier. Stihl realized that manufacturers were going in the wrong direction. He envisioned, right then, the future of the chain saw; he would take the basic idea of a power saw and make it smaller, rather than larger. It seems obvious now, but such is the stuff of genius. Stihl made up his mind, as he always said, to develop a motor-driven chain saw that you could carry and that would work reliably from morning to night: a light, portable chain saw that would be easy to handle.

Stihl had the idea and he worked hard and long. He carefully studied American, Swedish, Czech, and German crew-operated logging machines. He studied how

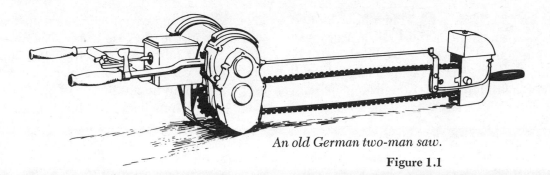

An old German two-man saw.

Figure 1.1

the power saws worked and why they didn't. His research was thorough, but it was that original brainstorm that really did the trick. "Make it little," was his inspiration. He sank all of his savings and all of his strength into his research. Word got around about Stihl's goals, and he soon found himself in hot water with the logging crew foreman and with the forestry officials. Certain of them opposed mechanizing the logging industry for personal, financial reasons. "Oh well," he thought, "every good inventor must face reactionary forces."

Charles H. Ferguson, meanwhile, was selling Homelite generators like hot cakes. Every American wanted to be ready for television.

In 1926, Andreas Stihl finally finished his invention. He had worked on his "Cut-off Chain Saw for Electric Power" for over two years but he still couldn't pick it up by himself. It was a chain saw, though. It looked like a chain saw, ran like a chain saw, cut wood like a chain saw, and sounded like several chain saws. All chain saws since then have been quite a lot like

it. Stihl sold a lot of them, too. It was the first portable chain saw.

The only trouble was, it had an electric motor. When his logger friends finally broke the news that there were no plugs in the Black Forest, Stihl almost felt like giving up. He didn't though. Who knows, maybe he read a magazine story about Ferguson's gasoline engine generator. Maybe he just remembered his washing machine.

In any case, it was 1927 when he finally hooked the gasoline engine and the chain saw together. He had to take them apart again in order to move them, but the job was done. He had invented and produced the world's first gasoline engine chain saw that could be carried into the woods and operated by a gorilla.

Stihl manufactured and sold his new invention for the next two years. Then, in 1929, he developed a new friction-reducing guide bar that greatly improved the machine. That design alone was critical to the development of the modern chain saw.

By 1930, Stihl was advertising his chain

saw as "The Midget." When he exhibited his new machine at the Leipzig European Trade Fair, in 1930, it weighed just 127 pounds and gained far-reaching recognition for Stihl and his young company with its sprouting sales offices in Europe and North America.

A year later, Stihl had it down to 104 pounds and the crowds were cheering. He was now clearly established as the leader of the race he had started, the race for a lightweight, powerful, dependable, portable chain saw. He started selling in Russia and opened a new factory that employed 200 of Germany's finest skilled craftspersons. By now, lots of loggers and forestry officials feared for their jobs. His old friends never turned against him, however.

In 1931, one of his old logger friends arranged for Stihl to meet and speak with the forestry officials and other opponents at a logging camp in the Black Forest. At that meeting, Andreas Stihl described the chain saw of the future with uncanny accuracy. All chain saw developments for years to come were sketched out for his skeptical audience. He described the light, powerful engines of the future and the metal alloys with which he was experimenting; he described the one-person operation that would be possible; he described the modern cutting chain, guide bar, and fuel system. He even specified and described the centrifugal clutch. He explained how the dreamy new tool would make life a pleasure for the beleaguered loggers, how they would be able to loaf and drink just as they do today. When he finished that talk, Stihl had their full support. They carried him back past his newest factory to his quaint little cottage. They even helped him hang out his clothes to dry.

Things were less cheerful back in the United States. The Great Depression had just about halted the lumber industry, as well as everything else. Stihl distributed and sold chain saws in North America all through the thirties, and he had very little effective competition. This was partly because of the depression itself, and partly because most of the crucial aspects of chain saw design were protected by Stihl patents. The desperate U.S. Forest Service began studying Stihl's saws, and in 1936 they established the U.S. Forest Equipment Development Laboratory in Portland, Oregon. Weren't they farsighted?

Demonstrations of Stihl chain saws were held at logging congresses, lumber mills, and forest logging camps everywhere. The depression and the Forest Service worked together and soon the government-employed loggers of the United States were all using Stihl chain saws and liking it. At last, the chain saw was fully accepted in the woods by the people who counted.

By now, Stihl almost never loafed in the woods. Before the end of the thirties, he had invented, developed, and incorporated most of the essential features of the modern chain saw. These included his lightweight alloys, the modern guide bar, an efficient cutting chain, an automatic oiling system for the chain and bar, and a decompression release. All of these features, together with critical aspects of Stihl's exclusive engine design, were protected by German, United States, and international patents. Stihl chain saws weighed 47 pounds by 1936. The competition was baffled and frustrated. The only important thing Stihl hadn't invented yet was direct drive and no one else had thought of it either.

This is where the war comes in. Stihl, of course, could no longer sell his chain saws in the United States. In fact, the market was pretty bad everywhere. As a result, companies like the Mill and Mine Supply Company of Seattle, Washington, began making chain saws instead of selling Stihl's. Because of the war, Stihl's saws were no longer protected by his patents. By the time of Pearl Harbor, at least six U. S. companies were mass-producing gasoline powered chain saws that were direct copies of Stihl models. Stihl paid the price of war and that part of our history is thoroughly understandable, but we should not pretend it never happened. Stihl's factories were completely destroyed, his markets cut off, and his patents released by the United States Government. If it hadn't been for that, the rest of the history of the chain saw would be very different and very much clearer.

Charles H. Ferguson was also affected by the war. He supplied 200,000 Homelite generators and helped power the war toward its end.

Sometime around in here, maybe 1942, a new company named Pioneer produced what it still claims was "the world's first one-person chain saw." It wasn't. Pioneer has done a lot since then, and they make fine chain saws, but they didn't do it first. They, uh, adapted Stihl's designs. Again, that's acceptable under the conditions, but claiming the saw was a first, and continuing to do so, is less understandable. This is just one example of the part pride played. False pride. Stihl's 1936–37 chain saw weighed 47 pounds and that put it definitely in the one-person class. Many other companies have made similar claims for the same period. That's partly because U. S. technology during the war was directed to produce lighter and faster chain saws. Not one company advanced beyond Stihl's 1936–37 models.

In 1947, a man named Joe Cox lived in Portland, Oregon. He became interested in the logging industry much as Stihl had before him. It is not known whether Cox loafed in the woods, but it is known that he watched bugs. He watched bugs while he was trying to develop a new saw chain design. He wanted to make a chain that would cut wood even more efficiently than Stihl's chain, which everyone had copied along with Stihl's saws. Joe tells about watching bugs.

"My first [saw chain] designs weren't working the way I thought they should. Knowing that nature usually figures things out better than man, I spent several months looking for nature's answer to the problem. I found it in the larva of the timber beetle.

"The larva has two cutters, but it alternates them. While one is cutting, the other acts as a depth gauge. Actually, I'd already figured out the alternating part and the depth gauge principle. It was the curvature of the cutters that the larva taught me. That's what made my chain cut better, last longer, file easier, and require less maintenance."

Isn't that interesting? Actually, the alternating cutters and the depth gauge principle were present in Stihl's original chain, but that really doesn't take away from Cox's discovery of the larva's rounded cutters. Joe Cox of Portland, Oregon, invented the first chipper saw chain, a chain that has been the standard ever since.

Joe showed his new chain to his old friend, Jack Jamieson, a professional logger from Lebanon, Oregon. Jack quickly found out that one chain saw equipped with Joe's chain "could do the job of two hand sawyers in a quarter of the time," and he still says so. Within a year, Jack had seven chain saws equipped with Joe's chain and with those seven saws he and his hired persons were doing the work of 16 fallers and 40 buckers.

Jack and Joe both did very well. In his first year of operation, Joe sold $300,000 worth of his new chain right out of his basement shop in Portland. Better than fixing toasters. Today, Joe's outfit is called Oregon Saw Chain and is the world's largest manufacturer of saw chain.

Now it was 1948. The war was over and lots of folks wanted to make chain saws. Why not? It was so easy with all those unpatented designs floating around. Dozens of companies converged on the old competitive battle field. Among the newcomers was the McCulloch Chain Saw Company. They got off to a good start with some really tough machinery. McCulloch still proudly announces the fact that they produced the first 50-pound chain saw in 1948. As we have seen, Stihl's 1936–37 model weighed only 47 pounds, so 50 seems more like a reasonably good try than a ground-breaking achievement. McCulloch's first die-cast magnesium chain saw, also in 1948, was more significant.

Although Stihl jumped fully back into the race in 1948, his position was not the strongest. He was, after all, coming from behind because of the war. Through 1947 and 1948 the United States manufacturers got really serious about chain saw development, and they had Stihl's designs to work from. Stihl's saws for 1948 were nevertheless the most advanced and, in fact, were dramatically close to today's saws in everything but size and weight.

One of the chief figures on the United States chain saw scene was Arthur Mall of the now legendary Mall Tool Company. Mall had been around for a long time and his contribution to machine and tool design is very significant. In the 1930s Mall made flexible shaft machinery. In 1937 he created a flexible shaft machine that drove a chain saw cutting attachment. Mall built chain saws from 1937 until 1956, when he sold his company to Remington Arms. Although still called Remington Chain Saws, that company was swallowed by Desa Industries in 1969 and is now best known for cheap electric chain saws.

The following quote is from a letter Arthur Mall wrote to Andreas Stihl in 1948.

"Through the showing of your original machine in Canada and the United States, you taught the [logging] industry the possibilities of using gasoline engines for cutting down trees as well as bucking them into log lengths. Throughout the United States and Canada, you were the first one to demonstrate a practical, lightweight gasoline-engine [chain] saw for this application. Today, there are at least 100,000 chain saws being used in Canada and in the United States for this work, all of which are more or less copies of your original machine."

Stihl was in no position to complain and he never did.

McCulloch's 1949 chain saw weighed just 25 pounds, half the weight of their 1948 model. Homelite entered the market and was suddenly producing a 30-pound chain saw. Pioneer and other companies also broke the 35-pound barrier, and no Stihl saw had done that yet. The year 1949 also saw the first all-position carburetor and fuel pump from McCulloch. These advances, predicted much earlier by Stihl but never developed, were essential to the modern chain saw.

The competition and the advancements continued all through the fifties. Everyone came up with something good. In 1953, McCulloch introduced a 21-pound, gear-driven chain saw. In 1954, Stihl introduced (and patented) his Mahle Long Life Cylinder, still used today. In 1955, McCulloch put bearings in their pistons. Homelite kept making good, lightweight chain saws. In 1956, Stihl produced the Stihl BLK, a professional 30-pound chain saw. Stihl Inc. now claims that that was "the world's first really lightweight chain saw." Thirty pounds is heavier than 21 pounds, but Stihl Inc. is taking a tip from the United States companies on how to achieve records—claim them.

In 1955, Charles H. Ferguson's Homelite Company was discovered and absorbed by Textron, a giant United States conglomerate that does anything from import chinaware to sell generators to the country folk. They still make great chain saws, but somehow it doesn't seem the same.

In 1959, the Stihl Contra appeared. It weighed 26 pounds, had a seven horse-power output, and was a direct-drive chain saw. The Contra was immediately accepted as the world's standard by loggers everywhere and it put Stihl back on top. The Contra is still used today and is now the Stihl 070, one of the very best heavy-duty production saws.

The appearance of Stihl's efficient direct drive system began to change the chain saw industry. In 1963, four years after the Contra and as a direct result of it, Homelite introduced the historic Homelite XL-12, another great saw that is still produced today. At twelve pounds (more or less), the XL-12 was 40 percent lighter than any other chain saw in existence. Consumer interest and extensive nonprofessional use of chain saws began with it. The pros continued to buy the Contra and other Stihl models, but everyone else grabbed up the XL-12's and a few McCullochs.

Later in the sixties, Stihl finally got into the consumer market. (By now he had completely forgotten how to get to his old loafing place in the woods.) In 1967 he came out with the first chain saw anti-vibration system; in 1968, the first chain saw with an electronic ignition. In 1970 he designed a new cutting chain. By 1971, Stihl Inc. was unquestionably the leader in both the professional and the consumer chain saw market and the comeback was complete. Stihl the man was 75.

In 1973, when Andreas Stihl died, he held over 400 international patents and 200 registered designs, all related to chain saws. He never sold out to a conglomerate and the company is still independent today. Parp hopes it stays that way.

Popular history has a way of cutting corners. If it didn't, we would never be able to name a single inventor. Nearly everyone really believes that Henry Ford invented the automobile. We like to pretend that inventions occur by miracle, a bolt of lightning in a brilliant brain. The truth is that inventions are created only by the need for them. No idea or machine ever appears without the need for it and without hundreds of contributions by people other than the inventor we name.

The history of the chain saw goes back from all of the present manufacturers, through Stihl, von Westfelt, Wolf, Muir, Smith, and all the others to prehistory. Still, we like to name our inventors and when we have trouble doing it, because of war, or pride, or prejudice, we behave badly. We start naming all the wrong people. Usually, Parp couldn't give two hoots, but in this case there's a responsibility. Parp does care about credit where it's due. Everyone connected with chain saws has always known who "invented" the chain saw and we should have named him long ago instead of ducking the issue and confusing it with false claims.

Andreas Stihl invented the chain saw in Stuttgart, Germany, in 1926. Parp has told as much of the story as he could get, but there was considerable resistance to its being told at all. All the facts presented here are accurate. If Parp added a bird singing here and a man loafing there, it's only because every good inventor deserves a little myth. It doesn't change the facts, at all.

WAS THE CHAIN SAW WORTH INVENTING?

Since the introduction of the Homelite XL-12 in 1963, the chain saw has become one of the most popular power tools. Partly, that's because of the lure of the woods. Mostly, it's because a chain saw is a practical and versatile tool.

Every year there are more attachments available to fit more saws: hedge trimmers, blowers, post hole diggers, drills, winches, cut-off saws, and so on. Every year there are more and more jobs that are easier with a chain saw.

In his 1948 letter to Andreas Stihl, Arthur Mall noted that there were over 100,000 chain saws in North America. Three hundred thousand chain saws were sold in 1963 alone and 800,000 in 1972. By 1975, manufacturers were selling over 2,000,000 chain saws each year and sales were increasing.

In 1963, the buying market for chain saws began shifting from professional users to home or "casual" users. Today, most marketed chain saws weigh less than 12 pounds and sell for less than $200. The manufacturers sell about 20,000 mini-saws each month and 20 percent of all chain saws sold since 1973 were purchased by women.

The retail sales for professional logging saws has increased greatly, also. Thirty-two thousand were sold in all of 1975. Not counting sales to corporations or governments, 105,000 professional saws were purchased in just the first half of 1976.

Such is progress, and so much for it.

WHO NEEDS A CHAIN SAW GUIDE?

Anyone who has or will ever have a chain saw. If you know little or nothing about chain saws, but need one or want one, this book will introduce them to you. It will then help you to select one, get it started, keep it running, and use it well.

If you've used chain saws quite a lot, it's likely you'll find some new and useful information in this book. Especially if you keep losing your owner's manual, or if you want to learn to do some repair work for yourself, or if you want to know about different kinds of cutting chains and attachments, or if you want to start using your saw to earn some extra income.

If you're a logger who can tear apart a production saw in the middle of a rainy night, make the parts you need from a beer can and the gaskets from a cracker box, and be ready to cut wood before dawn, you should have something to sit on. This book will do as well as anything.

The Basic Chain Saw •1

A chain saw is one of those machines that you could see a dozen times and never recognize. I have a foggy memory of seeing my first chain saw. I grew up visiting Goodwill stores and that's where it was. I remember moving a box away from a table in the back room of the store. Behind the box was an ugly machine covered with dust and oil. It had a mean-looking arm with a dangerous chain of claws circling it. I shuddered and went to look at old radios. I know now it was a chain saw.

If you look around a little, especially if you're shopping for a used chain saw, you might run into that monster from my foggy memory. If you do, let it rest in peace. It did its share and carries a curse or two.

THE BASIC COMPONENTS

The modern chain saw is a lightweight, well-designed, precision machine that can cut firewood or build cabins and can be used to power a growing number of very useful attachments. The modern chain saw is one of the most efficient products of industrial society. No other machine can match a good chain saw's power-to-weight proportion.

The chain saw has two major and obvious components. The cutting attachment is similar on all chain saws and Parp will have lots to say about it in a minute, and throughout this book. For now, let's look at the other component, the power unit.

This old-fashioned saw is a clumsy outmoded hunk of machinery in contrast to the light, simple, streamlined saws in use today.

Figure 1.2

1

The power unit of a chain saw is the part that has the handles. Most chain saws are powered by an electric motor or by a gasoline engine.

There's little to say, by way of introduction, about the power unit of an electric chain saw. You connect it to the cutting attachment, plug it in, and turn it on. You do need a place to plug it in, so you could use it in the basement but be careful, you need a dry place to stand.

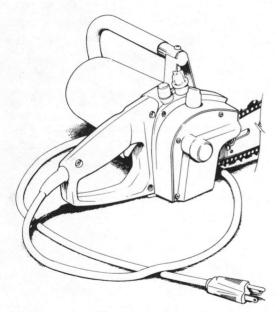

A lightweight electric chain saw for trimming backyard trees and cutting firewood near a convenient power source.

Figure 1.3

The other kind of power unit is a gasoline engine. This power unit doesn't plug in and it won't kill you if your pole house isn't finished when the monsoons come. But it's louder, and it smells some, and you have to learn how to feed and care for it or it'll snore its last sooner than a pheasant in a logging camp.

THE ENGINE: AN INTRODUCTION

In this first and basic chapter, we will limit our discussion to those aspects of the engine that will be of practical help to you in selecting and buying a new chain saw.

Most chain saws are powered by lightweight, portable, self-contained internal combustion gasoline engines.

In order to be efficient tools for their specialized jobs, chain saws must be capable of operating in various positions. In fact, chain saw users occasionally operate their machines upside-down, and anyone who is about to cut down a tree will realize that the chain saw must frequently operate on its side. A chain saw engine must be able to operate in all positions as well as it operates right side up.

If you could pick up the engine in your motor vehicle and carry it about, you would soon discover that it does not operate upside-down, or on its side. It doesn't operate that way because it's impossible for the engine to lubricate itself in any position except right side up.

As an engine operates, its pistons go up and down in their cylinders. In many engines, a flipper extends from the bottom of the mechanism connected to the piston, below the crankshaft. As the piston goes up and down, it causes the flipper to throw oil up onto the moving parts of the engine. Many small engines are lubricated in exactly this way. Your car's engine is somewhat more complicated than this, since it has an oil pressure system, with an oil pump and oil passageways. But the pump has to reach into a pool of oil, so the principle is the same. When the engine is tilted the flipper can't reach the oil. When the engine is upside-down, the situation is even worse.

Obviously, the oil pool kind of engine can't be operated upside-down or on its side. So how are we going to design an engine that we can carry around and run on its side or upside-down? Why don't we mix the oil with the fuel—just enough so that little drops of oil will fly around with the vaporized gasoline, in any position?

Since we're going to mix the oil with the gasoline, we won't need a place to store the oil in the engine. There are lots of other things we won't need—that flipper, for one thing.

That's exactly what the engineers did when they realized the need for a portable engine that could be operated in any position. They combined the lubrication needs with the fuel process itself. An engine that uses fuel mixed with oil is called a two-cycle engine. Unlike an automobile, many two-cycle engines have only one cylinder and only one piston. It's called a two-cycle engine because the piston transmits power on every downward stroke and compresses fuel vapor, including the oil, on every up-

ward stroke. Other engines are called four-cycle engines but there is no particular reason for us to bother with them here. They aren't used on chain saws. For a fuller discussion of two-cycle engines, see Chapter Nine.

COOLING

You will notice that, unlike most automobile engines, there is no radiator on a chain saw. That's because gasoline chain saw engines are air-cooled, for fairly obvious reasons. First, a radiator full of coolant is too heavy to add to a portable engine. Second, a radiator needs to be reasonably stationary in relationship to the engine in order to work properly. Like the oil pool system of lubrication, it won't work on its side or upside-down. So chain saw engines are air-cooled. That means, for one thing, that all that shiny metal surrounding the engine isn't just streamlined decoration; it's essential to the operation of the engine because it deflects air into currents that move around the engine and help cool it.

At this point you may begin to appreciate how efficient and precise a chain saw engine is. There's no fat because there can't be. Loggers wouldn't tolerate it. Every bit of weight on a chain saw has to do at least one essential job, often more than one.

DISPLACEMENT

We've already mentioned, several times, a piston in a cylinder. Throughout your experience with chain saws and other engines, you will encounter the term displacement. One of the reasons that this term is used in relation to chain saws is that displacement is a more accurate and informative measurement of a small engine's size and capability than is horsepower, the term often used in connection with automobiles.

Displacement is like any other semi-technical term—you have to become accustomed to it. But you grew up to understand the difference between 3 feet and 50 feet, and you will also understand the difference between a displacement of 2.0 cubic inches and a displacement of 3.0 cubic inches.

As the piston travels upward in the cylinder, it compresses the vaporized fuel-oil-air mixture that is trapped about it. At exactly the right time, the spark plug fires, causing the trapped and compressed fuel vapor to burn rapidly. The burning fuel produces gases that rapidly expand to force the piston back down, subsequently turning the crankshaft that transmits the power.

The power of the engine is largely determined by the amount of fuel-oil-air vapor that is trapped and compressed in the cylinder. The amount of vapor that *can* be compressed is determined by a combination of the distance traveled by the piston and the size of the cylinder itself. The figure resulting from the correct combination of these factors is known as displacement. This refers, simply, to the volume of space that is displaced by the piston during its upward stroke.

Stroke is the distance traveled by the piston from its lowest position, called bottom-dead-center, to its upper-most position, called top-dead-center. Bore is the term that refers to the diameter of the inside of the cylinder. Displacement is often incorrectly defined as the product of bore times stroke. It is sufficient to our purposes to understand that displacement refers to the total volume of vaporized fuel that is compressed by the piston on its upward stroke.

That's all there is to it. If you're curious or inclined, the formula for determining displacement is available, but it really isn't necessary to a working understanding of displacement. The important thing is to have an idea what the displacement figure represents, and allow your understanding of the term to grow naturally. You'll probably never have occasion to determine displacement mathematically, but stated displacement will come to mean more and more to you in terms of an engine's practical ability. Your response to particular statements of displacement will become increasingly intuitive as you go on.

The displacement of chain saw engines ranges from about 1.6 cubic inches to about 8.36 cubic inches. As you may suspect, either end of that range is quite extreme. A 1.6-cubic-inch engine is very small and has definite limitations when it comes to cutting up logs that are big enough to bother chopping. An 8.36-cubic-inch engine comes only on a chain saw that most of us would rather not carry around. The practical range is from about 2.0 cubic inches to about 4.0 cubic inches.

BAR AND CHAIN

We're back to that mean-looking arm with its chain of claws.

The guide bar, around which the chain travels, is made of a hardened and very strong steel, often with an even harder steel around the tip. The bar is grooved all along its edge, with rails standing up to form the sides of the groove. Chain saw guide bars come in various sizes, from a useless 8 inches to a very demanding 5 feet. The practical range of guide bars for most users is from 12 inches to about 20 inches.

The links of a cutting chain or saw chain are arranged in a specific pattern and in an endless loop. Each chain contains several different kinds of links. Certain pieces of the chain have tangs that fit into the groove in the guide bar. These pieces are called drive links. They receive the turning force from the engine and are the parts that move the chain around the bar. They also keep the chain from falling off the bar, and they help keep the guide bar groove clean so that dirt and sawdust don't completely clog it.

It's easy to see which of the chain parts cuts the wood as the chain speeds around the guide bar. It's the part that looks most like a claw and has a sharpened front edge. All the other parts are equally important and, indeed, the cutters couldn't cut if the other parts weren't there to do their specialized jobs.

The depth gauge is a part of the same link as the cutter and sticks up right in front of the sharpened edge. Coming right before the cutting edge, the depth gauge helps keep the cutter from digging too far into the wood and jamming. The depth gauge feeds the wood to the cutter, leads the cutter into the wood, and determines how deeply the cutter will cut.

The tie strap or side strap has several important jobs. First of all, it's the link that holds the rest of the chain together and keeps the cutters properly spaced. It holds the chain together with rivets between itself and other parts of the chain. It also acts as a bearing that helps the chain be flexible enough to bend around the guide bar. Finally, it acts as a shoulder that rides on the rails of the guide bar to keep the tangs of the drive links from hitting the bottom of the guide bar groove.

Now we need to know how cutting chains are measured.

PITCH AND GAUGE

There are two measurements to consider when determining the size of a cutting chain. One is pitch. Again, as you read this book and as you work with chain saws, you will consistently run across the word "pitch." In order to make an intelligent choice of a chain saw for yourself, and in order to repair or replace its chain, you will need to understand pitch.

Pitch is a measurement of a length of the chain from one point to another. Amusingly, the experts disagree about exactly where these points are. A measurement commonly is taken between the centers of the rivets of one of the drive links; scientifically, and more exactly, pitch is one-half the distance between the center of the second rivet in one drive link and the center of the second rivet in the next drive link.

As we will see later, the most common saw chain size is ⅜-inch pitch, although many popular mini-saws (or small chain saws for occasional users) utilize chain that is ¼-inch pitch. Again, pitch will become a familiar term and will come to mean more as you go along.

Chain gauge is another measurement that you will need to know when you replace or repair the chain on your saw. The gauge of a chain is predetermined by the kind of chain saw you use and so you will always find the gauge of your chain listed in the owner's manual. If that fails, any saw chain dealer, including a mail order company, can usually tell you what gauge chain or chain parts you need if you can tell him what kind of saw you have.

Gauge is a measurement of the thickness of a drive link tang, where it rides inside the grooves of the bar. Of the two terms, pitch and gauge, pitch is the one that will be important when you determine your needs and go out to buy a chain saw.

CONNECTING THE ENGINE TO THE BAR AND CHAIN

On almost all modern chain saws, a sprocket is connected directly, or almost

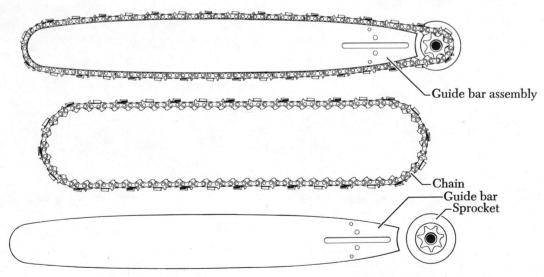

Assembled and disassembled guide bar, chain, and sprocket

Figure 1.4

directly, to the crankshaft. As the piston goes up and down, it turns the crankshaft. As the crankshaft turns, the sprocket turns, too. As the sprocket turns, it engages the drive links in the cutting chain and moves the chain forward around the bar, which is bolted to the body of the chain saw.

Some chain saws have a gear or set of gears between the crankshaft and the sprocket. This system allows the chain to turn slower than the crankshaft. Many early chain saws were gear driven. Most contemporary gear-driven chain saws are very large felling saws used by professional loggers.

OIL FOR THE BAR AND CHAIN

We've already noted that a two-cycle engine is lubricated by mixing the oil with the fuel and that this kind of engine doesn't require an oil storage tank or oil filler cap. A chain saw does have an oil tank and an oil filler cap, but the oil isn't for the engine.

As the cutting chain speeds around the bar, at 50 feet per second or so, it must endure several sources of extreme resistance with resulting friction, heat, and wear. The chain is in constant contact with the bar, of course, and then there are the moving parts of the chain wearing against each other and against the work itself. If the chain and bar weren't very well lubricated, they would burn up very quickly. Hence, all chain saws employ some method of lubricating the bar and chain.

Parp tells some scary stories of loggers with giant old saws, plunging the bar with its moving chain into a steel bucket full of dirty oil. Nobody should have to do that these days.

On many modern chain saws, bar and chain lubrication is automatic. As you depress the throttle trigger and increase the engine speed, a pump system shoots increasing amounts of oil out through a small opening in the side of the saw's body, next to the tail of the bar. The oil lands on the chain and in the groove of the bar that the chain's drive link tangs pass through. When you slow the saw down, the amount of pumped oil decreases.

A manual chain-oil system is similar, but you must depress a plunger or lever in order to operate the pump that delivers the oil to the chain and bar. When you use a chain saw with a manual oiler, you have to learn how to control the oiler so as to deliver the proper amount of oil for the work you are doing. In any kind of cutting you must pump the oiler often. When cutting dense, hard, frozen, or wet wood, you must pump more often. That is why more and more chain saws mass-produced for the consumer market have automatic oiling systems.

Some chain saws employ both systems. That is, a saw may have an automatic oiling system which is supplemented by a manual control. Many professionals prefer this combination. The current trend is toward adjustable automatic oilers with manual override controls.

FUEL MIXTURE

In order for a chain saw engine to operate properly, it must be supplied with fresh, regular-grade leaded gasoline which is premixed in the proper proportions with clean, new two-cycle engine oil. The fuel can't be high-octane or unleaded gasoline and the oil must be made especially for two-cycle engines. It can't be automobile engine oil; automobile engine oil is often as much as 50 percent additives, which may be good for automobile engines but are fatal to chain saw engines. We've already discovered that chain saw engines are air-cooled. As such, they operate at much higher temperatures than do automobile engines. Also, in a two-cycle engine, the fuel is mixed with the oil and so the oil is exposed to the high temperature of the inside of the combustion chamber. At these high temperatures, the "viscosity improvers" in automobile engine oil (or in additives such as STP) undergo a chemical change known as polymerization. They turn into something a lot like glue. A factory warranty is void if multi-viscosity lubricants or automobile additives are used. The evidence is always obvious and conclusive.

High-octane fuels are blended to burn more completely than regular-grade fuels. In order to accomplish this, an unburned portion of the fuel in the compression chamber reaches a point of self-ignition. This causes a second expansion in the compression chamber that has the force of an explosion. Since the two ignitions do not occur at the same time, the second has a hammering effect on the piston. This, together with the much higher temperature caused by the double ignition, quickly causes engine damage.

Always use the fuel and oil recommended by your manufacturer in your owner's manual and mix them according to the instructions.

WHO SELLS CHAIN SAWS?

Chain saws are available almost everyplace these days, including discount department stores, drug stores, gas stations, and automobile showrooms.

But Parp recommends two sources in particular, for good reasons. Your local hardware store is probably run by experienced, friendly people who back up what they sell and who know how to contact the people who make, and can repair, the chain saws they carry. It's good insurance.

Another good bet is the parts distributor or authorized factory service station for the chain saw you're most interested in. This will often be the local franchised dealer for that particular saw. If you're lucky enough to have one of these franchised dealers in your locality, give him your business on new saws and try him first for used ones. He will take good care of you in order to protect that valuable franchise.

Very often a farm machinery dealer will also be a franchised dealer for one or more brands of chain saws. If you're also in the market for a tractor or a tiller, ask your salesman for a package price. It's worth a try. Also, if you're about to buy a truck, look around the showroom for a chain saw display. You might get a good deal.

In this chapter we've seen and discussed the basic chain saw. Wilderness and farm life in many areas of the world now includes a chain saw, often even for people who don't have a motor vehicle or tractor. A chain saw is not quite a basic tool, and never will be unless we somehow develop a new fuel or power system less dangerous, cumbersome, foul, and expensive than using cans of gasoline or generating plants. But the chain saw is such a useful addition to a basic tool collection that it might be considered a basic convenience, like a stove to cook with in addition to your fireplace.

During pleasant and remote years without electricity, Parp has used his chain saw to supply both basics: fire and ice. Wood for the stoves, of course, and ice for the icebox, cut into manageable blocks from a nearby lake. And the chain saw made the boards that made the skids that got the ice home. It could have been done with basic tools, axes and hand saws, as it has been before, by Parp and by millions of others. But the chain saw saved a lot of time and time was what Parp was there to save, for himself.

BASIC CHAIN SAW SAFETY RULES

1. Wear protective gear, gloves, and snug-fitting clothing.
2. Keep chain sharp, sprocket new, bar in good condition.
3. Keep chain properly adjusted.
4. Keep chain thoroughly drenched with oil.
5. Keep exterior of saw clean.
6. Keep all screws, bolts, and nuts tightened.
7. Use correct fuel-oil mix.
8. No smoking.
9. Start saw at least ten feet from fueling area.
10. Clean air filter frequently.
11. Start saw on the ground, braced safely with one foot.
12. Don't walk with a running saw.
13. Hold saw firmly with both hands. Keep thumbs curled around handles. Keep left arm as straight as possible.
14. Keep spectators well back out of your way and well out of danger.
15. Prevent tip of bar from touching anything.
16. Move only with saw turned off and guide bar pointing behind you, unless you are walking down a steep incline, in which case the guide bar should point forward.

17. Don't race engine "in the air" or when not cutting.

18. Don't allow chain near metal, stone, or ground.

19. Use advised cutting techniques.

20. Keep body to one side (left) of plane of chain rotation.

21. Don't bore the end of the bar straight into the work. Use advised boring techniques.

22. Don't raise saw above chest height.

23. Stand uphill from work.

24. Keep your eye and your attention on the saw and the work.

25. Wear gloves when handling or sharpening chain.

26. When felling, clear the area, watch for dead branches, plan your escape.

27. Don't operate a chain saw in a tree.

28. Don't get too confident.

29. Foresee the unforeseeable.

30. Never loan your chain saw.

How to Buy a New Chain Saw • 2

Most old-timers experience great anxiety when faced with the prospect of selecting and buying a new chain saw. That's understandable. People who've used chain saws for years believe that they are temperamental, unpredictable beasts and that each saw has its own innate personality which will only reveal itself after the warranty has lapsed. Many old woodsmen have this mystical view of their chain saws because the performance of their saws reflects the treatment they've received. You just can't take the common wisdom of truck mechanics from the 1940s and apply it to the high-performance, lightweight chain saws of the 1970s, either in selecting or in using these machines.

It is true, of course, that not all chain saws are equal. Many manufacturers produce machines that are dependable, with proper care and maintenance, year after year; and, unfortunately, there are companies that produce saws that are simply not well engineered, made of components that will not stand up to hard use. But, for the most part, today's new gasoline chain saws are remarkable examples of the highest standards in manufacturing technology. The problems develop with use and much of this book is concerned with how to avoid the problems.

Right now you need to determine what you need from a chain saw. In order to do that, you need to know about the various types and sizes of chain saws that are available, the jobs they were designed to do, and the various features you may expect to find on certain models.

You should take the time to be careful. You should immediately start gathering information on specific brands and models. The chain saw industry is very young, and brilliant changes come quickly in a young industry. Those of us who've been watching have seen incredible changes in chain saws over recent years and we tend to think of the machines as completely developed. But we may well see many more valuable innovations over the next few years.

You should learn what kinds of saws are available now, and from which companies. Write to the major chain saw manufacturers, as listed at the back of the book, and request product information. Many of the most excellent chain saws are not easily accessible and this is the only satisfactory method of learning about them. While you're waiting for the responses, visit all the chain saw dealers in your area. Examine the saws and become as familiar with them as you can. Ask all the questions you want, both in the dealer's showroom and in the repair shop out back.

You should also consult your local library or bookstore for any recent articles on chain saws in any of the consumer information publications, such as *Consumer Reports*. At this writing, the most recent *Consumer Reports* information on chain saws appeared in the "Buying Guide Issue" for 1972. According to Parp's spies, the next report will appear in 1977 or 1978, about the same time that this book will appear. Parp says that the report in *Moneysworth* wasn't worth the money.

The accessories and extra features of a product are often emphasized both in that product's advertising and in the publications that determine ratings. Remember that the presence of a chain brake system, or a heated handle, or an automatic chain-sharpening system, or a trim design does not necessarily indicate a guttsier engine, or a stronger bar and chain, or serviceability. Some of these features, like automatic sharpening systems and electric starters, are disparaged by woodspersons in general and Parp in particular. Remember also that no safety feature makes chain saw work safe, and no manufacturer would say otherwise.

We'll discuss some of these features in more detail later.

GUIDE BAR SIZE

Gasoline chain saws are commonly avail-able in bar lengths from 10 inches to 36 inches. There are some 8-inch bars available, especially on electric chain saws, but they are obviously not very practical, even for trimming the hedge. And there are professional saws that are available with 60-inch bars. They're very practical for the work they're intended to do, but not otherwise.

The common and most useful lengths for most of us are 12, 14, 16, and 20 inches. Lots of people who cut a great deal of wood, year-round, keep two saws, one lightweight with a 14-inch or 16-inch bar, and one medium-duty or light production with a 20-inch or 25-inch bar. In general, anything longer than 25 inches is too awkward for most users, and therefore unsafe.

Most people find that a 16-inch bar is sufficient for nonprofessional use. In areas where you're likely to cut a lot of large wood, you may want a 20-inch or 25-inch bar. If you're only cutting wood for your fireplace, however, you can do fine in almost any area with a smaller bar. All you have to do is find wood that your saw can cut. There's always plenty of that: dead brush, stands of small aspen or birch, and good-sized logs up to 32 inches in diameter.

Whatever size bar you decide you need, be sure that your saw's engine is more than adequate in power. In other words, look up the specifications for any saw you're considering. Find the bar lengths available for that saw. If you're buying anything larger than a mini-saw, get the bar length you want on a saw that can take a

TYPES OF GASOLINE CHAIN SAWS

	Mini-Saws	Lightweight	Medium-Duty	Production
Dry weight[1]	6-9 lbs.	9-13.5 lbs.	12.5-20 lbs.	18-28+ lbs.
Displacement[2]	2–2.5 cu. in.	2.5-3.7 cu. in.	3.5-4.8 cu. in.	4.5-8.5 cu. in.
Fuel capacity	.7-.85 pints	.85-1.1 pints	1.2-2.0 pints	2.0-2.6+ pints
Bar lengths	8"-14", av. 12"	14"-18", av. 16"	15"-20", av. 18"	16"-60", av. 21"
Chain types & sizes	¼" pitch or ⅜" pitch low profile	⅜" pitch standard	⅜" or .404" pitch standard	.404" or ½" pitch standard
Chain oil capacity	.30-.50 pts.	.55-.65 pts.	.65-1.0 pts.	1.1+ pts.
Chain brake system[3]	uncommon	common	common option	some models
Auto. chain/oil system	common	common	common	some models
Manual chain oil control/override	uncommon	uncommon	common w/auto	common w/auto; manual standard
Bumper spike	inadequate	adequate	good	professional
Vibration control	uncommon	some models	common	common
Heated handles	uncommon	some models	common	common
Hedge trimmer	uncommon	common	some models	no
Brush cutter	no	some models	common	some models
Bow bar	no	no	common	common
Cut-off attachment	no	no	common	some models
Earth auger	no	no	some models	common
Ice/wood drill	no	no	some models	some models
Auto. sharpening	no	too common	some models	no

(1) Power unit only. Most manufacturers list chain saw weight less cutting attachment.

(2) Horsepower is not an accurate or convenient measurement for small engines, especially chain saws. See Chapter One.

(3) Homelite has recently developed and introduced a unique, removable bar tip guard designed to prevent kickback. Available on mini-saws and lightweights.

bar at least one size larger. If you want a 20-inch bar, don't buy a saw that can only take up to a 20-inch bar; get one that can take a 25-inch or a 28-inch bar. This is important for two reasons. First, if your engine's power is more than adequate for the bar and chain you're using, you have an extra margin against strain and wear. And, if you later decide you need more reach, you simply replace with the next size bar and chain. My own idea, for heavy use, is to get as large an engine *as is practical* and combine it with a medium-length cutting attachment. Parp uses a saw that can take a 25-inch bar but equips it with a 16-inch bar. He suggests that this configuration makes a very useful and versatile all-around chain saw. On the other hand, if what you need is a mini-saw, then what you need is a mini-saw.

MINI-SAWS

If you're about to buy your first chain saw and you expect to use it casually and infrequently, mostly around your home, and if you can obtain a supply of small logs or poles, such as birch or aspen, to cut up for your fireplace, you may well choose one of the many mini-saws that are available.

The mini-sized gasoline chain saw has an engine displacement of about 2 cubic inches and is available with a 10-, 12-, or 14-inch bar and chain. It weighs about 6.5 or 7 pounds and has a fuel capacity of about ⅔ pint. In spite of their size, many of these saws are professionally dependable

and are often used, as they were originally designed to be, by tree surgeons who must climb trees with chain saws clipped to their belts and then hold them in one hand to cut small limbs. (Don't try that yourself.) If you're going to buy a mini-saw, it might be a good idea to find a friendly local tree surgeon for advice on a new saw. They all disagree with each other, but the advice could be useful anyway.

Mini-saws have some very real advantages over larger saws and often really are the best choice for light-duty use around the home or in the orchard. Many of the advantages are obvious. They are light, easy to handle, and inexpensive. Surprisingly, they also hold their value very well and often bring more on resale or trade-in, dollar for dollar, than do medium-duty or production saws.

Mini-saws utilize a special type of saw chain, commonly called mini-saw chain or low profile chain. New mini-saws come equipped with a small size chain (¼-inch pitch, or .315-inch or .325-inch on a few European mini-saws) but this chain may be replaced with low profile chain in ⅜-inch pitch. Replacement chains of low profile ⅜-inch pitch are considerably less expensive than ¼-inch pitch replacement chains. This is because ¼-inch-pitch chain requires more pieces—drive links, cutters, and side straps—per foot of chain. The ⅜-inch-pitch low profile chain was developed as a lower cost replacement that can still pass the close quarters of a mini-saw.

Low profile chain or ¼-inch-pitch chain

is not as strong as full size ⅜ or .404-inch-pitch chain, simply because the side straps holding the chain together are lighter and thinner. For the average homeowner or part-time woodsperson who uses a chain saw only occasionally, this chain is adequate, but the user must be extra careful of hazards such as stones or nails. A ¼-inch-pitch chain may cut a thinner slice, but the slice can be just as deep and just as deadly. Be especially watchful of the small stones and other debris that often collect on top of log or brush piles.

Most mini-saws look radically different from larger saws. The handle, trigger mechanism, and other controls of a mini-saw are usually mounted on top of the engine housing. Many smaller models have no bumper spikes for grabbing the wood, or have so-called integral bumper spikes that are very small and are structurally a part of the saw's body, rather than separate parts that may be removed or replaced. That is a disadvantage when cleaning or repairing the saw.

At the upper end of the mini-saw range are the professional models. As indicated earlier, these saws are designed for use by tree surgeons, nursery workers, orchard pruners, landscapers, park and road crews, and other professionals who use chain saws less than constantly and who require mini-saw size and weight. The engines are the same size on these models, and other differences are few. Sometimes the fuel capacity is increased, and the handles on these professional models are often mounted behind the saw, in the conventional manner. They may also be available with a chain brake system, as well as with hand guards and larger bumper spikes. "Pro-minis" may also come with 16-inch bars.

Except for these professional models, all mini-saws are designed for light, casual, and occasional use. All mini-saws do best on light to medium hardwoods (emphasis on light) and softwoods. They don't do very well when you're cutting down trees unless the trees are little.

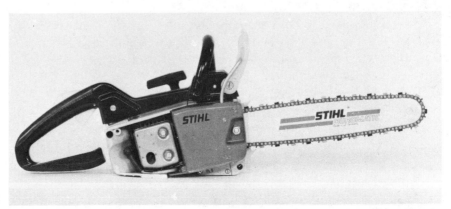

Stihl 020 AVP, a "pro-mini"
Figure 1.5

LIGHTWEIGHT CHAIN SAWS

Chain saws classified as lightweight or light-duty actually have much more in common with medium-duty or production saws than they do with mini-saws. They are not just "big mini-saws"—they are the beginning of the line of traditional chain saws. The lightweight chain saw is actually a smaller and lighter version of the logger's tool that most of us think of when we hear the words "chain saw."

If you'll be using your new chain saw somewhat more than for small, weekend fireplace wood, or if you'll be cutting medium hardwoods or dense, wet, or frozen softwoods, and if you don't need a professional mini-saw for a specific application, you'll do well with a quality lightweight.

Good, professional-quality lightweights are produced by most manufacturers. They usually weigh between 9 and 12½ pounds and have a displacement of 2.5 to 3.0 cubic inches. You usually have a wide choice of bar lengths from about 14 to about 20 inches, though these saws do best when equipped with a 14-inch or 16-inch bar. Lightweights usually hold around one pint of fuel. That means, very roughly, that the average user will refuel only once while cutting a pick-up load of softwood. A saw classified as lightweight will run about one-third again as long as a mini-saw on a tank of fuel. That can be a very significant advantage if you work with your saw for an entire afternoon or longer.

A quality lightweight has all the advantages of a mini-saw, including high resale and trade-in value, with only a slight increase in weight. And the slight increase in weight is countered by the improved balance resulting from the rear-mounted handle. There is a great increase in power and performance. The common mini-saw displacement is 2.0 cubic inches and the common lightweight engine displacement is 3.0 cubic inches.

A lightweight chain saw is quick to start and easy to maneuver. It is large enough, usually, to start in a safe position on the ground with one foot holding down the handle. A ⅜-inch-pitch cutting chain, pretty much the standard of the industry, is supplied on all models.

There are several optional features that may be available on a lightweight saw, including a chain brake system, manual override for the automatic chain lubrication system, and vibration control. Some lightweights will accept a few attachments, such as a hedge trimmer or a brush cutter.

In addition to good, solid home or farm use, these saws may be put to work on the construction site to cut boxing boards, moldings, or fence posts. You can do a great deal with a lightweight gasoline chain saw and it doesn't take a great deal of getting used to. (See chart, page 246)

MEDIUM-DUTY CHAIN SAWS

Chain saws are classified as medium-duty if they are built for medium-duty logging and heavy pulpwood cutting. They usually weigh between 12½ and 16 pounds and have a displacement between 3.0 and 4.9

John Deere chain saws, made by Echo: mini-, lightweight, medium-duty, and production saws.

Figure 1.6

cubic inches.

Medium-duty saws offer the greatest versatility in model choice, attachments, and optional features. In addition to standard bar and chain cutting attachments from 14 inches to 25 inches or more, the owner may add a brush cutter, a hedge trimmer, an earth auger, an ice or wood drill, a bow bar for clearing or pulpwood cutting, or a cut-off attachment, which is a large circular-type saw for cutting stone, asphalt, and tile.

Medium-duty saws are used by such professionals as loggers, firewood suppliers, pulpwood cutters, construction workers, road crews, and rescue crews. They are widely used on large farms and in small private timber operations. Most people who earn part of their living by cutting and selling firewood use medium-duty saws

exclusively. They are entirely satisfactory for any kind of chain saw work up to, and sometimes including, the heaviest professional logging application. And there is no reason at all that a homeowner or occasional user shouldn't have the best medium-duty saw that fits the budget and the muscles, although they sometimes take a little getting used to.

If you anticipate cutting a lot of wood every year, especially hardwood, either for your own use or to sell by the truck load, a good-quality medium-duty saw will pay its way as a good investment and, with proper care and maintenance, such a saw will give years of dependable service. They are better made and easier to service and repair than smaller saws.

Medium-duty saws are, of course, heavier and larger than mini-saws or lightweights. But any healthy person with average coordination can get used to these saws, especially if you've chosen a quality machine with good balance. A 16-inch or 20-inch bar will, in use, balance the heavier engine weight; and if the chain is sharp the work will go much easier than with an inadequate saw. Also, these saws have the very considerable advantage of a much larger fuel capacity. If you're selling firewood, that factor will make the difference between profit and loss.

PRODUCTION CHAIN SAWS

Professional heavy-duty or production chain saws are produced by several United States and Canadian companies and by every major European manufacturer.

They are just what it says: heavy duty. They are not for everybody and they are not the only professional-quality saws you can buy. Most medium-duty saws, lots of lightweights, and several mini-saws are also high-quality machines designed for professional use. Get one of those.

Production saws are simply bigger, heavier, and louder. Of course, if you're going to do contract logging for the Forest Service, or if you're going to operate an outpost in the far North or in the tropics, or if you're going to produce a lot of rough lumber, or if you fell giant trees every day for some reason, then maybe you do need a production saw.

But for almost all of us who use chain saws, even very extensively, a production saw is much more than we need. And since they are heavier and have huge cutting attachments, they are considerably more dangerous than medium-duty saws. Nothing is so awesome as a giant production saw with a 40-inch bar running at high speed with its throttle lock stuck, jumping all over the ground after being dropped. Even if you can easily afford it, be sure you need a production saw before you decide to live with one.

A top-of-the-line production saw, like the Stihl 090, has a displacement of 8.36 cubic inches and its power unit alone weighs 27.8 pounds. The smallest bar available with that saw is 21 inches with a .404-inch-pitch or ½-inch-pitch chain. A smaller bar and chain would probably not be properly balanced. That saw is the standard of the logging industry.

ELECTRIC CHAIN SAWS

Chain saws that are powered by electricity rather than by a lightweight, two-cycle internal combustion gasoline engine are far less expensive to manufacture. They can also be just plain cheap. The cheap ones are pretty obvious and you should avoid them. They have plastic parts that wear and break very quickly and often cannot be repaired.

A quality electric chain saw, and there are many available, will cost a fair amount —roughly 35 percent to 50 percent of the price of a comparable saw with a gasoline engine.

As well as being inexpensive, electric chain saws are light, easy to start, quiet,

Stihl 090. This heavy-duty production saw is the world's most powerful one-person chain saw.

Figure 1.7

and much less messy. They can be used in a closed area without danger from fumes and so suggest good construction possibilities if the saw's strength is adequate to the job.

But the greatest potential for the electric chain saw is seldom mentioned. It's the backyard woodpile. It's strange that this obvious application of the electric chain saw is so often ignored. Parp has greatly enjoyed the peace, convenience, and quiet of working close to the cabin on a still and snowless winter day, cutting huge amounts of kindling and small wood, effortlessly and pleasantly, without disturbing the atmosphere or the surrounding communion of nature. If you're looking for a chain saw to use exclusively around the yard, house, or shop, a quality electric chain saw will be a far better investment than a cheap gasoline mini-saw. And you can make things with it in the basement.

Until recently most electric chain saws could be easily damaged severely if the chain bound or jammed in the cut. Most new models, however, are equipped with a special centrifugal clutch to help prevent both motor damage and dangerous kickback. When the chain encounters extreme resistance, this clutch acts to disengage the motor. Because of the delicacy of electric motors, Parp advises against investing in a used electric chain saw unless you know the owner and know that the saw is almost brand new and a recent model.

In general, electric chain saws are equipped with small bars. That is, almost all consumer-type electric saws are available with 8-, 10-, or 12-inch bars and mini-saw-type ¼-inch-pitch cutting chain. Don't buy an 8-inch model. Unless you have a very specific need for such a saw (such as electric chain saw carving or craft), you'll be better off with a good $10 hand-powered bow saw.

There are professional models, made by several companies, that are available with 16-inch bars. Again Stihl gets the individual attention for an exceptional line of electric saws, the E-10, E-15, and E-30. The Stihl E-30 is a powerful electric chain saw available with a wide range of bar sizes from 17 inches to 48 inches. It weighs 31.3 pounds (and that's without the bar and chain) but the E-30 is great for construction where 220 volts and lots of muscle power are available.

Other quality electric chain saws are produced by Skil, Sears, Solo, and Wen.

THE FINAL CHOICE

From the preceding description of the general types and sizes of chain saws, and from your own research and investigation, you should now have a pretty good idea what kind of chain saw will best suit your needs. Now you can shop in earnest.

Try to find chain saw dealers that have demonstration models or used saws that will give you some idea of the feel of working with particular saws. You might decide to invest a few dollars by renting a saw of the desired model from a rent-all shop. Work with it for an entire afternoon. This is worthwhile for several reasons. If you've never used a chain saw before, you'll get some valuable practice without risking your own brand new saw and chain. You'll also soon decide if the saw you're considering is capable of, or too much for, the work you're likely to be doing. And you might decide that you never want anything to do with a chain saw again.

"Feel" is an important consideration and will often be the determining factor in your final choice. If you can't actually start and use a chain saw, and if you can't rent the model you're considering, spend some time in the dealer's showroom. Pick up the saw and hold it a while. Get the heft of it and try holding and moving it in all directions and from several angles. Simulate cutting stances and imagine working in the woods, with your feet on the natural ground. After you consider reputation and everything else, when it comes down to a decision between two different saws, get the one that feels better.

There are many brand names of chain saws produced both in the United States and in other countries. The United States is not the only country where trees grow, nor the country where the trees are largest or thickest. It is not the only country with an important forest products industry, nor, as a matter of fact, the country where chain saws first appeared.

There are huge forests in Germany, Sweden, Norway, and other European countries, and this is the area the chain saw comes from. There are many outstanding manufacturers whose names are unfamiliar to most Americans. If you just started looking for a saw when you picked up this book, you've probably already heard of Homelite, McCulloch, Pioneer, Poulan, and other United States chain saw manufacturers. You may never have heard of Husqvarna, Jonsereds, Solo, or even Stihl. That doesn't mean that you shouldn't choose one of these saws, or another saw from an unfamiliar manufacturer. If you hang around chain saws a while, or read this book, you'll soon know which names have been around and which are newcomers.

As a matter of fact, Parp believes that for the vast majority of chain saw users, especially occasional users, a lightweight saw or mini-saw from any of the companies mentioned above will be entirely satisfactory and will hold up well with proper care and maintenance.

Parp also believes that the European manufacturers produce the best and toughest professional-quality chain saws in all sizes and all price ranges.

TOOLS AND ACCESSORIES

There are many tools and accessories that you will need in order to do chain saw work and in order to keep your saw in good condition. Several of these items should come with your saw and you should make sure you have them all when you leave the store. You should also purchase all the others, either before or just after you pick up your saw, so you won't be unnecessarily delayed from using your saw. If you get home without the tools to adjust the chain

tension, for example, you could damage your new saw in your enthusiasm.

Parp's Best Advice: DO NOT START your new saw until you have carefully read your owner's manual and Parp's An Ersatz Owner's Manual (Chapter Five) and Using Your Chain Saw (Chapter Eight).

You can put off Parp for a while, if you're in a real hurry to fire up that bright and powerful machine, but don't try to put off a thorough reading of your owner's manual. If you do, you'll offend your saw for sure and you may injure yourself, or the garage, or the neighbor's tree. And, of course, you can easily damage your machine with an incorrect chain adjustment, or an incorrect fuel mix (chain saws differ greatly in this), or by making a hundred other potential errors. All of this will seem very elementary to many readers, but people ruin new saws every day and then expect the dealer to take them back. Of all the tools and accessories, your owner's manual is certainly the most essential.

Here's a list.

TOOLS AND ACCESSORIES

* 1. Owner's manual and warranty information in writing.

*† 2. Spark plug wrench.

*† 3. Wrench to loosen nuts on sprocket cover.

*† 4. Screwdriver *to fit* chain-tensioning screw.

* 5. Other special tools peculiar to your saw or recommended by the manufacturer. Check owner's manual.

* 6. Grease gun and grease if required for roller nose.

? 7. Chain-sharpening device or file holder.

* 8. Round file to fit your chain. Not tapered.

* 9. Depth gauge or jointer.

10. Flat safety edge or triangular file for depth gauge.

? 11. Chain repair kit. (Extra cutters, drive links, rivets, etc.).

12. Chain repair tool.
13. Extra chain.
? 14. Spare air filter.
15. Plastic wedges for felling and bucking.
? 16. Chain guard or chain saw carrying case.
17. Chain and bar lubricant.
18. Two-cycle engine oil.
19. Regular-grade leaded gasoline.
20. Safe gas can with filter nozzle.
21. Fuel funnel with screen filter.
22. Small funnel for bar lubricant.
23. Clean SAE 10-weight oil for chain bath.
24. Kerosene or commercial cleaner for parts and body.
25. Small tub or flat dish or pan for soaking chain.
26. Small cleaning brush or old toothbrush.

27. Safety gear: hard hat, ear and eye protection, good, well-fitting leather gloves, safety shoes for tough work.

---

* You may expect these items to be supplied with your new saw.

† Most manufacturers supply a combination tool designed to perform all these functions. You may want to replace it with separate, higher-quality tools but the combination can come in handy if you tromp off into the woods, away from your tool-box.

? The question mark is used advisedly. You *might* be able to convince the salesman to "throw in" any of these items, especially with an expensive saw, or with a new "last year's" model.

ADDITIONAL NOTES

The need for, details regarding, and proper uses of the above tools, fuels, and accessories are covered in other chapters, but a few essential hints now may save you some time and trouble. (Numbers refer to the above list.)

1. If it doesn't have a warranty, it isn't a new saw.

5. Some manufacturers supply a crankshaft locking screw, or a special wrench for unlocking the clutch shoes or pulling the clutch. Check the owner's manual. There should be a list of included tools at the end of the manual. Check them off since they sometimes get lost in the store or repair shop.

6. Ask your salesman and check your owner's manual. If you've decided on a saw with a roller nose, you probably already know that it needs grease *daily.*

7. Even if you receive a file holder with your saw, Parp advises that you further invest in a clamp-on type sharpener such as the Granberg FILE-N-JOINT. Sears sells a less precise clamp-on sharpener that will do. These sharpeners are hard to find so you may want to order one through your dealer or direct from Granberg or Zip Penn (addresses are in the Appendix). Many old woodspersons will snort at this advice but they will also go on, year after year, getting less than maximum service from their cutting chains and saws. And it takes a lot of practice to be able to hand-sharpen as well as they do. Get started with good habits, habits as modern as your new saw. You'll still have plenty of opportunity to field-sharpen or touch up your chain by hand, and then you can correct the mistakes with your clamp-on sharpener before they get out of hand.

8. & 9. If these items don't come with your saw, check your owner's manual for the manufacturer's recommendations.

12. Parp recommends Granberg BREAK-N-MEND, from Granberg or Zip Penn.

13. Everyone except the most casual user should have an extra chain on hand when cutting. It can save a lot of time.

17. Don't take that old mechanic's advice and use worn-out automobile crankcase oil in your new chain saw. Oil wears out—it loses its slickness—and your bar and chain need maximum lubrication. Old crankcase oil will ruin your saw quickly, no matter what anyone says. Use the special bar and chain oil sold by dealers, or use new motor oil according to the weather.

18. Any good two-cycle engine oil will do, provided it matches the SAE requirements stated in your owner's manual (usually SAE 30). Sold by dealers or hardware stores. NOTE: Outboard motor oil is usually SAE 40. Check your manual.

20. One-gallon can for casual and mini-saw users. Five-gallon can for frequent users, or at the start of a heavy season. NOTE: Gasoline goes stale, especially when mixed with two-cycle engine oil.

27. Listen to ole Parp. He wants you to have lots of fun with your new saw and many pleasant evenings in front of the fireplace instead of bad hours in some sawbones' office getting your fingers or scalp repaired. And if you're going to cut trees, you've got to be able to see them. At least wear a hard hat and eye protection and good, snug-fitting leather gloves.

BE SURE TO GET THE BOOK

The importance of the owner's manual can't be overstated. If you buy a new chain saw, get the book. If the dealer doesn't have the book, don't close the deal until he does. It may take a long time, even though it "only takes two weeks." It may take forever. Most saw manufacturers are good about supplying owner's manuals *if* they have them and *if* you can get the manufacturer's correct, up-to-date address. That is often amazingly difficult. One more thing. If you plan to keep your saw for a long time, take steps *now* to obtain the expensive and hard-to-get shop or technical manual from the manufacturer or distributor.

ANOTHER WORD ABOUT SAFETY

Again, read your owner's manual before you start your saw. And you should read the first part of this book, through Chapter Six, before you actually cut any wood. If you can't wait, get a large log—the bigger the safer—and practice cutting only one-third of the way through with the entire log well supported, preferably by the ground. Don't hit the ground with your saw. Stand uphill from the log. Good luck, have fun, and cut those utility bills.

Accessories and Features • 3

DESIGN

At first glance, most modern gasoline chain saws appear to be very much alike. It is interesting that they all share the same basic design. The modern chain saw demonstrates the modern idea of good design: form follows function. If the term "chain saw" didn't exist to express our need for it, neither would the chain saw.

When that need arose, it arose in context. It was very clear to the pioneers of the early chain saw that loggers needed a portable saw they could carry into the woods and work with all day. A few of the early developers of the chain saw could see that the possibilities were not limited to felling trees. Some inventors, especially

Andreas Stihl, had a very early vision of the ultimate development of the chain saw, and could foresee a portable saw that would be light enough for one person, and able to cut at any angle—in other words, a saw that could be used for bucking and limbing, as well as for felling. That early vision of the function of the chain saw resulted in its present form.

When you consider buying a chain saw, used or new, you can determine some important matters on the basis of appearance. You can often spot a flimsy chain saw just by the way it looks. If the finish is chipped you know that the paint won't prevent corrosion. If there are sharp corners or exposed metal parts, they will catch on clothing and brush and will be a safety

Homelite Super
EZ Automatic

Figure 3.1

hazard. If the power head is large, awkward, or crude, you know that that particular manufacturer has failed to progress from the chain saw designs of 1948. All of these considerations bear directly on the saw's balance and ability to perform. When you're limbing a fallen tree, you don't want a chain saw that's always getting hung up in the work.

Finally, design reflects the manufacturer's concern and progress. After you've spent some time working in the woods, you'll realize that a designer of chain saws must carefully consider the work that the user is going to do. Chain saw design has come a long way since 1948 and it has come that far only because the inventors and designers have understood the work that has to be done by a chain saw. A chain saw's design is the first indication of its quality.

ANTI-VIBRATION SYSTEMS

Maybe you think that tools should be kept as trim and light as possible, free of any gadgetry or extra weight that isn't absolutely necessary. Parp sympathizes with this attitude and likes the clean feel of a precision tool, one that incorporates nothing that isn't directly related to the function of the thing. Good sense tells us that good design is exactly that.

But chain saws are not simple hand tools. They are complex and potentially dangerous machines that have hazards and side effects that are not immediately apparent. TVD, for example. If you're a logger,

you might know that this is what most of your friends call "white fingers." TVD, or traumatic vasospastic disease, is a common and extremely uncomfortable problem for many loggers. It's caused by operating a vibrating tool for long hours. If an operator already has trouble with TVD, any work with a chain saw that does not have an anti-vibration system will aggravate the TVD beyond endurance. Besides being sheer torture, it can put the strongest logger on unemployment. (There are some recent medical theories that indicate that TVD and long periods of operating a vibrating tool may be related to early arthritis.)

The average healthy chain saw owner who uses a saw less than constantly doesn't have to worry about TVD. But you do have to worry about comfort, and the safe efficiency that comfort promotes. For several years, many chain saw manufacturers have incorporated special designs to isolate the vibration of the engine and prevent the vibration from reaching the operator's hands. In general, this is accomplished by cushioning the handles with rubber blocks. There are other, more complex systems but the rubber mounting blocks work as well as anything.

Anti-vibration systems do add some weight to chain saws, and the rubber blocks do need to be cleaned often and replaced occasionally. It's well worth the trouble. Even if you don't have TVD, the vibration of an unequipped saw will wear you out very quickly. Parp says that if you're buying anything larger than a mini-saw, don't buy any chain saw that doesn't have an anti-vibration system.

HEATED HANDLES

Even with good gloves, the cold steel of unheated chain saw handles is very uncomfortable in the winter. The rest of your body may be overheated from exertion but those handles can freeze to your gloves and will dangerously sap the warmth from your hands, clear to the bone.

And that brings up TVD again. If a vibrating tool is held by hands that are cold or wet, TVD is more likely to occur. And if the operator already has TVD, cold hands will aggravate it quickly, even with a machine equipped with an anti-vibration system.

If you use your chain saw less than full-time, you won't need heated handles, but Parp says good, rubber-insulated handles are a must for everyone. If you're going to be cutting a lot of wood all day in the winter, heated handles will be a welcome accessory. They should probably not be a deciding factor in your choice of a chain saw, but if they're an option on the saw you want, and if you live or work in a cold area, get the heated handles.

There are two common heating systems for chain saw handles. The first and oldest is exhaust heating. In this system, exhaust from the saw's engine is channeled through passageways in the handles. This can cause problems. The exhaust leaves carbon deposits in the tubing of the handles and also makes the handles oily and sooty after a while. When the carbon deposits become extreme, the engine's exhaust system is impaired. This heating system is also very difficult to regulate.

The other method is a modern electrical heating system with heat rods or coils permanently installed in the handles. The current is usually supplied by a separate generator that is an intregral part of the ignition. You can usually turn such heating systems on and off.

Heated handles are not available, so far, on most chain saws for the consumer market.

AUTOMATIC OILING

It used to be true that no logger would buy a chain saw with an automatic oiling system. Now, however, few loggers would buy a saw without one. Automatic oiling systems have become much more durable and dependable in recent years. The development of adjustable automatic oiling systems has done a lot to overcome professional prejudice against them. On any saw above the mini-saw class, the automatic oiler should be adjustable for different kinds of cutting under different conditions. If you buy a chain saw with an adjustable automatic oiling system, you should study your owner's manual before changing the preliminary setting. Some of these adjustments are ridiculously delicate and it is possible to damage some automatic oilers with an incorrect adjustment or by forcing the adjustment.

Automatic oiling systems are directly or

indirectly connected to the crankshaft of the engine. Sometimes the connection is a worm gear and sometimes it's an eccentric, a sort of lopsided circular device attached off-center to the crankshaft. As engine speed increases, the worm gear or eccentric automatically operates the oil pump and increases the amount of oil delivered to the chain. On some saws, notably the European makes, these systems are easy to replace or repair. On other saws, they are almost impossible.

Parp still prefers to have that manual override when the going gets rough, but an automatic oiling system sure saves a lot of thumb work. It also saves chain.

ANTI-KICKBACK DEVICES

Parp happens to believe that no industry works so hard to minimize or eliminate hazards as the chain saw industry. Completely on their own, with no governmental or private pressure, chain saw manufacturers began safety research very early in the history of chain saw development. It would have been easier to have said that the chain saw is an inherently dangerous machine

Safe-T-Tip installation
Figure 3.2

and let it go at that.

But long before Detroit ever heard of Ralph Nader, Andreas Stihl was already dreaming of ways to make a safer chain saw, a lightweight machine that would be safe enough for the average backyard woodsperson. And Stihl wasn't the only one. Very significant safety innovations have been achieved by Jonsereds, Homelite, McCulloch, and Husqvarna.

All together, these companies have introduced or improved a very impressive array of mechanical and design features intended to minimize the hazards of cutting wood. Operating a chain saw today, in Parp's opinion, is no more dangerous than operating an ax, and considerably less dangerous than driving one of those Detroit monsters. Most chain saw manufacturers do care, and do try.

Homelite, for example, introduced a beautifully simple device called the Safe-T-Tip. This innovation made everybody else wonder why they didn't think of it first. It is an extremely effective device that really does eliminate kickback when it is properly installed.

Kickback happens when the chain hangs up as it speeds around the upper nose of the bar. The chain catches in the wood and the whole saw then makes an upward arc, back toward the operator.

When you're running a chain saw, engine torque is transferred to the chain. This is the turning energy that cuts the wood. If the chain hits a solid object unintentionally, or if the chain takes too large a cut, it stops for an instant. The engine torque is then transferred to the guide bar and the chain saw, as a rotation around the center of mass. Since this mass includes you, it can make a mess out of your mass. That's what this kickback fuss is all about.

Homelite's Safe-T-Tip is a one-piece steel guard that fastens to the nose of the bar and prevents the chain from hitting anything as it passes the nose. It is an effective device and is especially useful when you're cutting single logs on your woodpile. It can easily be removed when you need to

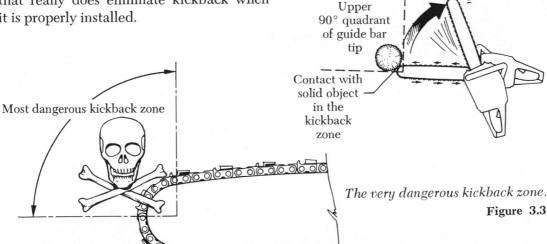

Most dangerous kickback zone

Upper
90° quadrant
of guide bar
tip

Contact with
solid object
in the
kickback
zone

The very dangerous kickback zone.

Figure 3.3

use the full length of the bar, but shut off the engine first. The Safe-T-Tip does not prevent the push or pull that occurs when the chain catches at the center of the bottom or the top of the bar.

The most common anti-kickback devices actually do not prevent kickback. For several years, most manufacturers have offered optional brake systems for most chain saw models. These brake systems prevent kickback from resulting in injury, by stopping either the chain or the engine or both within a split second after kickback occurs.

These brake systems typically comprise a hand guard or lever mounted immediately in front of the front handle. The lever is connected to a device, usually a steel band or a brake block that contacts or surrounds the clutch. When kickback occurs, the operator's left hand bumps the lever. The lever then activates the brake and instantly stops the chain.

Some brake systems stop both the engine and the chain. In that case, the lever must be reset before the engine can be started again. Other systems stop only the chain.

Some engineers say that a system that stops both the engine and the chain is safest. However, a brake system that stops only the chain may be used as a convenience. This system allows the operator to lock the chain and move more or less safely with the saw while the engine is still running. (Once in a while, technology outmodes a basic safety rule, but Parp is still cautious.)

HAND PROTECTION

Chain breakage is not a common experience for the occasional chain saw user,

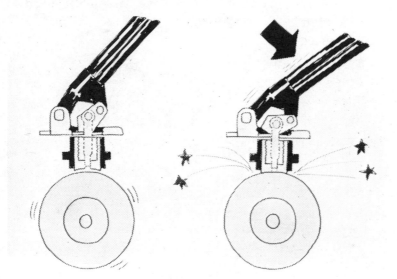

Chain brake in action
Figure 3.4

especially if good chain-sharpening and maintenance procedures are practiced. But when a chain does break, it breaks in use, while speeding around the guide bar. The broken ends then snap viciously toward the operator and can do a great deal of damage to the operator's unprotected body or hands.

Most of today's chain saws include a left or front hand guard as standard equipment. Often, this handle is also the chain brake lever. A broken chain can snap back to reach the operator's left hand at the front handle but a front hand guard will prevent this.

A broken chain is more likely to injure the operator's right hand because the chain is already moving down and back when it breaks. Some saws incorporate a chain-catcher pin that prevents the end of the bottom half of a broken chain from reaching the operator's body. This safety item should certainly be standard equipment on all saws and probably will be soon.

But even with a chain-catcher pin to stop the chain from reaching the body, the end of the chain can still snap across the operator's right hand. Only a right or

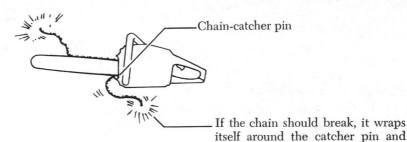

Chain-catcher pin

If the chain should break, it wraps itself around the catcher pin and cannot reach the operator.

Left hand guard; in some models this is also a chain brake lever in case the left hand slips off during kickback.

Right hand guard; in case the chain may still reach the right hand.

Three safety features
Figure 3.5

rear hand guard will absolutely prevent this. And a right hand guard is doubly useful during limbing operations.

Photo of Jonsereds 90 showing front and rear hand guards
Figure 3.6

Parp urges the combination of an anti-kickback device together with a chain-catcher pin and front and rear hand guards for maximum user protection.

TRIGGER INTERLOCK

Another good safety feature that has become common is the trigger interlock system. A trigger interlock is a safety catch that theoretically makes it impossible to unintentionally rev the engine speed above idle, to cutting speed.

Most trigger interlocks consist of a latch or locking lever mounted on the top of the rear handle, above the trigger. When the latch is locked, the trigger cannot be moved. To move the trigger, you have to squeeze the latch at the same time. Theoretically, this makes it possible for the operator to carry an idling chain saw without fear that a branch or something will catch the trigger and accelerate the engine to cutting speed. It also makes it safer to adjust the carburetor while the engine is running.

Parp certainly recommends selecting a saw with a trigger interlock safety system, but he also cautions that it will not always

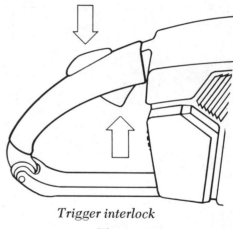

Trigger interlock
Figure 3.7

prevent the chain from moving accidentally. Two-cycle engines are given to erratic behavior, especially when they get old. Your saw may appear to be idling smoothly and perfectly, with the chain absolutely still, when a movement or a change in humidity or a passing cloud suddenly gives the engine a slight rev that makes the chain jump. If the chain happens to be resting against your leg or side, it will cut. And it can cut incredibly deep, incredibly fast, with one short burst of the engine.

Even with a trigger interlock system and a chain brake, Parp says don't walk with a running chain saw.

ELECTRONIC IGNITION

Every year, more and more high-quality chain saws are available with optional electronic ignition. Soon, Parp predicts, all chain saws from major manufacturers will include electronic ignitions as standard equipment.

Until the development of the electronic ignition, all hand-start chain saws incorporated the standard breaker point ignition. This kind of ignition needs frequent service. To service a standard ignition you replace the points and condenser. Whenever the points or the breaker plate are moved or altered, the timing of the spark is also altered and must be readjusted. Furthermore, in order to replace the breaker points and condenser, you must open the assembly that contains them. Not only is this assembly susceptible to dirt and contamination when it's open, it's also susceptible to dirt at all other times simply because it can be opened. And there is always a lot of dirt around a working chain saw.

The electronic or breakerless ignition is a one-piece unit with no moving parts. You never need to do anything inside, so the unit can be permanently sealed against dirt, moisture, and temperature changes. Also, the timing of the spark is electronically controlled, permanently. All of this represents a great improvement in chain saw design, especially for the occasional user who would rather not do any tune-ups.

Electronic ignition should not be confused with electric start. A few years ago, a number of leading chain saw manufacturers experimented with electric starting systems intended to replace the standard, hand-crank rope-pull starters. It didn't work. The electric start system proved to be grossly inconvenient and inefficient. Manufacturing of these systems has been virtually discontinued.

DECOMPRESSION VALVE

A decompression valve, or compression release, is another convenience feature that appears on large displacement chain saws.

This handy accessory allows the operator to open a valve in the engine to release some pressure during cranking. If an engine has a displacement of five cubic inches or so, it can be very hard to pull the starter rope against the pressure that builds up in the combustion chamber. If the saw includes a compression release, you just push a button that stays in until the engine fires. When the saw is running, you pull the button out to allow full compression. Or you pull and then you push. Some compression releases are automatic and release when the engine fires or when the throttle trigger is squeezed.

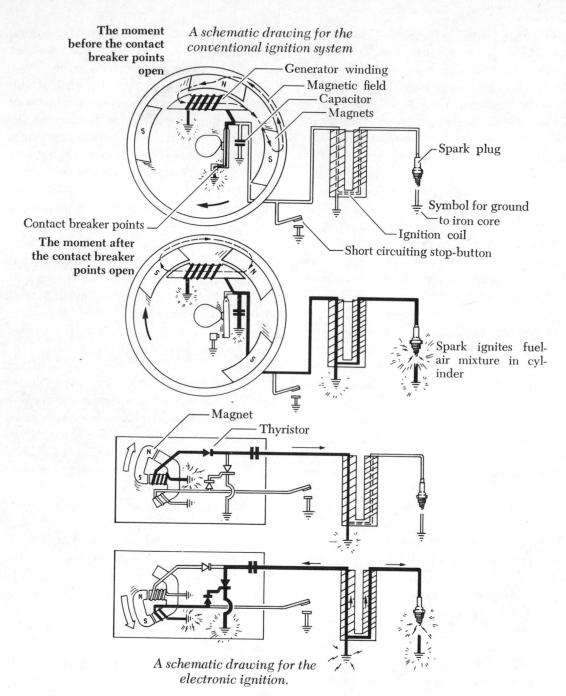

The moment before the contact breaker points open

A schematic drawing for the conventional ignition system

Generator winding
Magnetic field
Capacitor
Magnets

Spark plug

Symbol for ground to iron core

Ignition coil

Short circuiting stop-button

Contact breaker points

The moment after the contact breaker points open

Spark ignites fuel-air mixture in cylinder

Magnet
Thyristor

A schematic drawing for the electronic ignition.

Figure 3.8

REPLACEABLE SPROCKET NOSE

One of the most consistent, troublesome, annoying, and expensive problems for professional loggers is the broken guide bar. Guide bars must be made of a steel that withstands the heat of chain friction and the heat that builds up in the log being cut. But any steel that can stand heat is a hard steel and is therefore susceptible to chipping and breaking.

Almost all guide-bar breaks occur at the nose of the bar. A few years ago, the Windsor Machine Company, a large manufacturer of guide bars, decided to tackle this problem. They developed a guide bar with a replaceable sprocket nose. When a break occurs at the nose of the bar, only that part is replaced, at considerably less expense then an entire bar. The sprocket itself, enclosed in the replaceable nose, also lengthens chain and bar life by accu-

rately guiding the chain around the nose of the bar. This increases the speed and efficiency of the saw, and decreases the heat buildup in the bar and chain. It also decreases the drag on the engine and provides better all-around performance.

Several companies now produce replaceable sprocket nose bars and Parp suggests that they are a good investment if you use a bar longer than 16 inches and if you do a lot of cutting in heavy timber or under rough conditions.

AUTOMATIC SHARPENING

Well, most of the features and accessories mentioned in this chapter are items that Parp would want in a new saw of his own. But automatic sharpening?

Parp has no serious objection to letting machines do his hand work—if they are able. But a built-in automatic sharpening system adds weight right where you don't

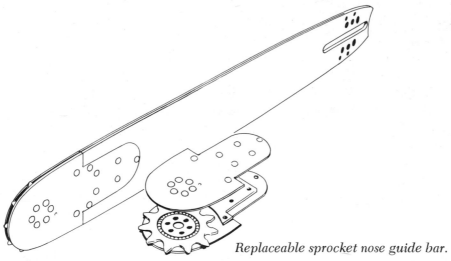

Replaceable sprocket nose guide bar.

Figure 3.9

need it. It also adds another gadget that can go wrong—easily, according to the expert repair people.

Furthermore, an automatic sharpening device doesn't begin to replace hand sharpening. At best, it saves a few seconds of on-the-job touching up. Is that worth even an extra ounce? Even the manufacturers of these things say you shouldn't use them very many times before you sharpen the chain correctly, with a file and special file guide. If the chain is not the correct tension, the system will actually dull the chain.

Parp says don't go for this one. Buy a high-quality saw with no extra weight and carry a good clamp-on file guide so you can control the sharpening for the wood you cut and the age of your chain. You'll come to know your saw better, and to understand why so few professionals would even borrow a saw with an automatic sharpening device. It isn't worth its weight.

CHAIN GUARD, CARRY-CASE, AND TOOL KIT

Any new chain saw should come with a good tool kit that includes a combination wrench for the bar nuts, spark plug, and chain-tensioning screw. Ideally, the tool kit should also include some kind of device for locking the crankshaft when you change the sprocket, and a clutch wrench. If the saw has a sprocket nose or roller nose, the manufacturer should supply a special grease gun designed to meet the daily lubrication requirements. The tool kit should certainly include a file guide and depth gauge, files, chain repair kit, and an extra air filter. And the owner's manual.

Now it helps a lot, says Parp, if you have a saw carry-case with room enough for all this stuff, plus the extra items you can't ask a chain saw manufacturer to supply. Keeping it all together, and portable, is far better than having separate tool boxes or an overflowing glove compartment. A large carry-case is a good investment, especially if you can also use it to carry all your accessories, replacement parts, and field service tools. For long-term storage, nothing beats a case designed especially for your saw.

In addition, a chain guard will make your saw safer to carry or leave around without the case. A chain guard slips over the chain itself and leaves the rest of the saw visible for service, cleaning, or showing off. A combination of a carry-case and chain guard is the best idea, but, so far, only one manufacturer, McCulloch, has produced such a thing as a unit combination. It's easy, however, to buy the two items separately and use them together. Even with a good storage case, you should also have a chain guard. They're very inexpensive. If your dealer doesn't sell them, order one from Zip Penn.

MANUFACTURING STANDARDS

Obviously, the most important of the features and accessories mentioned in this chapter are those that make chain saw work safer. In Sweden, a study of saw-caused injuries among professional loggers showed that saw-related injuries decreased remarkably over the five years (1967 to 1972) that the significant safety features appeared on most chain saws.

But the relative safety of a chain saw doesn't depend entirely on the safety devices it includes. Good balance, in Parp's opinion, is a very significant safety consideration. If a saw is lightweight, well-balanced, and easy to operate, you get a lot less fatigued and frustrated while you're working. A good weight-to-power ratio and good balance are qualities found only in the best chain saws. Again, good design is an important indication of these qualities. Parp suggests that if you look for high standards of manufacturing quality in chain saws, you'll find the saws that are the safest and easiest to handle.

How to Buy a Used Chain Saw • 4

SHOULD ANYONE BUY A USED CHAIN SAW?

If you ask a logger for advice on buying a used chain saw, chances are he'll tell you not to do it. Unless he happens to have one for sale. Nearly all old-time professionals say the same thing: never buy a used chain saw. And, in the world of the professional, that's excellent advice.

When a logger discards a chain saw, it is indeed used. It's been used at least eight hours a day, at least five days a week, for an average of 18 months or more. Trees have fallen on it, it's been dropped in a lake, an apprentice has burned the bar, or it's just been run to death. And, of course, all the "professional" mistakes have seriously contributed to the saw's demise. Used crankcase oil has been reclaimed to lubricate the bar and chain. It's been stored in a semidry state or with its gas tank full of stale fuel. It has been hand-sharpened too often by an over-confident expert. Obviously, the professional advice to avoid used chain saws is good advice, considering the treatment most saws receive from most professionals.

But very few used chain saws are discarded refugees from a logging camp.

Those saws are usually junked or tossed in a spare-parts can, never to be touched again.

Most of the used chain saws that you're likely to run across were traded in on newer models, or on an electric fireplace. Most used chain saws are found in new saw dealer showrooms, sharpened, thoroughly cleaned, possibly even reconditioned and ready for many hours of average use.

Other serviceable saws can be found at farm or estate auctions, garage sales, pawn shops, or through the want ads. Often, these saws were hardly used at all and the original owner didn't have time to do any serious damage. Now, damage can occur very quickly, with very little use, and you will have to learn how to identify saws that have been improperly used, even if it was only for an hour or so. We'll cover the most important symptoms later in this chapter.

As it happens, Parp himself has considerable experience with used chain saws and, as a result, tends to agree with the professional advice against them. But not everyone is in a position to buy a new chain saw, and all the advice in the world won't change that. There are beginning farmers who need to clear brush, and young homesteaders who need firewood, and there are others who, feeling the energy crunch, want to supplement their fuel usage with a little fireplace wood. Many of these people simply can't spend the bundle required to buy a really dependable new chain saw in the size and class they require.

A used chain saw that works can change or even save your life now, but the dim prospect of a savings account large enough for a new chain saw will do nothing to keep you warm meanwhile.

So how do you buy a used chain saw?

DETERMINE YOUR NEEDS

If you didn't read Chapter Two, How to Buy a New Chain Saw, you might do so now. It will give you a good idea of the types and sizes of saws available, and their best uses.

In any case, you've decided to look for a used chain saw and that is a considerably different and more complicated matter than buying a new saw.

At this point, Parp is busting me in the ribs to caution you against used electric chain saws. Since new electric chain saws are so much less expensive than gasoline models, and since electric saws are fatally damaged so easily, let's take Parp's advice and avoid them altogether. We'll confine our discussion to used gasoline engine chain saws.

Do you need a used chain saw in order to fell standing dead trees, and then to cut the trees into logs to load into your pickup, and then to cut them at home to fit your stoves? Are you a homesteader or something like one?

If you heat and cook with wood a great deal, then you will use your saw a great deal. You will at very least use it solidly for a month in the summer and for at least one day a week through the rest of the year. You will certainly need a full-sized saw with an engine displacement right around 3½ or 4 cubic inches, or more. And you will need a saw that has a fuel capacity of more than one pint so that you won't have to refuel twice for each pickup-full of wood. You will also want a bar 16 inches or 20 inches long.

No matter how much or how little you expect to use your chain saw, you must first consider the wood you'll be cutting. The best advice is get the smallest and lightest saw suitable to the work you'll encounter most. But that's not very complete or satisfactory advice. How can you know how small a saw might be acceptable? On the other hand, you won't need or want a bar as large as the diameter of the largest tree around, since hopefully you won't be felling that tree anyway. You want a bar long enough, and an engine strong enough, to conveniently cut most of the logs you'll be handling. Remember that a chain saw will cut a tree or log twice the size of its bar. Also remember that, as you're working on your woodpile cutting long logs into short pieces for chopping, your work will be doubled if your bar isn't long enough to cut most of the logs in a single pass.

You're shopping for a used chain saw, so you're not likely to have as much choice as a new saw shopper would—all the more reason why you should determine your needs within general guidelines before you begin to shop. Otherwise, you could end up with a real bargain on a fine, well-kept saw that's all wrong for the work you need to do. There are some really surprising used saw bargains, and they can be hard to resist if you haven't determined your needs first.

COMPARATIVE VALUES OF USED CHAIN SAW MODELS

The next section of this chapter contains information on particular chain saws, arranged by class or type. If you've determined that you need a saw classified as lightweight, look at the list of models that Parp has classified as lightweight. This list includes the chain saws that you're most likely to run across in the second-hand market. If you encounter a used chain saw from a manufacturer that doesn't appear in this chapter, take a very close look.

Mini-Saws

Saw Model*	Displace-ment, cu in.	Dry weight, lbs.	Standard bar, in.	Current list[1]
Allis-Chalmers 65	1.86	8.2	12	$135.00
Allis-Chalmers 75	2.3	8.75	14	$153.75
Allis-Chalmers 75A	2.3	8.5	14	$161.75
Danarm 36 AV	2.2	7.6	12	$159.95
John Deere 81	2.1	6.5	12	$134.95
John Deere 91	2.1	6.5	14	$142.95
Echo CS 302	1.83	9.3	12	$149.95
Homelite XL	1.6	7.1	10	$114.95
Homelite XL12	1.6	7.1	12	$139.95
Husqvarna 35	2.2	6.75	12	$139.95
Jonsereds 36	2.2	6.75	12	$139.95
McCulloch 25	1.8	7	12	$ 89.95
McCulloch 30	1.8	7	12	$109.95
McCulloch 35	2.0	7	14	$149.95
Partner Mini II	2.2	6	12	$139.95
Poulan 20	1.86	8.1	10	$114.95
Poulan 20 D	1.86	8.1	12	$134.95
Remington Bantam	2.1	6.5	10	$ 99.95
Remington Weekender	2.1	6.5	12	$109.95
Remington Mighty-Mite Auto	2.1	6.5	12	$134.95
Remington Mighty-Mite Delux	2.1	6.5	14	$144.95
Remington Mighty-Mite E	2.1	8.5	14	$149.95
Roper C110 79	1.9	8.3	12	$109.95
Roper C121 47	1.9	8.3	14	$119.95
Sears 35082	1.9		10	$ 97.95
Sears 35094	2.1		14	$157.95
Sears 35096	2.3		16	$217.95

As a shopper for used chain saws, you now have sufficient information to come to an informed decision regarding the approximate value of many different models. And by now you should have a pretty good idea what saws will best suit your particular needs.

You should now make a list of several of these saws and become familiar with the pertinent data regarding each. You may, on your first try, have a chance to buy your first choice at a good price. It's more likely that you'll have to look for quite a while before you find your first choice and, in the meantime, you may well run across a very adequate substitute at a real bargain price. Searching for a used saw is different from choosing a new saw and going to a dealer to pick it up. The usual way that most people buy second-hand things is to take the first buy that's offered in the want ads. That's not the best approach. Make a list of several acceptable models and then keep searching until you find what you want, at your price or close to it.

Midrange Values[2]						
One year old		Two years old		Three years old		
Whole-sale[3]	Retail[4]	Whole-sale	Retail	Whole-sale	Retail	Comments
$75	$105	$50	$75	$35	$50	
$85	$115	$55	$80	$40	$60	
$90	$120	$60	$85	$45	$65	
$90	$120	$65	$90	$30	$60	
$60	$90	$45	$70	$35	$50	
$65	$95	$50	$75	$40	$55	
$65	$95	$50	$75	$35	$50	+
$70	$85	$55	$70	$45	$65	+ +
$80	$110	$65	$80	$50	$75	+ +
$75	$95	$50	$70	$40	$55	+
$75	$95	$50	$70	$40	$55	+
$55	$80	$45	$55	$30	$45	
$60	$85	$50	$65	$40	$55	
$85	$115	$60	$85	$45	$55	
$75	$95	$50	$75	$45	$65	+
$70	$90	$50	$75	$40	$50	+
$75	$95	$55	$85	$45	$60	+
$45	$65	$35	$50	$25	$35	
$50	$70	$40	$55	$30	$40	
$60	$90	$45	$70	$35	$50	
$65	$95	$50	$75	$40	$55	
$70	$100	$55	$80	$40	$55	
$50	$75	$30	$50	$20	$35	
$55	$80	$40	$65	$30	$45	
$45	$70	$35	$50	$25	$40	
$75	$100	$55	$65	$35	$50	
$100	$145	$85	$110	$60	$75	

Mini-Saws
(Continued)

"Pro"-Mini-Saws

Lightweights

Saw Model*	Displace-ment, cu in.	Dry weight, lbs.	Standard bar, in.	Current list[1]
Skil 1705	2.1	7.4	10	$114.99
Skil 1712	2.1	7.4	12	$124.95
Skil 1614	2.2	7.4	14	$139.95
Skil 1616·	2.2	7.4	16	$149.99
Solo 600	1.95	9.7	12	$149.50
Solo 610 VA	2.14	10.5	14	$223.80
Stihl 015	1.9	7.5	10	$135.00
Stihl 015 L & E	1.9	8.1	12	$168.50
Stihl 020 AV	2.0	8.4	12	$201.50
Wards 30000	2.1	6.5	12	$108.95
Wards 30004	2.1	6.5	12	$128.95
Wards 30008	2.1	6.5	14	$148.95
Wards 30012	2.1	8.5	14	$179.95
Dolmar 118	2.3	12	15	$307.00
Homelite Super 2	1.9	7.2	14	$159.95
Homelite 150 Auto	2.6	9.25	16	$194.95
Jonsereds 361 AV	2.2	6.75	14	$169.95
McCulloch Power-Mac 6A	2.0	7.3	14	$179.95
McCulloch Super Pro 40	2.3	9.8	14	$194.95
Pioneer 1073	3.1	9.8	14	$149.95
Poulan S25D	2.3	8.6	14	$159.95
Poulan S25 DA	2.3	8.6	14	$169.95
Solo 615VA	2.75	11	14	$308.50
Stihl 020 AVP	2.0	8.5	12	$215.90
Allis-Chalmers 95	3.6	13.25	17	$195.50
Allis-Chalmers 195	3.6	12.5	17	$227.75
Danarm 55	3.3	11.75	16	$249.95
Danarm 76	3.7	11.4	17	$249.95
John Deere 18	3.6	11.75	16	$212.95
Echo CS 451 VL	2.7	11.6	16	$229.95
Homelite Super EZ Auto	2.5	9.5	16	$239.95
Homelite XL 12	3.3	13.25	16	$234.95
Husqvarna 140 S	2.5	10	14	$279.95
Jonsereds 52	3.0	11.5	15	$279.95
Jonsereds 52 E	3.0	11.5	15	$289.95
Jonsereds 521 EV	3.0	11.5	18	$329.95
Jonsereds 621	3.4	13.5	16	$329.95
McCulloch Pro 10-10A	3.3	13.4	16	$234.95
McCulloch Pro Mac 55	3.5	13.2	16	$264.95
Partner F55	2.8	10.5	15	$224.95
Partner R16	3.4	10.5	15	$249.95
Partner R417T	3.4	10.5	15	$289.95

| Midrange Values² | | | | | | |
| One year old | | Two years old | | Three years old | | |
Whole-sale¹	Retail	Whole-sale	Retail	Whole-sale	Retail	Comments
$65	$85	$45	$75	$40	$55	+
$70	$90	$55	$80	$40	$55	+
$80	$115	$65	$90	$50	$75	+
$85	$125	$75	$100	$60	$85	+
$85	$125	$75	$100	$65	$95	+ + +
$120	$155	$95	$125	$85	$110	+ + +
$85	$115	$75	$100	$65	$90	+ + +
$95	$125	$85	$115	$75	$100	+ + +
$125	$145	$105	$125	$85	$125	+ + +
$50	$70	$35	$50	$25	$40	
$60	$85	$45	$60	$35	$50	
$75	$100	$60	$80	$40	$55	
$95	$125	$75	$95	$50	$75	
$150	$205	$135	$175	$100	$150	+ + +
$95	$115	$85	$100	$65	$85	+ +
$125	$150	$95	$125	$75	$100	+ + +
$80	$100	$70	$85	$65	$80	+ + +
$90	$120	$75	$95	$50	$75	+
$100	$145	$85	$110	$65	$85	+ +
$75	$100	$60	$85	$40	$55	+ +
$80	$105	$65	$85	$50	$75	+ +
$85	$110	$70	$90	$60	$80	+ +
$165	$220	$145	$195	$125	$175	+ + +
$135	$150	$110	$135	$95	$125	+ + +
$100	$135	$85	$125	$65	$100	
$120	$160	$95	$135	$75	$110	
$125	$165	$95	$135	$85	$125	
$125	$165	$100	$135	$80	$115	+
$110	$150	$85	$115	$65	$95	
$110	$150	$90	$120	$80	$110	+
$135	$180	$100	$150	$85	$125	+ +
$145	$175	$100	$135	$85	$115	+ +
$140	$185	$115	$165	$95	$125	+ + +
$140	$185	$115	$150	$65	$90	+ +
$150	$195	$125	$160	$75	$100	+ +
$165	$220	$145	$190	$115	$155	+ +
$165	$225	$145	$195	$125	$165	+ + +
$120	$180	$100	$145	$85	$125	+
$140	$200	$120	$165	$105	$145	+
$110	$155	$85	$125	$75	$100	+
$120	$180	$95	$130	$75	$100	
$140	$195	$120	$150	$85	$115	

Lightweights
(Continued)

Medium-Duty

Saw Model*	Displace-ment, cu in.	Dry weight, lbs.	Standard bar, in.	Current list[1]
Pioneer P20	3.1	10.2	14	$179.95
Pioneer P25	3.1	10.25	16	$194.95
Poulan S25CVA	2.3	9.4	16	$189.95
Poulan 361	3.6	13.25	17	$224.95
Poulan 306A	3.6	12.5	17	$234.95
Remington SL9	2.8	9	14	$189.95
Remington SL9 Auto	2.8	10	15	$199.95
Remington SL14 Auto	2.9	10	14	$184.95
Remington SL16 Auto	2.9	10	16	$194.95
Remington SL4 Auto	3.6	13	17	$234.95
Roper C6 3667	2.5	10.5	15	$194.95
Sears 35177	3.7		17	$237.95
Stihl 031AV	3.0	11.5	14	$246.50
Stihl 041AV	3.7	12.5	14	$306.00
Stihl 041AVE	3.7	12.5	16	$360.00
Wards 30016	2.8	9	16	$197.95
Wards 30020	3.6	13	18	$247.95
Allis-Chalmers 295	3.6	12.75	16	$257.55
Danarm 1-71-SS	4.3	16.5	16	$349.95
John Deere 19	4.0	13	19	$237.95
Dolmar 122-S	4.3	15	17	$384.00
Dolmar 122-SL	4.3	16	17	$405.00
Dolmar KMS-4	3.5	17	17	$598.00
Echo CS-601 S	3.65	13.64	16	$279.95
Echo CS-601 SVL	3.65	16	16	$294.95
Echo CS-701 SVL	4.25	16.7	16	$324.95
Homelite SXL AO	3.5	14	16	$265.00
Homelite 350 AO	3.5	13.2	16	$300.00
Homelite 450 AO	4.5	16.5	16	$380.00
Husqvarna L65	4.0	13	16	$249.95
Husqvarna L77	4.7	13.2	16	$329.95
Husqvarna 163 S	3.8	14	16	$339.95
Husqvarna 263CD	3.8	14.4	16	$359.95
Husqvarna 280 S	4.7	16	16	$394.95
Husqvarna 380 CD	4.7	16	16	$409.95
Jonsereds 801	4.9	16	20	$384.95
McCulloch Super-Pro 70	4.3	13.6	16	$349.95
Partner R420	4.0	11	15	$368.95
Partner R421T	4.0	12	15	$427.95
Pioneer 1200A	3.5	13.8	16	$233.95
Pioneer P40	3.97	14	16	$299.95
Poulan 245 A	4.5	13	17	$264.95
Poulan 4200	4.2	16	17	$329.95

Midrange Values[2]						
One year old		Two years old		Three years old		
Whole-sale[1]	Retail	Whole-sale	Retail	Whole-sale	Retail	Comments
$125	$145	$95	$115	$75	$100	+ +
$135	$150	$105	$130	$85	$115	+ +
$90	$125	$80	$110	$75	$100	+ +
$110	$135	$95	$125	$85	$115	+ +
$125	$175	$100	$135	$75	$100	+ +
$95	$130	$75	$100	$50	$75	
$100	$135	$80	$105	$55	$80	
$90	$130	$75	$100	$50	$75	
$100	$135	$80	$105	$55	$80	
$120	$165	$85	$120	$65	$95	
$95	$125	$75	$100	$55	$75	
$115	$150	$95	$125	$75	$100	
$145	$180	$125	$155	$95	$125	+ + +
$165	$215	$150	$185	$135	$165	+ + +
$190	$260	$175	$200	$165	$185	+ + +
$95	$125	$75	$100	$50	$75	
$125	$165	$95	$125	$65	$85	
$135	$180	$115	$145	$85	$125	+ +
$175	$225	$145	$190	$125	$175	+
$120	$170	$100	$135	$75	$100	
$170	$255	$155	$200	$135	$175	+ +
$200	$275	$165	$220	$150	$195	+ +
$275	$400	$225	$325	$175	$225	Sachs Wankel Engine
$135	$185	$95	$145	$75	$100	+
$140	$195	$115	$165	$95	$125	+
$160	$215	$135	$185	$120	$145	+
$145	$200	$125	$175	$115	$135	+ + +
$155	$230	$135	$195	$125	$150	+
$185	$290	$165	$240	$135	$180	+
$125	$165	$100	$135	$75	$100	+ +
$160	$220	$125	$170	$95	$135	+ +
$165	$225	$130	$175	$115	$145	+ +
$180	$240	$150	$195	$135	$175	+ +
$185	$265	$165	$225	$145	$185	+ +
$200	$275	$175	$235	$155	$195	+ + +
$185	$255	$165	$215	$145	$185	+ + +
$175	$265	$160	$230	$115	$165	+ +
$180	$245	$145	$200	$100	$150	
$200	$285	$165	$225	$115	$165	
$115	$165	$95	$135	$75	$100	+ + +
$155	$210	$135	$175	$115	$145	+ + +
$135	$185	$115	$150	$95	$135	+ +
$165	$235	$135	$185	$100	$140	+ + +

Medium-Duty
(Continued)

Production Saws

Saw Model*	Displace-ment, cu in.	Dry weight, lbs.	Standard bar, in.	Current list[1]
Remington SL 4	3.6	13	17	$234.95
Remington SL 11	4.0	13	19	$274.95
Roper C33237	3.7	11	15	$214.95
Roper C34337	3.7	11	17	$239.95
Roper C35437	3.7	11	21	$249.95
Sears 36212	3.7		17	$277.95
Skil 1631	4.2	13.5	16	$239.95
Skil 1645	4.2	13.7	16	$259.95
Solo 620 VA	3.36	15.5	16	$319.85
Solo 650 VA	3.78	15.5	16	$333.65
Solo 660 VA	4.94	16.5	20	$373.55
Stihl 08-S	3.4	13.5	17	$301.50
Stihl 045 AV	4.6	17	16	$403.50
Wards 30024	4.0	13	20	$297.95
Danarm 110	6.7	18.4	16	$389.95
Danarm 125	7.6	19.4	20	$419.95
John Deere 23	5.0	15.5	21	$316.95
Dolmar 152	6.1	19	21	$452.00
Dolmar CT	7.2	23	21	$580.00
Echo 1001 VL	6.08	21	21	$449.95
Homelite SXL295	5.0	16.7	15	$380.00
Homelite CL 72	4.9	19	14	$315.00
Homelite 650 AO	6.1	21.5	20	$485.00
Homelite Super Wiz 66	4.7	22.75	19	$420.00
Husqvarna 1100 CD	6.0	19.4	16	$499.95
Jonsereds 90	5.5	16.25	23	$429.95
Jonsereds 111	6.7	19.5	27	$504.95
McCulloch Super-Pro 81	5.0	16.4	Power Unit only	$339.95
McCulloch Super-Pro 125C	7.5	23.8	Power Unit only	$539.95
Partner R435	5.2	16	15	$408.95
Partner R440T	6.1	16	15	$437.95
Pioneer P50	5	16.25	16	$369.95
Poulan 5200	5.2	16	17	$379.95
Poulan 6000	6.0	20	21	$424.95
Remington SL55A	5.0	14.5	21	$339.95
Remington SL7A	5.7	18	21	$349.95
Solo 635	5.61	22.0	17	$357.70
Solo 642	6.47	22.0	17	$370.75
Stihl 051AVE	5.5	18.5	17	$411.50
Stihl 070	6.5	22.5	17	$469.95
Stihl 075AVE	6.7	18.5	21	$462.50
Stihl 090G	6.5	26	17	$539.95
Stihl 090 (090 AV)	8.5	23.5	21	$543.75

| Midrange Values[2] | | | | | | |
| One year old | | Two years old | | Three years old | | |
Whole-sale[1]	Retail	Whole-sale	Retail	Whole-sale	Retail	Comments
$115	$165	$85	$135	$65	$95	
$135	$195	$115	$165	$85	$125	
$95	$145	$75	$100	$50	$75	
$105	$160	$85	$105	$55	$80	
$115	$165	$95	$115	$65	$85	
$135	$185	$100	$135	$75	$100	
$115	$170	$95	$135	$65	$95	+
$125	$180	$105	$145	$75	$105	+
$155	$210	$135	$195	$115	$175	+ + +
$170	$225	$150	$200	$135	$185	+ + +
$195	$250	$175	$225	$165	$210	+ + +
$155	$210	$145	$195	$140	$190	+ + +
$210	$290	$195	$275	$185	$255	+ + +
$145	$195	$125	$150	$85	$125	
$185	$260	$150	$200	$110	$150	
$200	$280	$175	$250	$125	$175	
$165	$220	$135	$180	$95	$125	
$240	$300	$215	$275	$140	$175	+ + +
$295	$385	$265	$350	$175	$200	+ + +
$225	$300	$200	$275	$150	$195	+ +
$195	$290	$175	$240	$150	$195	+ +
$165	$240	$145	$195	$100	$150	+ +
$255	$370	$210	$300	$175	$235	+ +
$225	$320	$195	$255	$165	$225	+ + +
$255	$335	$225	$275	$185	$245	+ + +
$215	$285	$185	$245	$155	$195	+ + +
$255	$335	$225	$285	$185	$250	+ + +
$215	$305	$175	$235	$125	$165	+ +
$285	$410	$235	$330	$165	$225	+ +
$200	$275	$165	$225	$125	$165	+
$225	$295	$185	$245	$155	$195	+
$185	$260	$155	$195	$125	$175	+ +
$195	$270	$165	$210	$145	$195	+ +
$225	$300	$185	$250	$165	$225	+ + +
$155	$240	$125	$180	$100	$135	
$165	$250	$135	$190	$110	$140	
$185	$265	$165	$220	$155	$195	+ +
$190	$270	$170	$225	$160	$200	+ +
$250	$300	$225	$275	$175	$195	+ + +
$300	$350	$255	$285	$195	$225	+ + +
$300	$350	$275	$325	$210	$250	+ + +
$325	$385	$285	$335	$225	$265	+ + +
$335	$395	$295	$345	$235	$275	+ + +

NOTES

*   Only the most commonly available standard production gasoline chain saws are represented in these pages —the ones that are likely to stay around. A few companies, notably Sears, Wards, and John Deere, buy their saws from another company. They change the model numbers every year but they should be easy to recognize from the specifications. For the popular standard models from the major chain saw manufacturers, this information should be reasonably accurate for years to come, requiring only minor adjustments for the changing price of peanut butter.

1.   "Current list price" is based on advertised retail prices circa 1977, with standard-size bars and standard equipment.

2.   "Mid-range value" refers to average wholesale and retail prices for used saws one, two, and three years old. Saws in poor condition are worth less, saws in excellent condition are worth more.

3.   "Wholesale" is what you may expect to receive for a trade-in.

4.   "Retail" is what you may expect to pay for a used saw that a dealer has accepted as a trade-in.

+   means "a good, high-quality machine."

++   means "a really fine and dependable saw with a good reputation among users and professionals."

+++ is Parp's personal superior rating.

HOW MUCH SHOULD YOU PAY?

The gasoline chain saw is still a relatively new consumer item, and the modern chain saw incorporates many recent technical advances. This means, for one thing, that used chain saw prices are still arbitrary, unpredictable, and unstable. The generally accepted rule is that any used power tool in good condition is priced at about 50 percent or 60 percent of its original retail value.

In various parts of the country, Parp has run across one particular used saw, a model of his choice, at prices ranging from $85 to $225. The original retail price of the saw was $411.50. Each saw was of the same model year and in reasonably good condition. The relative figures given in the preceding chart will serve as a general guide to prices, but may be better used to indicate comparative value. In other words, you can get a pretty good idea just how much a lot of other people feel a particular saw should cost, compared to a lot of other saws.

Also, bear in mind that used chain saw prices and values are definitely affected by season. Fall is certainly the worst time to buy a used chain saw. That's when the prices are highest, obviously. That's also when the average person will discover that that saw that was stored in the garage all winter is full of varnish. Lots of other people will decide for other reasons that last year's saw isn't good enough for this year. They'll all trade them in. The cheap ones and the best ones go first, but they're all over-priced. The saws that are left until spring, or not traded in until spring, will cost a lot less than they would have in the fall. And many of the saws that are passed up in the fall will be good medium-duty saws, ignored by most shoppers because of their weight, but well maintained by the previous, probably serious, owners.

Weight is another important consideration that affects the price of a used chain saw. Almost universally, a lighter chain saw retains more of its original value than does a heavier one. There are several reasons for this. Chiefly, most people simply prefer lighter saws. Also, most dealers automatically assume that a heavier saw has been harder used than has a lighter saw. Very often this is true, and you should test and examine any large used saw before you buy it. But it's also often true that larger saws were owned previously by more serious (though not professional) woodspersons, or at least by people who are experienced with power tools. Some of these people do maintain their equipment well and most of them know enough to avoid the worst and most obvious mistakes.

If you've decided that you need a used chain saw in the medium-duty class, and if you shop for it in late spring or early summer, chances are you'll get a better deal than most. Except for that particular situation, however, the best bargains in used saws cost the most. That's because the saws that are well maintained are owned by people who realize their value. They usually won't sell cheap.

To review briefly, we've seen that mini-saws and lightweights cost more, comparatively, than do medium-duty or production saws. On the other hand, medium-duty saws in good condition are often the best deals because they're less popular. Parp again urges caution regarding used production saws. And avoid older chain saws —those huge monsters with the 25- or 30-pound bodies and long, wide bars. The best bargains cost the most, and the more it weighs, the less it's worth. And then there's the occasional steal.

Chain saws are designed for one specific purpose: cutting trees. And if that isn't scary enough, there's the whole business of a portable gasoline engine that you're supposed to hold between your hands while it sputters and coughs and explodes. They're not very delicate tools and many people, rather than appreciating the chain saw as a really admirable design achievement, have a different and more sensible reaction. They're scared to death of the things, whether they're running them or somebody else is.

Once in a while one of these people somehow ends up with a new chain saw. Often the saw never sees use at all. Parp has a friend who found one at a garage sale in the original package with the bar and chain still disassembled. Whenever you have this kind of situation, you have all the signs of a steal.

So the first thing you do in shopping for a used chain saw is tell all your most unlikely friends about your interest. Mention it to the relatives, also, and to the mailman.

And put notes on the bulletin boards in the laundromat, grocery store, drug store, and hardware store. All of your sane friends will pretend they didn't notice.

SOURCES

New Saw Dealers

As noted before, most used chain saws are trade-ins and so will be found in new chain saw dealer showrooms. Most dealers at least clean and sharpen a used saw before offering it for sale, and if you find a used saw in a dealer's showroom that is dirty and has a dull chain, you should try another dealer. Dealers are usually well informed on the true market value of a used saw so you may expect to find that the dealer's prices are not too far off, one way or the other. Very few dealers will ask $100 for a saw worth $50, and a dealer's showroom is no place to expect a real steal, though it does happen. A good bargain is common.

If you do shop in dealers' showrooms, you might keep in mind that if one is satisfied with a particular saw, one is more likely to trade it in on another from the same company. Obviously, there are exceptions to this, and reasons other than lack of satisfaction cause people to switch brands. It's still a good rule.

There are several real advantages to buying a used chain saw from a dealer. Again, such a dealer is likely to be very well informed about saws in general. A dealer is also likely to be a chain saw mechanic, or to have one in the shop. It's a great help to be able to take a limping chain saw to the person you bought it from and pick it up later that day, or in just a day or two. They know the saw when you bring it in, especially if they sell the same saw brand new. The dealer or the mechanic is also familiar with repair methods for that particular saw, and will have the most commonly required parts in stock. Specialized chain saw dealers are surprisingly established in almost all areas, including many areas where a wild tree hasn't been seen alive in decades.

If it should happen that there is not a specialized chain saw dealer in your area, the next best bet is the local hardware store that sells chain saws, either from stock or on special order. Most hardwares that deal in new saws also accept trade-ins. Most hardwares that sell chain saws also carry cutting chains, chain-sharpening tools, two-cycle engine oil, and other parts, tools, and accessories, in stock or by order.

Hardly Used Homeowner Types

Your local newspaper publishes ads for estate auctions, farm auctions, neighborhood sales, and garage sales. These are the most likely places to buy hardly used chain saws, especially mini-saws, at reasonable prices.

Many people buy or are given chain saws who have very little or even no use for them. In recent years, mini-saws and lightweight saws have become popular Christmas presents and retirement gifts. Something around 20 percent of the chain saws sold every year are purchased as gifts. An amazing number of these saws are never used at all, and some never even have fuel in their tanks. These are the saws to watch for.

You can spot them immediately at garage sales. If the chain is sharp and the bar is clean and new looking, you can bet on the saw being as good as new. If there are the slightest scratches, or if the chain has been sharpened, you can judge how much it has been used by examining the chain, and by the little tests that we'll cover soon. Parp has turned up some amazing values at garage sales, including one $250 professional lightweight in new condition, with all new accessories, case, and owner's manual, for $85. Don't expect to find such buys very often, especially as more people become aware of the value of chain saws as tools. And it takes only one serious mistake to ruin a new chain saw. If the owner only used it once but failed to use the proper fuel or two-cycle engine oil, the saw may appear to be in excellent condition but may be full of varnish. Don't buy a used saw without starting it.

Rental Shops

Rental shops, those large stores that rent everything from sick-room equipment to backhoes, usually rent chain saws as well. These shops generally operate under one of two opposite philosophies. One rental philosophy assumes that people are unintelligent and destructive. This kind of shop carries the cheapest equipment available, figuring that it won't last anyway. Consequently, their chain saws, if they

have them, aren't much good to start with and are no good at all after a few customers have used them. This kind of shop will also do only minimal maintenance and service to their equipment. Chain saws require good care in order to go on working. You should be able to identify these shops by the merchandise they have on hand.

The other kind of rental shop buys the best equipment it can find and then maintains it with adequate to excellent care and service. When a saw comes back, it is cleaned, sharpened, tuned if necessary, and tested before it goes back out. This kind of shop tries not to let equipment turn into junk. Accordingly, they will offer chain saws for sale constantly, at reasonable prices based on estimated hours of use. These shops can be excellent sources for good, dependable used chain saws.

Rental shops price used chain saws primarily according to age and weight. Weight is an especially significant factor here. In a rental shop, large medium-duty saws with few hours of service will frequently sell for as little as a used mini-saw. Rental shop mini-saws, on the other hand, are often sold at 80 percent or 90 percent of the original retail value. Shop around and be careful. Rental shops don't have a fast turnover in used equipment for sale, so a saw that you're considering may well sit there for several weeks, giving you plenty of time to be sure it's what you want.

Incidentally, a few rental shops surveyed stated that they don't sell their equipment at all. They wait until it's just about gone. When a saw fails, they give it to the last customer who rents it. Something to remember, says Parp.

Local Government and Businesses

Many government agencies use chain saws. County road crews use chain saws for clearing new roads or for removing fallen trees. Chain saws are used for rescue work, construction, building and clearing trails, and for maintaining forests, parks, and agricultural projects. Some colleges have chain saws in storage rooms and occasionally they turn up in surplus sales. Utility companies and other semigovernmental organizations use chain saws extensively. All of these sources periodically hold public auctions at which one may buy a used chain saw for very little money. These auctions are always well advertised and the public usually has a chance to examine, but not operate, the equipment to be sold. Bidding is subsequently held on a number basis and you just take your chances.

Private businesses or professionals that use chain saws as a main tool nearly always have one for sale. Tree surgeons and nursery persons are notable for used mini-saws or lightweights. Obviously one must be very careful here, but there are tree surgeons who maintain their saws at peak performance and sell them all at the end of each season as a matter of policy. If you don't have much capital, and you want a lightweight saw, this can be an excellent source.

On the other hand, some tree surgeons are extremely casual in their maintenance. Even that can work to your advantage. Parp tells of some professionals who don't clean spark plugs. When their saws fail, they sell them or drop them in a barrel in the back of the shop. You can gamble on a junker like that and sometimes do very well.

And then there's the real professional castoff, a logger's used saw. Many loggers use medium-duty saws so we're not necessarily talking about huge 25-pound saws with 40-inch bars. The Stihl 051 is a very popular logging saw, and it is even on the light side of the medium-duty class. Homelite's 650 and Solo's 660 are two other examples. You'll be able to tell if the saw is a little too tired for professional use but just fine for your woodpile.

GETTING THE MOST FOR YOUR MONEY

When you consider a used chain saw, look first at the type and size. Don't hustle yourself into something you don't need just because it's available. Determine what you need first, as discussed earlier in this chapter, and don't buy anything that isn't pretty close to your conclusions.

Next, look at the general condition of the saw. If it obviously hasn't been kept clean you can stop right there. A chain saw that's been run dirty is sure to have other, much more serious problems. The dirt and grease will cause the saw to overheat, for one thing.

If the saw is clean and appears to have been well cared for, look more closely for signs of improper use or poor maintenance. Examine the chain, bar, and sprocket. If the chain cutters are dull or have not been filed uniformly, or if the bar is bent or burned, or if the sprocket is badly worn, you can bet the owner hasn't taken good care of the saw and you don't want it, except maybe for parts. Any single problem, like a bent bar, might be easily remedied, but the point is that you're looking for signs of bad maintenance or improper use. If you find them, the chances are that the saw is ruined.

There are other little things to look at before you even start the engine. First, look carefully for stripped or missing bolts or nuts. If any bolts or nuts are missing, try to determine if it's because of stripped threads. If not, replace them and be sure they stay put while operating the saw. If threads are stripped, consider whether or not you will be able to correct the problem yourself or if you can afford to have a mechanic do it for you. If you can't correct the problem one way or the other, look for another saw.

Sometimes the screw that adjusts the tension for the chain becomes stripped or misshapen. If so, you won't be able to keep the chain properly adjusted. On most saws, it's an easy job to replace the entire chain-tensioning mechanism, or just the screw itself. On other saws it's a job for a master mechanic or the factory itself. In either case, a damaged chain-tensioning mechanism indicates hard use and possible abuse

so, if you're not gambling on a junker, forget it.

Next, remove the top plate that covers the area of the carburetor. Inside, there should be a fine-mesh filter screen. This is the air filter. If it's missing, don't buy the saw except as junk. The filter should be there and it'll probably be a little dirty, maybe even clogged. Don't be concerned about normal dirt and slight clogging. Just clean the filter before you start the saw. But if the filter is very clogged, and if the incoming dirt and dust seems to be collecting around the sides of the air box and below the air filter, gross neglect is indicated and you can bet it isn't limited to the air filter. The air filter of a chain saw must be cleaned every working day, or more often, with kerosene or air pressure. The air entering the carburetor has to be clean or the abrasive effect of dust, dirt, and sawdust will clog and choke the machine or grind it to death.

Another little thing to look at is the oil used for chain lubrication. Get some on your finger and see if it feels gritty. If it feels gritty and old, it's probably used crankcase oil. In itself, that may not be so serious—you could easily just start using new oil yourself. But we're looking at little things, indications of improper use or lack of maintenance. All these factors will affect whether or not you want the machine, and for what price. Of course, you can also ask the owner specific questions about the machine. "What kind of oil do you use?" If the questions are specific, most people will be honest.

Examine the condition of the spark plug cover or connection, and the spark plug cable. If the material appears dry, frayed, or damaged, it will have to be replaced and may indicate that other ignition problems are present or will soon develop. Also look at the starter pull rope. If it is hanging loosely from the saw, either the rewind spring was improperly installed or it needs to be retensioned. If it's frayed, figure that the saw has either been run for many hours, or else that it's hard to start.

Chain, Bar, and Sprocket:
A Closer Look

For complete information on how to sharpen, maintain, and replace the chain, bar, and sprocket once you have a chain saw, see Chapter Seven. For now, we're going to look for specific problems that have already developed and at symptoms that indicate abuse of a used chain saw. If you do find a used saw with a damaged or badly worn or improperly maintained cutting attachment, you must then decide if the problem is severe enough to stop you from buying the saw, or if the saw itself is still good enough, and reasonable enough, to justify replacing the attachment entirely. Very minor abuse or error may be corrected with proper care and filing, but it has to be pretty minor.

The first thing to look at is the bar. The chain is still on, so you can't see the grooves, but you can see the hard tip and blade portion. If you see any chips or cracks, the bar is no good and it is dangerous to operate it as is. Chips or cracks

at the tip or near the sprocket indicate that the chain was run too tight or the bar was used to pry logs apart. Damage along the top or sides of the rails indicate that the chain was run too loose.

If you see signs of burning (dark blue or black streaks or stains), the saw has probably been forced through wood with a dull chain, or run without oil, or both. A burned bar is a very serious symptom that nearly always indicates a junker. If the bar is badly burned, the engine or clutch may be damaged also.

If the bar has a sprocket nose or roller nose, find out if it has been properly greased and maintained. Ask the owner how often you have to grease a thing like that. If he says "Once in a while," he's wrong. It's every day. For a final look at the bar while it's still on the saw, set the saw down so you can look directly at the end of the bar. See if it's bent or twisted. If you buy it anyway, you'll have to replace the bar, chain, and sprocket, all together, to correct the problem. There's no cheaper way.

Now let's take a closer look at the chain itself. Using a ruler, measure the length of several cutters on each side. If the cutters on one side are longer than the cutters on the other side, the chain has not been sharpened uniformly and the saw will not cut straight. Then find the shortest cutter. To make the saw cut straight again, you'll have to file all the other cutters back to match the smallest one. You'll probably have to file the bar rails square, too. Also check the depth gauges with a depth-gauge tool to be sure they are uniform. If they're all too high, the chain has not been cutting efficiently and has caused drag that has worn on the engine. If they're not uniform, that's even worse and it's a sure sign of bad maintenance. In any of these cases, certain parts or pieces of the chain itself may have cracked or may soon break.

Now remove the bar and chain from the chain saw. While you're at it, double-check those studs and nuts that fasten the bar to the saw. Be very sure they're not stripped or loose in the casting. And look at the outside of the nuts. If they appear chewed or rounded, the wrong tool has been used on them. It's a very common problem, and quite easy to correct, but it does again indicate abuse. Don't use anything on those nuts except a quality wrench that's exactly the right size. Pliers or adjustable wrenches or cheap open-end wrenches will ruin them fast. Use a socket wrench, or a good box wrench, or (last choice) the tool that came with the saw.

When you have the bar and chain removed from the saw, look at the sprocket. If the sprocket is chewed or worn or damaged, it must be replaced; even minor wear on the teeth (particularly the tips) changes the pitch of the sprocket. Look for dirt around the sprocket, in the groove of the bar, and on the parts of the chain you've just exposed. Here's where a superficial cleaning job will be revealed.

Now hold the bar up without the chain and examine the grooves. At the tail end, where the chain enters the grooves, they should be funneled out so the chain won't

catch on them. Except for this funneling, the rails should be straight, parallel, and uniform all around the bar. Filing, of course, is a part of normal maintenance but the filing must be uniform and accurate. If it isn't, other problems will be present. Check the depth of the rails against the drive link tangs of the chain. The chain should ride *on* the rails with clearance below the tangs. Now hold the bar up without the chain to double-check for bends, or pinched-together sections. The groove should be of equal width all around. Remember that you must replace or repair a bent bar in order to cut efficiently, safely, and accurately.

While the bar is off the saw, look at the hole in the saw that delivers oil to the bar and chain. If the saw has a manual oiler, or an automatic oiler with manual override, push the oiler control button. You should see a strong spurt of oil come from the hole. Don't look too close. If the saw has only an automatic oiling system, you'll have to wait until the saw is running before you can check the pump.

Finally, take a look at the entire chain. Check the drive links for damage. If you find any problems, compare them to the Saw Chain Troubleshooting Guide on pages 122-23. That way you can determine the probable cause of the damage and decide if it indicates a problem too serious to correct. And look for any parts of the chain that may have been replaced. Notice if they have been properly filed to match the old pieces. This is essential.

If you find you must replace the chain,

bar, and sprocket, figure that cost as part of the price of the saw.

ENGINE PERFORMANCE

First, read Chapters Five and Six and familiarize yourself with the proper way to start a chain saw. Have the owner start it first, to show you any little tricks for that particular model. If it doesn't start, we're talking about a junker, more than likely. If it does start, it should run fairly smoothly, while both idling and running faster. Don't race a chain saw when you're not cutting.

Chain saw exhaust is normally dark, and a steady, popping sound is also normal with two-cycle engines. But the engine should sound steady and dependable and should not smoke or pop excessively. If you've never heard a chain saw run before, it may be hard to tell if it's running properly or not. Hopefully, you've prepared by having a friend or dealer demonstrate a new saw first.

There are three major concerns that you should try to check out during your examination of this used saw. You need to determine if the ignition is working properly and is delivering sufficient spark; you need to know if the saw still has enough compression to last for a while; and you need to know how well the saw performs under load. If you have time to do a complete check, study Chapter Nine and become familiar with troubleshooting techniques. If not, proceed as follows.

If the saw starts easily, it is getting sufficient spark and you can probably count on the ignition parts lasting for a while. If it doesn't start, refer to troubleshooting procedures or go back to the want ads.

Now let the saw warm up for a while. Before you cut, check the chain oil system with the engine running. Lean a piece of cardboard or something up against the log. Aim the front of the chain saw directly at it, about six inches away. If the saw has an automatic oiling system, just rev the engine moderately. If the saw has manual oiling, push the oiler, rev moderately, and push the oiler again. If the oiler system is working properly, a fine spray of oil will leave the end of the bar where the chain speeds around the tip. The oil will appear on the cardboard. If the saw has an automatic oiling system with a manual override, test both functions separately, as above.

Now do some cutting on a 10- or 12-inch log. If you're not used to a chain saw, only cut about one third of the way into the log. From idle, increase the speed of the saw just as the chain touches the wood. It's like engaging the clutch and stepping on the gas at the same time. Do several cuts until you're satisfied that the saw operates under load as well as it does at idle. If it doesn't, serious problems are indicated that go anywhere from bad timing to carburetor problems to worn rings. If you're still interested in the saw, refer to the Appendix.

If the saw started easily and ran well under a load, you can assume that most of your worries about performance are answered. Lots of things could be wrong, or could soon go wrong, but at this point you can take a chance that the saw will be satisfactory. If you have time, however, you should now turn the saw off and let it sit for a few minutes. Then start it again, following the instructions outlined in Chapter Six (page 75). It should start easily, if you don't flood it, and it will probably start unchoked and with the throttle at idle. It should continue to run smoothly at idle and with slight to moderate revving as long as the fuel holds out. If it does all this satisfactorily, you just might have found a dependable used chain saw. If you have any reservations at all, you should not buy the saw—or offer a lower price, or follow the troubleshooting procedure in order to determine the probable trouble and roughly estimate the cost and difficulty of repair.

It may, at this point, be worth your while to take a quick compression test as a final check, especially if the saw seemed a little weak or rough at high speed and under a working load. There's an easy way to do this.

With most chain saws, it's easy to remove the starter housing and flywheel cover. If the fuel tank is also built into this assembly, as it is on many saws, you only have to be careful not to damage the fuel line. Remove the flywheel cover, and disconnect the fuel line if necessary. Then turn the flywheel until you feel pressure. Then give the flywheel a quick spin. If it snaps back strongly, compression is good. If it keeps going or stops weakly without

snapping back, the compression is low; or, the compression could be normal but the compression release valve is not seating properly. If the saw passes this test satisfactorily, and if it starts easily cold or warm, and if it runs well under a load, and if the chain, bar, sprocket, and general appearance of the saw are satisfactory, it's still a gamble, but the odds are decent.

GAMBLING ON A JUNKER

You can improve the odds by looking for saws that have been worn out but not beaten to death. The condition of the chain will often give you enough information to decide which of these baskets a particular saw goes into. If the chain has been used very little and treated very badly (see "Saw Chain Troubleshooting Guide" at the end of Chapter Seven), the poor saw was probably beaten to death. If the chain is worn out but still looks as if it has been well cared for, filed uniformly, and kept sharp, chances are the saw is just tired and a reconditioning will wake it up. If that's the case, and you can get it cheap enough, that's the junker to buy.

To recondition the saw, you'll need to be able to buy parts. The more recent the model is, and the more common, the more likely it is that you'll be able to complete the job and then keep the saw running for a year or two afterwards. Parp says that five years old is a maximum in most cases. If it's a production saw that's popular with loggers year after year, it might be a little older. It's a junker anyway, and you're a gambler.

In many cases, you should be able to obtain a shop manual for the saw from the saw manufacturer. That will make the recycling infinitely easier. Plan on storing the junker for up to three months while you wait for the book, which will cost about $10.

While you're waiting, take the saw completely through the troubleshooting procedure in Chapter Nine, and study all the repairs covered in this book. Also obtain the *Chain Saw Service Manual* (Intertech Publishing Corporation) and any other repair book that seems appropriate. Then practice dismantling the saw and putting it back together, going a little further each time. As you're doing this, clean, repair, and replace *all* the parts that you possibly can.

It's at this point that you'll wish you had a barrel of saws for spare parts. If you can find a government garage, county shop, or tree surgeon who has used that kind of saw for a few years, you just might be able to buy a never-used parts barrel or even a few identical junkers. If so, you'll probably have everything you need except gaskets, rings, and some ignition parts. These you can buy or mail-order from a parts distributor or from the original manufacturer. Some dealers will sell you "used parts assemblies," including starter assemblies, carburetors, oil pumps, and mufflers.

Many saw users make no repairs whatsoever, and do very little maintenance. It is not uncommon to find an otherwise serviceable saw that's been discarded be-cause of a broken starter spring. In almost every parts barrel, you can find a good saw. It might be in the form of a piece here and a piece there, waiting to be assembled. If the starter spring was broken, you can pull the entire starter assembly and housing off another saw of the same model that has worn rings. If the bar is broken as well, that's only a little more trouble. If you're interested and determined, it is entirely possible to scrounge enough parts in almost any town to put together two or three good saws and start a firewood business. Familiarize yourself with the major components of all chain saws, study this book and the *Chain Saw Service Manual,* and you will be an expert scrounger-restorer in no time.

ACCESSORIES FOR A USED CHAIN SAW

Not only is it easy to find substitutes for the tools that come with a new chain saw, but Parp says it's necessary as well. A good ⅜-inch drive socket set is a very reasonable investment in any case. And with it you'll be able to work efficiently on any chain saw. Almost any large screwdriver is better than the screwdriver end of the "scrench" that comes with new saws. And a good hex wrench set is very inexpensive.

If the saw has a roller nose, get a small grease gun with a small needle adapter at your local hardware store. Zip Penn (see Appendix) sells an inexpensive one. The depth gauge that comes with saws is exactly the same as the model in the hardware store. Just get the right size. File guides are generally not supplied with new saws anyway and, if they are, they're the hand-held type. Invest in a high-quality clamp-on type and get used to it. Other than an electric power shop grinder, built especially for saw chain, a clamp-on hand-powered sharpener is the best.

Chain guards are very inexpensive and will protect you, your saw chain, and the backseat. A full case isn't necessary. Just get a chain guard and cover up the saw when it's stored.

Getting the owner's manual is not always easy. The big chain saw companies are pretty good about this and will supply the book if they have it. If not, start calling the professional chain saw users in your area. When you find one that uses your brand of saw, ask if he has any old manuals lying around. He probably will. You can sometimes substitute with one covering a similar model of a different year, as long as it's from the same company.

If you have trouble obtaining parts and supplies from the chain saw's original manufacturer, you may have to write some letters or visit the older established parts distributors, warranty stations, or dealers for that particular saw. They will often have some odd, really old stuff in stock.

The entire subject of used chain saws can be a fascinating pursuit in itself. It can also be a way of making a living, either with a business that puts used saws to work selling firewood, or with a business that deals in used chain saws.

A little shop, some piles of wood, some open space.

An Ersatz Owner's Manual • 5

Don't start it yet. First, let's cover a few more basics and make sure that your new or used saw is complete, and in good condition for safe operation. We're going to check it in as if we'd just received it on a job where it has to perform professionally.

Your saw's first days at home are important. It is all too possible to ruin a new chain saw's career in just one day of improper use. But this chapter is short and in a few minutes we can go on to Chapter Six, which is where we fire up that new machine and finally mingle the smells of gasoline and oil and fresh sawdust. Ah, says Parp. The very thought takes him back to the woodpiles of yesterday and away from the typewriter of this week. He sees the standing dead beckoning their widow makers in the green forests of tomorrow, where this book becomes a thing to carry instead of a full-time job.

INSPECTION AND ASSEMBLY OF A NEW CHAIN SAW

First, of course, unpack your saw, the bar and chain, and the owner's manual. Take time to read your owner's manual thoroughly. Much of this chapter is intended to supplement your owner's manual or to

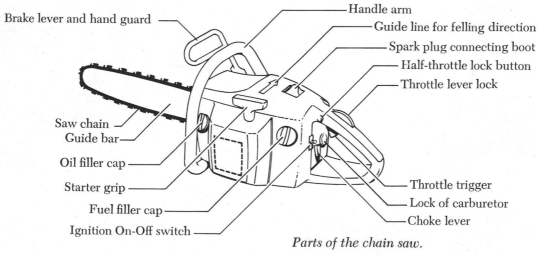

Brake lever and hand guard

Handle arm
Guide line for felling direction
Spark plug connecting boot
Half-throttle lock button
Throttle lever lock

Saw chain
Guide bar
Oil filler cap
Starter grip
Fuel filler cap
Ignition On-Off switch

Throttle trigger
Lock of carburetor
Choke lever

Parts of the chain saw.

Figure 5.1

serve as a general substitute. With new saws, your owner's manual should contain a list of components, parts, supplies, and tools that the manufacturer intended to include with your saw. Carefully check in each of these items, and examine them for breakage or flaws. Especially check the outer edges of the bar and all parts of the cutting chain for burrs or roughness. Wear gloves when handling the chain. You can smoothly file any slight roughness or minor burrs, or you can remove them with emery cloth, being careful to work in the cutting direction. If you find large burrs, steel slivers, or a lot of roughness, refer to Chapter Seven for proper filing techniques and file the chain and bar as if they had been through a hard day's work. The chain and bar of a new saw should, of course, be perfect.

Inside the fuel tank of most chain saws, there is a fuel pick-up tube with a filter in the open end. If your owner's manual indicates such a filter on your saw, remove the fuel tank filler cap. Then, using a piece of bent wire, carefully fish out the end of the fuel pick-up tube. It's usually bell shaped or cylinder shaped and made out of black rubber. If yours is a new saw, we're only checking to be sure the filter is there and that it's properly secure. If yours is a used saw, remove the filter by twisting it free. Clean it with solvent and be sure it's dry before you put it back. If it seems clogged or at all greasy, you should replace it with a new filter. Do not attempt to clean it with water. When you replace it, push it in with a twisting motion. Never

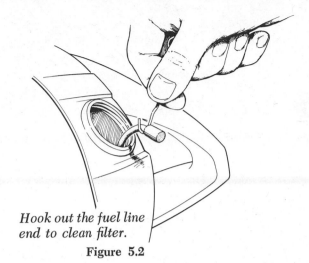

Hook out the fuel line end to clean filter.

Figure 5.2

operate a chain saw without a fuel filter installed.

Inside the chain oil tank there is a similar device. It is the oil pick-up tube and filter. Used-saw owners should also remove and clean the oil filter. Don't twist or break the oil line.

If you are checking in a used chain saw, you should read this chapter and follow *all* maintenance procedures before using your saw. Be especially careful to thoroughly clean all sawdust guards and cooling fins, the spark arrester, muffler, and the exhaust ports, according to the recommended procedures.

Whether your saw is new or used, you should now check *all* screws, nuts, and bolts to be sure they are tight. Don't forget to check the screws that secure the handle. These are often loose on new saws and a loose screw that flies out during your first cutting session can make you wish you'd bought a propane space heater.

Now, just as we checked the fuel filter, let's make sure we have a clean air filter. First, be very sure that the entire top or cover plate of your saw is perfectly clean and free of all sawdust, loose screws, tools, oil, grease, and so on. If it's a used saw, be sure you have completely cleaned the entire saw. Then remove the top cover plate by loosening the large hub that holds it in place. Use your fingers on this—not any kind of tool. Then, under the top cover plate, clean very carefully all around the air filter and the air box. If dirt gets into the air box, it can do a lot of damage very quickly. If your saw is new, you shouldn't have to do any cleaning, but it's best to be certain. If your saw is new, you should only have to glance at the filter to be sure it's there and clean and securely in place. If your saw is used, remove and clean the filter with kerosene and blow it out with compressed air or allow it to dry before you replace it. Always keep two or three extra air filters on hand. You'll need them. Make sure all fasteners are tight as you replace the air filter and the top plate cover. Never operate a chain saw without a clean air filter properly installed.

Air filters and the like are often best cleaned by blowing them out with compressed air, and you can make your own source of compressed air easily and cheaply. Obtain an old truck tire that is worn out but will still hold air. Attach an air hose, which you can buy at most hardware stores and large service stations. You can either attach a hand-operated valve or you can use the push valve that comes with the hose. Just hold the hose against the work so that the valve needle is pushed in. This method is every bit as effective as using an air compressor. You should never, of course, blow out an air filter while it's on the saw since you'd be blowing the dirt through the air filter and straight into the carburetor.

Parp's cautions regarding the fuel filter and the air filter are not just echos from an owner's manual. Dirt is the first enemy of the small engine. Most of the really first-rate professional small-engine mechanics that Parp knows work in atmospheres of laboratory cleanliness that remind one of a surgeon's operating room. There are good reasons for this. The smallest amount of dirt that enters the air box will go straight to the carburetor and clog its tiny passages. Also, dirt coming from the fuel line or air box can eventually build up in the crankcase or in the cylinder. There, its abrasive effect will quickly score the sides of the cylinder and burn out the piston rings. All of this is mechanically very serious indeed. Mechanics is nothing more than making things work together properly in the way in which they touch each other. Anything else that gets in the way or interferes or causes wear is bad mechanics. Dirt is the number-one bad mechanic.

INSTALLING BAR AND CHAIN

After you've found that you have all the components, parts, tools, and supplies that you need for your saw, and after you've read the owner's manual if you have one, and after you're satisfied that your saw is clean and in good condition, it's time to install the bar and chain and do the first adjustments, called "cold-tensioning."

(It is a good idea, however, to first soak the chain overnight in a covering bath of clean, new 10-weight nondetergent oil. This will assure maximum chain lubrication during the crucial break-in period. Used chains should be cleaned in solvent first, to remove all pitch, and then soaked in oil overnight before using.)

There is a plate attached with a nut or nuts to the lower right-hand front side of your saw. This is the clutch guard and chain sprocket cover. Remove the nut, or nuts and washers, and remove the clutch guard. Oops. Switch the ignition switch to OFF. If your new saw has fiber or cardboard spacing washers on the bar bolts, remove and discard them.

Now locate the inside bar protector plate. Mini-saws often have only one bar protector plate, the inside one, and the clutch guard serves as the other. Almost all other saws have two bar protector plates that sandwich the bar and chain. Very

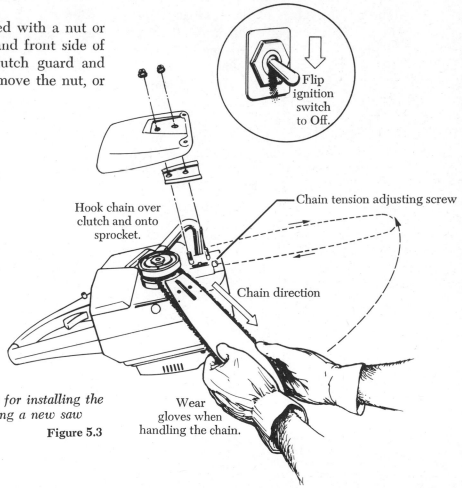

Flip ignition switch to Off.

Chain tension adjusting screw

Hook chain over clutch and onto sprocket.

Chain direction

Wear gloves when handling the chain.

The fundamental procedure for installing the bar and chain when preparing a new saw

Figure 5.3

few saws have none at all so if you don't find one, check your owner's manual. It should be easy to identify the inside plate if there are two. It is the one with more holes in it. One of these holes is for the chain oil. In any case, one will fit over the bolts with the flanges facing the saw's body and the other won't.

Install the inside bar protector plate over the bar bolts with the plate flanges away from the bar and the edges pointing toward the saw's body. Now, straighten any kinks in the chain and lay it out in a loop. The cutting edges of the teeth must face in the direction of the chain rotation. On the bottom of the loop, the teeth must face the engine. On the top of the loop, the teeth must face away from the engine, toward the nose of the bar.

Lay the bar in the loop of chain with the nose pointed away from the saw. Put the chain's drive link tangs into the grooves of the bar so that the chain is snug around the nose and sides of the bar. This will make a loop at the tail of the bar. This loop will go over the sprocket as you install the bar and chain.

Now hold the chain in place on the bar as you pick up the bar and loop the chain over and onto the sprocket. The bar bolts should now be through the mounting slot on the bar. If there is only one bar bolt, there will also be a fixed pin that will come through the long slot in the bar. Turn and fit the bar and chain so that the chain-tensioning pin fits into its proper hole in the bar. The hole will often be distinguished by shape, i.e. a square pin takes a square

hole. In any case, it should be apparent. If necessary, turn the chain-tensioning screw until you can mount the bar properly. Be sure that the bar is mounted flush against the inside bar protector plate and mounting pad. Now, hold the bar flush and place the outside bar protector plate, or the clutch cover/chain guard, over the bar bolts. Replace all washers and nuts and tighten just enough to hold the bar snugly in position. Some saws, notably certain models made by Skil, have the chain-tensioning screw and mechanism built into the outer chain and clutch cover, rather than in the main part of the saw's body. In this case, you have to move the bar as you install the chain cover in order to properly position the chain-tension pin through the hole in the bar. The chain will slip around awkwardly, but it can be done.

An alternate method of installing the cutting attachment is to install the bar first and then put the chain on while the bar is on the saw. You may find that this makes it easier to handle a large bar and chain. To use this method, first turn the chain-tensioning screw until the tension pin is almost all the way back. Then place the bar over the bolts with the tension pin through the proper hole in the bar. Hold the bar in this position while you loop the chain over the sprocket. Then start the chain in the top groove of the bar. Continue thus with the chain until all of the drive link tangs are properly seated in the grooves of the bar. You may have to turn the adjusting screw until the chain is positioned at both ends—over the sprocket and over the nose of the bar. Then replace the outer bar protector plate and the clutch guard and chain/sprocket cover. Tighten the nuts to hold the assembly and proceed to adjust the chain tension as follows.

COLD-TENSIONING

You adjust a cold chain differently than you do a warm chain. Ideally, you should always adjust the chain when it's cold but that's not always possible, as we shall see. In any case, the most important chain adjustment is the cold-tensioning procedure. This first adjustment will determine how well your chain will hold tension later, and how long it will last.

First, be sure the bar-mounting nuts are loose enough to allow the bar to move by hand. For now, we're going to adjust the chain quite snugly. Hold the nose of the bar up as you tighten the chain-adjusting screw with a good long screwdriver that fits the screw. Get the chain as tight as it can be and still move freely along the

bar. Pull the chain in your gloved hand forward and along the top of the bar. Adjust the tensioning screw until the chain is taut but moves without binding. To remove any kinks, snap the chain by pulling it away from the bar and letting it go. Do this several times and, if the chain develops slack, readjust the tension until it is snug. The tie straps should be just touching the bottom of the bar. When all the tie straps are just touching the bar along the entire lower edge of the bar and the chain moves freely, the tension is correct.

While still holding the bar nose up, tighten the bar nuts to lock the cutting attachment securely at this cold setting. Then double-check the tension by moving the chain in the proper direction of rotation. Again, it should fit snugly but should move freely with no binding. When you use the saw you will have to readjust the tension for warm chain as in the next chapter.

You've got it together.

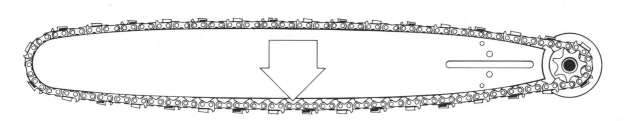

Too much chain sag!
Figure 5.4

Adjusting pins positioned in the corresponding holes in the guide bar

Clutch guard nuts

Bar flush against mounting pad

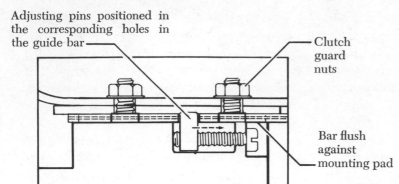

Turn the mounting nuts down until snug but loose enough that the bar can still slide.

Tension the saw chain by turning the screw clockwise while holding up the bar nose.

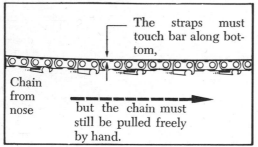

The straps must touch bar along bottom,

Chain from nose

but the chain must still be pulled freely by hand.

This "cold-tension setting" is complete when the clutch guard nuts are tightened securely.

Figure 5.5

INSPECTING YOUR USED SAW FOR WORN PARTS

Sprocket

We've already discussed the air filter and fuel filter. When you bought your used saw, you probably took a good look at the sprocket. If not, you should inspect it now, and new saw owners should inspect the sprocket often. A worn sprocket will ruin a new chain fast, will make it impossible to keep your chain sharp, will cause excessive wear on the bar, and will make your cutting inefficient and unsafe. Check the sprocket carefully. If there are any grooves or scars on it, you'll have to replace it. Chain manufacturers recommend that you change the sprocket with every second chain. The best thing is to start with two chains and alternate them. When you replace the chains, get a new sprocket. You should always have at least one extra sprocket and chain on hand.

REPLACING SPROCKET

One of Parp's few gripes against chain saw manufacturers is their occasional tendency to behave like Detroit's car manufacturers. The whole business of sprocket replacement is a typical example. Chain saw manufacturers understandably want you to visit their authorized repair centers often. Not so understandably, many of them attempt to force you into this by making it seem very difficult to replace your own sprocket. Some companies say, in their official owner's manuals, that you must take your saw to an authorized service outlet to have a sprocket replaced.

All this is because, in order to replace the sprocket, you have to lock the crankshaft against turning. Some companies make this relatively easy. Skil, for example, provides a simple hole in the bottom of the saw below the flywheel. To lock the crankshaft, you insert a small punch or steel rod through the hole and into the flywheel.

The European manufacturers are generally more considerate when it comes to things like this. Jonsereds gets the kudos for a simple and ingenious device they call a counterhold. It's a tool made of shaped, flat steel that locks the crankshaft easily at the clutch side of the machine. Other companies, notably Stihl, provide a free crankshaft-locking screw with every chain saw. To use this kind of device, remove the spark plug and insert the locking screw in the cylinder at the spark plug hole. Screw it in by hand until it butts against the piston. This locks the crankshaft. Professional mechanics often accomplish the same thing by using a spanner wrench to hold the clutch.

Whatever kind of saw you have, there is some easy way to lock the crankshaft. It's not always easy to find out how to do it, however. Parp suggests you simply ask around, for your particular saw, until you find someone who does know how and is willing to tell you. Often the service dealer himself will be willing to do this.

To replace the sprocket, set the ignition switch to OFF. Then remove clutch cover, bar, and chain. Pull out the starter rope far enough to wrap the rope three times around the handle; this protects the rope from breaking when you tighten the clutch. Lock the crankshaft according to the manufacturer's recommended procedure, or use a spanner wrench and socket set. Then remove the clutch nut by turning it *clockwise.* It has a left-hand thread. Then remove the clutch, sprocket bearing, and sprocket from the crankshaft. Take careful note of the exact assembly of all these parts as well as any retaining washers. You can now install your new sprocket.

Before you reassemble your saw, clean the crankshaft, the bearings, and all exposed parts with a clean oil-soaked cloth. You must also repack the clutch bearings with a high-quality waterproof grease. Inspect the bearings carefully and replace if necessary. Put some oil on the crankshaft behind the clutch. Then reassemble in exactly the reverse order of disassembly.

GUIDE BAR

Very often the bar of a used chain saw is worn and needs to be filed to proper shape.

Place the bar in a vice and use a flat file to make the rails of the bar straight, flat, and uniform. When you're done, be sure the chain's drive link tangs still have clearance inside the grooves. The chain should ride on the rails and the tangs should be above the bottom of the groove.

There isn't much you can do, usually, with a badly worn bar. If, however, you happen to be starting a chain saw-related business such as logging or selling firewood, you may want to buy an expensive machine for rebuilding bars and regrinding the grooves, from Specialty Motors, Inc. The address is in the Appendix.

An inexpensive but brand new bar, chain, and sprocket set is far better than a once-high quality cutting attachment that has been ruined. And don't be shocked at your own mistakes. Unfortunately, almost everyone goes through at least one cutting assembly—if not an entire chain saw—before learning good maintenance and uniform filing techniques. That's one good reason to start with a used chain saw.

SPARK PLUG

The spark plug, like many modern mechanical devices, is an amazingly durable item. A new spark plug is also a real bargain but, as long as your saw is running well, you should leave the spark plug in place. It'll let you know when it needs cleaning or, if you like schedules, you can remove, inspect, clean, and regap or replace the spark plug after every 50 hours of use.

If the saw begins to run roughly, remove the spark plug and carefully clean it with a medium-hard hand brush, hand file, or with a hydro-hone process. Never sandblast or powerbrush a spark plug—the residue will ruin your engine. Use a spark plug wrench or a good deep-well socket to remove the spark plug. Do not use any other kind of tool. When you replace the spark plug, start it with your fingers and screw it in by hand to be sure you don't strip the threads. You can tighten it, moderately, with your wrench. After cleaning, set the spark plug gap. Most chain saw spark plugs are gapped either to .025 or to .030. If you're not sure which it should be, call a dealer who sells your brand of saw. A new saw, of course, comes with all specifications in the owner's manual.

To gap a spark plug, you need a high-quality set of feeler gauges. This tool has dozens of uses and is essential for chain saw maintenance and repairs. A feeler gauge is a set of either wire gauges or flat metal or plastic blades of precise and marked thicknesses. The gauges are used for measuring the distances between parts. Whenever you clean or install a spark plug, even a new one, you must set the gap between the electrodes. The gap must be precise.

To set a spark plug gap, insert a feeler gauge of the proper thickness between the electrodes. The gauge must be held straight to get an accurate reading. If your set does not have a blade of the required thickness, use two smaller blades that, combined, add up to the correct thickness. Carefully bend the outside electrode, the L-shaped one, until the feeler blade just touches both electrodes. It should move freely even though it is touching surfaces on both sides. Once the gap is set, be careful not to bump the electrode or disturb the setting.

In an emergency, an old spark plug may sometimes be reused if you clean it well and reset the gap. Often, however, the spark plug will be fouled in such a way that you can't detect the problem visually. Considering how cheap they are, it's always best to install a new plug.

Before you replace your spark plug, test the ignition system as follows. Insert a metal rod or screw into the spark plug boot to connect with the spring or contact inside. Hold this together firmly, with your fingers well protected by the insulation. Hold the rod or screw close to the metal edge of the muffler or some other bare metal contact or engine ground on your saw. Let there be an air gap of about ¼ inch between the rod and the metal. Then with the switch ON, pull the starter rope to crank the engine. (Be sure electronic systems are properly grounded and that the spark can jump. Electronic systems can be ruined if the spark generated has nowhere to go. Protect yourself from shock, since electronic systems pack a tremendous wallop.) You should see a strong blue or white spark. If so, your ignition system is probably good. If the spark is weak, or if there's no spark at all, your ignition system needs service and the problem is probably in the magneto.

When a spark plug fails and must be replaced, you should try to determine the cause. They are pretty tough little gadgets but poor maintenance or improper fuel can kill them fast.

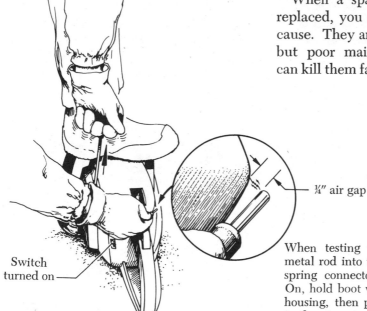

Switch turned on

¼″ air gap

When testing the ignition system, insert a ¼″ metal rod into the spark plug boot to contact the spring connector inside; turn starting switch to On, hold boot with rod in it ¼″ away from metal housing, then pull starter cord to create a spark in the air gap.

Figure 5.6

Look at the electrodes to find the symptoms. If the electrodes are black to dark gray or even tan, the plug is just old and indicates no problems. If the electrodes and the bottom of the plug show heavy oily or sooty black deposits or are heavily carboned, something is wrong. Either the fuel mix is incorrect, or the ignition is weak, or it's the wrong spark plug. If the deposits are light gray and the plug porcelain looks blistered and the electrodes or other parts appear melted or burned, the engine is running too hot. This may be caused by defective engine seals or by an air leak in the fuel system or by an incorrect carburetor setting. If the deposits are yellow and ashy and are bridging parts of the plug, it's very likely that improper ingredients containing additives have been used in the fuel mix.

In any of these unusual situations, you should avoid using the saw until the trouble is identified and corrected.

STARTER ROPE

The hardest part is getting to it—and that's not hard. Disassemble the saw only as much as is needed in order to remove the starter housing. That's where the rope goes in. On some saws, you'll have to remove the front handle. On others, the fuel tank may be built into the starter housing. If so, just be careful not to damage the fuel line; it will have a fitted plastic connection that you can take apart easily once the housing is unscrewed and partly removed from the body of the saw. Take care not to get dirt into the fuel line.

Remove whatever screws are necessary in order to lift off the starter housing assembly. If necessary, remove the front handle. Also, if necessary, disconnect the fuel line. The ignition switch should be OFF.

Inside the housing, you will see the pulley or rotor that the rope attaches to. In the center of this, you see the starter axle. The rotor or pulley is usually secured to the starter axle by a small circular clip. (You must release the tension on the starter spring before attempting to lift off the rotor or pulley. The energy contained in a wound spring is tremendous. Either untie the knot in the starter grip to release the cord, or unwind the cord from the drum.) Hold the pulley down while you remove the clip. Then very carefully lift the rotor ½ inch or less from its proper position. The object is to avoid releasing the starter spring that is just under the pulley. Use a screwdriver to push the spring down firmly and hold it there. Now you can lift the rotor or pulley clear off the axle. Remove the old rope, and thread in a new rope, using a single, simple overhand knot to secure it in the pulley (a figure-eight knot is better if there is room for it in the rotor cavity). Thread the other end out through the cord hole in the housing and through the starter grip. Secure it with a double knot. Wind most of the rope onto the pulley and replace it. Then rotate the pulley until it engages the rewind spring. Then lock it all in place with the circular clip or lock washer.

REWIND SPRING

To replace a rewind spring, remove the rope and pulley as described above. Then dislodge the old spring by giving the back of the housing a sharp blow. Discard the old spring safely, either taped up securely or wrapped in a rag. Put the new spring into place. The proper installation will be obvious from the shape and direction of the die-cast portion of the housing that holds the outer end of the spring. You'll only be able to put it in one way. Just be sure to keep the spring in place, especially after you remove the wire loop or clip that holds it together. If the retainer is a wire loop or clip, it will come off *as you force the spring into place*. Don't remove it first. Rewind springs have tremendous stored energy and release it explosively. Some mechanics prefer to wear eye protection when working with rewind springs. If the spring should come loose, you can still use it. Just install it clockwise from outside to inside and then get the bandages.

When the spring is in place, reassemble the rope pulley and retaining clip as above. Oil the spring lightly with an AFT-type oil. Then set the tension for the spring.

Tensioning Spring

To reset the proper tension, have the rope wound onto the rotor and hold the rotor in place. Pull out the starter handle to put stress on the spring. Then make a loop in the rope inside the housing, using a screwdriver as a lever if necessary. Now wind the rope twice around the pretensioned rotor. The tension is correct if the rotor still has about a half of a turn left after the rope is pulled all the way out. Too much tension will deprive the spring of a long life.

STARTING CLEAN

And speaking of long lives, your chain saw won't have one unless you keep it clean. Not only will dirt and debris get into the engine, as Parp said before, but it will also cause your saw to overheat and it will cause the bar and chain to burn up by preventing proper lubrication.

Since this chapter is serving as an ersatz owner's manual, Parp will detail some basic cleaning procedures here so that you can refer back to them and so you can get started clean.

We found in Chapter One that the chain saw is an air-cooled machine. Every single piece of the shining metal that covers your saw's body is an essential part of the cooling system. So are all those funny looking fins and vents and ports and vanes that you see here and there. All of that has to be kept as clean as possible, inside and outside.

Exhaust Guards and Cooling Fins

All around the starter housing you'll see holes and vents of various sizes and shapes. This whole assembly is intended to allow cooling air to reach the engine and to keep out sawdust and other foreign matter. To clean the assembly, remove the housing from the saw and use an old toothbrush, a wooden scraper, and a soft cleaning brush. When all the sawdust, wood chips, and dirt are scraped out, use a dry, soft cloth to wipe the entire assembly, inside and out. Reach as far as you can and do as good a job as you can. Compressed air is a real help here.

While the housing is off, thoroughly scrape any cooling fins on the cylinder that may be exposed. This is essential. The slightest amount of dirt on those fins will increase the running temperature of the engine dramatically. Similarly, clean all the vanes on the flywheel and any other engine parts that are exposed. Get into the habit of thoroughly cleaning anything you can reach every time you remove or disassemble any part of the saw.

Exhaust System

Back at the other end of the saw is the muffler or spark arrester. You should frequently disassemble and thoroughly clean all the parts in this area.

Remove the screws holding the muffler or exhaust area cover and spark arrester. Clean off all carbon deposits with a scraper, or by washing with the toothbrush and solvent, or by soaking the metal parts in clean solvent.

While the muffler is removed, clean the exhaust ports in the engine, but first slowly pull the starter rope (ignition OFF) until the piston completely covers the exhaust port from inside. You'll be able to see it. Use only a wooden scraper to clean the ports. Anything metal will scratch the

piston or the rings. When you're done, turn the saw so the exhaust ports are down and blow away the dirt and scrapings. Be very careful not to allow any dirt or scrapings or loose particles to stay on the ports or to enter the cylinder. Finish up with the toothbrush, carefully.

Decompression Valve

If your saw is equipped with a decompression valve, it will have to be serviced occasionally. If it fails to close during acceleration, it needs attention. While you're at it, you should also clean the decompression passage. Remove the valve. Remove any loose particles or dirt. Then remove the decompression passage plug screw. Using the starter rope, slowly move the piston until the piston skirt blocks the passage from the inside. Use your wooden scraper to remove all carbon deposits. Then blow away all the dirt and particles. Do not disturb the saw after cleaning until it is fully reassembled. Clean the valve seat and the valve assembly (metal parts only) with solvent. Again, blow away all dirt and particles and reassemble.

Chain Oiler

It's very easy to clean the little hole behind the tail of the bar where the oil comes out. Give a little push on the oiler control to clean any clogs. Then clean out the hole with a bent wire or stick.

It's a good idea periodically to clean the oil strainer screen if your machine has one, and the oil tank itself. If there is an oil strainer screen, it will probably be accessible through an assembly in the side of the oil tank. Drain the oil tank, remove the screws and the cap, gasket, and screen. Clean the screen with kerosene and replace it. Then half-fill the oil tank with kerosene and shake to clean out the tank itself. Fill it up with fresh bar lubricant and test to be sure the system is working properly.

The bar holds the real secret of proper chain lubrication. The holes at the tail of the bar and the groove of the bar itself must be frequently and thoroughly cleaned. Use a bent wire or stick for the holes and a toothbrush for the bar grooves. Be especially careful to get all the oil-soaked sawdust out of the grooves, paying special attention to the tail of the bar. That groove and the funneled tail should be immaculate when you're finished. Those grooves should gleam. And, of course, the chain itself should be carefully cleaned with solvent and soaked in clean 10-weight nondetergent oil after every use. Parp knows it sounds like a lot of trouble. But, as Stihl said recently in one of their in-house publications, "Never buy anything with a handle on it. It means work."

LONG-TERM MAINTENANCE AND STORAGE

Whenever you store your chain saw for a long period of time, 30 days or more, you must protect it against rust and corrosion, inside and out.

The first thing you should do is completely clean your saw and perform all maintenance procedures. Never store a saw that's in bad running condition without correcting the problem first. And since you're going to store your saw after it's cleaned and inspected, drain the fuel tank first.

When your fuel tank is drained, start the saw and run it at idle speed until the engine stops. This will remove almost all the remaining fuel from the fuel system. Fuel stabilizers do not protect a stored saw against corrosion, moisture absorption, or varnish for very long.

When all the fuel has been run out of the system, remove the spark plug and pour a teaspoonful of two-cycle engine oil through the spark plug hole into the combustion chamber. Then pull the starter rope slowly several times to distribute the oil evenly throughout the engine. Replace the spark plug tightly. Drain and clean the chain oil tank.

After sharpening, remove and clean the bar and chain. Store the chain in a covered container completely covered by clean, 10-weight oil. An empty coffee can with a plastic top is ideal for chain storage.

Apply a heavy coat of bar oil over the entire bar and be sure plenty of oil gets into the chain groove. The bar, of course, must be cleaned first. Wrap the bar in heavy paper like butcher's paper, or in cloth.

Clean the outside of your chain saw's body with automotive cleaner and then apply a good protective coat of automotive body wax. If you don't have a saw case, cover and wrap the entire saw with a lightly oiled cloth. Store the saw and the bar in a cool, dry place. Never store near any heat source, chemicals, or fuel supplies.

To take the saw back out of storage, remove the spark plug and briskly pull the starter rope to clear the excess oil out of the cylinder. Clean and gap the spark plug, or install a new spark plug. Fill the fuel and chain lubrication tanks and follow the standard starting procedure.

Even with all the precautions mentioned here, it's best not to store any gasoline power tool longer than 60 days without removing it from storage and working with it for a while. In any case, most of us are glad to get out the old chain saw every month or so and spend a pleasant afternoon cutting wood. Whenever you do that, take your saw all the way through the complete cleaning and maintenance procedures before you store it again. It's the only way to keep a chain saw in good condition.

A FOND MEMORY

Parp has an inexplicably fond memory of one of his early used chain saws, a particularly temperamental model. He was wintering far from any chain saw dealer and badly wanted to keep his little monster running. He used it every day and every day it had to be completely cleaned or it would go on strike.

So there was Parp, long after dark, on a mountain that should have been peaceful, with his old toothbrush and various scrapers and rags and kerosene, surrounded by little tiny chain saw parts, cleaning, cleaning, cleaning. That saw had to be completely disassembled and thoroughly cleaned and reassembled every night. Every night. Parp got so he could even do it sober.

Making It Go • 6

Let's start out with still more attention to the hazards and dangers of operating a chain saw, and to the safety precautions that can help protect you from those hazards.

HAZARDS

The problem is that the many aspects of chain saw work present many different kinds of potential threats to your health and safety. First, of course, is the obvious danger of the cutting attachment itself. It is meant to cut wood. It will also cut meat. When you operate a chain saw you must constantly be alert to the potential of that cutting attachment and you must take whatever precautions you can. Lots of things can go wrong.

Kickback is the most common cause of wounds. It causes 30 percent of all chain saw injuries. Kickback occurs when the chain, as it speeds around the upper part of the nose of the bar, comes into contact with something solid. When the chain is at the upper third of the nose, it can't cut efficiently. Since it can't cut, the power of the chain's movement forces the bar back and up, in the direction of the operator. Whenever you use the nose of the bar,

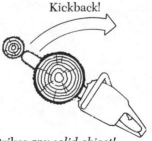

Kickback!

When nose strikes *any solid object!*

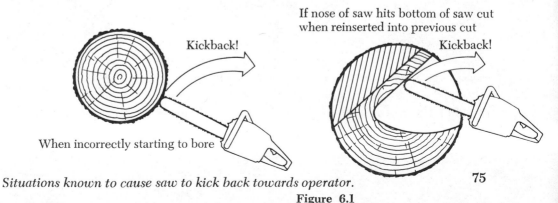

Kickback!

When incorrectly starting to bore

If nose of saw hits bottom of saw cut when reinserted into previous cut

Kickback!

Situations known to cause saw to kick back towards operator.

Figure 6.1

75

either accidentally or intentionally, the risk of kickback is highest. If you have to cut with the nose of the bar for any reason, be sure to start the cut with the lower part of the nose and be sure the saw is running at high speed as the chain touches the work. You should definitely avoid boring or using the nose of the bar before you are familiar with operating chain saws.

There are various anti-kickback devices available for many chain saws. Most of these devices can be back-fitted; in other words, if you own a McCulloch chain saw without a McCulloch chain brake, you can take your saw to a McCulloch dealer and he can install a chain brake for you. This is true of most brands of chain saws, and most anti-kickback devices.

But the best way to avoid kickback is to be aware of its causes and avoid those circumstances. When you operate your chain saw, be alert for kickback at all times. Always cut with your left elbow locked, or with your arm as straight as possible. Cut only one log at a time. Take every precaution to be sure that the nose of your bar does not touch anything. Always cut as close to the engine end of the bar as possible. Use your saw's bumper spikes to grip the wood and provide pivot and balance for your saw.

Another problem caused by the chain itself is the pull or push that occurs as the chain catches in the work at the middle of the bar. Push occurs when the top of the bar hits the work. The chain catches in the work and the saw is forced violently back toward the operator. Similarly, pull occurs

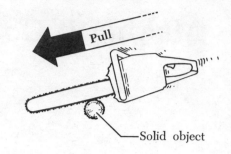

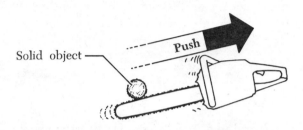

Push and pull reactions
Figure 6.2

when the work is forward of the bumper spike. The chain catches in the work and violently pulls the saw forward until the spike hits the work. These two hazards are most likely to occur if the saw is not running at full speed as the chain hits the work, or if the operator isn't holding the saw firmly.

Certain safety precautions can help prevent chain-caused injuries. Competence and alertness are the operator's best protection. Next is proper clothing. Safety clothing is available, chiefly from the European chain saw manufacturers. Such clothing is limited in its ability to protect the operator if a fast-running chain actually hits the clothing. It can absorb the first shock and give you time to react. Euro-

Safety clothing and gear
Figure 6.3

pean loggers always wear these protective garments. For most of us, however, ordinary snug work clothes are best. You should certainly avoid wearing bulky or loose coats, sweaters, or gloves when you're working with a chain saw. Trousers should be snug and cuffless. Parp prefers ordinary jeans. Those Scandinavian loggers in full dress look like Martians, even if they don't get hurt as often as U.S. loggers do.

The cutting chain can also cause injuries when it breaks. A chain-catching pin built into the saw can protect the operator by stopping the chain before it flies into the body. Hand guards for the front handle and for the rear handle also help. Even when a chain catcher stops the broken chain, the end can still reach the operator's right hand. Many recent chain saw designs incorporate a large guard to protect the right hand. Snug leather gloves can also help. Goggles or face mask and hard hat

protect the operator's eyes, face, and head from flying chain.

In addition to the cutting attachment, other aspects of the chain saw present hazards to the safety and health of the operator. Noise and vibration can be much more serious than they might seem. The best modern chain saws all incorporate designs that are intended to minimize vibration and noise. But you should take further precautions. Any prolonged session of chain saw work increases the chance that vibration and noise will endanger your health. You should, if possible, avoid working for more than six hours in one day. For most of us that's no problem. The wood still has to be split and stacked, and there are valleys to look at, fish to catch, things to think about. And that's good. On those rare occasions when you must operate your saw for extended periods, or if you're about to become a logger, at least be sure

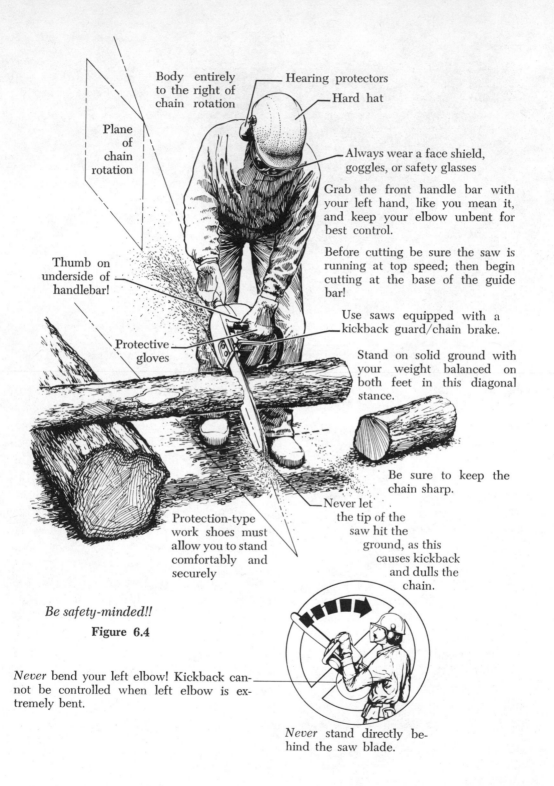

Plane of chain rotation

Body entirely to the right of chain rotation

Hearing protectors

Hard hat

Always wear a face shield, goggles, or safety glasses

Grab the front handle bar with your left hand, like you mean it, and keep your elbow unbent for best control.

Before cutting be sure the saw is running at top speed; then begin cutting at the base of the guide bar!

Use saws equipped with a kickback guard/chain brake.

Stand on solid ground with your weight balanced on both feet in this diagonal stance.

Thumb on underside of handlebar!

Protective gloves

Be sure to keep the chain sharp.

Never let the tip of the saw hit the ground, as this causes kickback and dulls the chain.

Protection-type work shoes must allow you to stand comfortably and securely

Be safety-minded!!

Figure 6.4

Never bend your left elbow! Kickback cannot be controlled when left elbow is extremely bent.

Never stand directly behind the saw blade.

to wear ear protection and take frequent breaks. Parp tells of getting that awful ringing in his ears and not being able to get rid of it for three days. It really is extremely unpleasant and it can do a lot of damage before you know it. Good, inexpensive, professional ear plugs are available from Bailey's (see Appendix).

As for the vibration, when it starts to bother you (after four or five hours or so), stop working. Never operate a chain saw when you're fatigued. Even if there's no danger of "white fingers" in your case, that vibration can cause your muscles to turn to jelly without warning. It's a temporary condition, of course, similar to writer's cramp, but it can be very dangerous if you and your saw are in a bad position, or if kickback catches you by surprise.

Other dangers from the saw itself are related to the fuel. Obviously, the fuel is extremely flammable. Always move your saw at least ten feet from the fueling point before you start it. The heat of the saw and unexpected sparks from the saw or the chain can start a big fire fast and the saw can explode. Don't take that lightly. It has happened. Always store fuel in properly marked containers that are designed for that purpose. Keep the containers tightly sealed and safely stored away from any open fire or heat source. If you spill fuel on your clothing, don't operate your saw until you change. If the fuel cap should come off while you're running your saw, immediately switch the ignition OFF, or kill the engine by choking it to full choke. Never use gasoline for cleaning.

Another potential danger from the fuel is the poisonous exhaust. No one should ever operate a gasoline chain saw in a closed area. The poison gases are odorless, tasteless, and invisible.

Not all of the danger comes from the saw itself. A whole new list comes from the wood. Before you cut any wood, you should study the techniques described in this book, in your owner's manual, and in other available literature. Pay special attention to the pictures and memorize the theories. A lot of research and experience are behind them.

Proper cutting techniques can help protect you from most of the dangers coming from the wood. They can help keep trees from falling in the wrong direction, stressed limbs from snapping your head off, and rolling logs from crushing your legs. But proper cutting techniques can't protect you from the falling limbs that we call widow makers. Obviously, large dead limbs are dangerous. The vibration of your saw in the tree's trunk can cause these large dead limbs to fall down on you. Parp's only suggestion is to avoid cutting under limbs that might fall, or to have a watching helper warn you when one falls. You can rehearse signals to facilitate your escape.

Small falling limbs are the ones that can surprise you with their speed, power, and deadly sharp points. They come down like spears and they can penetrate several inches of frozen ground, or anything else that happens to be in the way. All Parp can say, faintly, is that cutting trees down is dangerous. If you're not up to it, buy logs or slabs and use your chain saw to cut them up on saw bucks. If you are going to cut down trees, you should most certainly wear a hard hat at all times, study the tree, use recommended cutting techniques, and stay alert. When you hear something snap and start to fall, leave your saw and retreat quickly.

MIXING THE FUEL

Two essential ingredients comprise the fuel mixture for gasoline chain saws. They are gasoline and two-cycle motor oil. Never operate a chain saw on gasoline alone. The engine receives its only lubrication from the two-cycle engine oil that you mix with the gasoline. Running a chain saw without oil burns it up and causes its parts to seize.

Start with a container designed and labeled for gasoline. If you're not going to do a lot of cutting, a one-gallon can will probably be enough. If you're beginning a season of wood gathering or a lot of clearing work, you may want a five-gallon container. Parp recommends that the container should be equipped with a removable, flexible pouring spout that is properly fitted with a clean, fine-mesh filter. Clearly relabel the container CHAIN SAW FUEL and avoid using it for anything else.

You should have two clean, rust-free funnels. One is for the fuel and one is for the chain and bar oil. Use these funnels when you fill the saw's fuel and oil tanks. The fuel funnel should be fitted with a filter. Do not switch the funnels. Label or mark them in some permanent way.

The gasoline must be clean, fresh regular-grade gasoline and should be about 85 to 90 octane. Never use white gas or high-octane gasoline, or any other substitute fuel.

You should also know that there is a difference between summer fuel and winter fuel. In the summer, petroleum companies blend their fuel so that it doesn't evaporate quickly in warm temperatures. The tendency of a fuel to evaporate is called volatility. Winter fuel is more volatile than summer fuel in order to make it easier to ignite. If you use summer gasoline after the weather turns cold, your chain saw will be much harder to start. If you use winter gasoline after the weather turns warm, you will lose a great deal to evaporation and your saw will run slightly hotter. The only real control over fuel volatility is to buy it for the season, in small quantities, and keep it stored properly.

The engine oil must be clean, new two-cycle engine oil and really should be exactly the kind and type specified by your saw's manufacturer. Manufacturer's specifications vary widely, especially between United States and European machines. If you have an owner's manual for your saw, you should ignore Parp's mixing instructions and follow your owner's manual to the letter. If you don't have an owner's manual, try to determine the manufacturer's fuel mix recommendations some other way. Call a dealer who sells that kind of saw, or ask the previous owner, or find someone else who knows. As a last resort, you can follow the general guidelines presented here.

For Homelite, Skil, and most other U.S. chain saws, the proper mix is 16:1—that is, 16 parts of gasoline to 1 part two-cycle engine oil labeled SAE-30-MS. If you use so-called premium two-cycle engine oil, you must adjust accordingly. If you use Homelite Premium SAE-40, the proper mix is 32 parts of gasoline to 1 part engine oil. If your saw requires a 16:1 mix, that means you add ½ pint of any SAE-30-MS two-cycle engine oil to each gallon of gasoline. If your saw requires a 16:1 mix and you use a *premium* oil, you add ¼ pint of premium SAE-40 two-cycle engine oil to each gallon of gasoline.

McCulloch chain saws and some other U.S. saws require a 20:1 mix. McCulloch recommends that you use their McCulloch 40:1 Two-Cycle Custom Lubricant. This, again, is a premium two-cycle engine oil and you must adjust the mixture accordingly. If you use that oil, you add 3 ounces of McCulloch 40:1 oil to each gallon of gasoline. If you can't get McCulloch's premium oil, they want you to use a good SAE-40 two-cycle oil. In that case, you add 6 ounces of oil to each gallon of gasoline.

Stihl and most other manufacturers outside the United States specify a 25:1 mixture if you use SAE-30-MS two-cycle engine oil. That means you add ½ pint of SAE-30-MS to each 1½ gallons of gasoline. If you use Stihl's own oil, the proper mix is 40:1. That's 3 ounces of oil to every gallon of gasoline.

Never use anything other than two-cycle engine oil in the engine of a chain saw. Other oils contain additives that turn into glue at high temperatures.

Now that you have your fuel container and two-cycle engine oil, partly fill your container with gasoline. Add the precisely measured amount of oil for the amount of fuel you're mixing, and shake well to mix the oil with this partial quantity of gasoline. Then add the rest of the gasoline. Cap the container and shake it well to thoroughly mix the ingredients, giving an extra few shakes in cold weather. Never attempt to mix the oil and the gasoline in your chain saw's fuel tank.

Your fuel is mixed.

STABILIZING THE FUEL

If you'll only be using your chain saw occasionally, or if you're going to store it for a month or two, you should stabilize the fuel now, while it's still fresh. Unstabilized fuel will separate quite rapidly and can, in time, cause corrosion and gummy deposits. If you're going to store your saw for a long period of time, follow the long-term storage procedure described in this book. Some people do simply stabilize the fuel before storing a saw, but a saw containing stabilized fuel must be started periodically and run for a few minutes to adequately protect the internal parts. Incidentally, if a saw has been sitting more than 20 minutes, always give it a good shake before starting it.

There are several products on the market that help stabilize two-cycle fuel for short periods of storage. These are ideal if you use your saw occasionally but regularly. They keep the oil and gasoline from separating. They do not keep the gasoline fresh, and that's why Parp doesn't recommend them for long-term storage.

Make sure your ignition switch is OFF. Use your clean filter funnel to carefully fill your saw's fuel tank. Close the fuel container, tighten the saw's fuel filler cap securely, and move away from the area. Wipe off your saw to clean away spilled fuel. Your saw is now half-ready to use.

LUBRICATING THE BAR AND CHAIN

Hopefully, you have already soaked your chain in clean 10-weight, nondetergent, nonadditive oil or in commercial bar and chain lubricant. It should be clean, sharp, and well lubricated. Used-saw owners should clean, sharpen, and reclean the chain before using it.

Your bar and chain are now properly installed on your chain saw. See the previous chapter for instructions. The chain's side straps are touching along the bottom edge of the bar but the chain moves easily by hand. Now, squirt enough oil on the bar and chain to thoroughly drench it. Don't get it all over the saw.

Now fill the chain oil tank with oil. Parp urges you to use good chain and bar lubricant. It costs a lot less than a new cutting attachment or a new chain saw.

Never use reclaimed or used oil, or crankcase oil, no matter what anybody tells you. Crankcase oil is worn out and contains shavings, additives, and dirt that can ruin your chain. Parp is starting to repeat himself so he mumbles to refer you back to Chapter One. You don't have to use the bar and chain lubricant that has your saw's brand name on it. Any good bar and chain lubricant will do, and so will any new nondetergent, nonadditive motor oil. In the chain oil tank, use SAE-30 when it's warm (over 40°F.) or SAE-10 when it's colder. In extremely cold weather, mix two parts chain oil with one part kerosene and use 30 percent more lubrication mix per work minute than you would use if it were straight oil. Make it a *habit* always to fill both tanks at the same time. If your chain is being properly lubricated by the oiling system, the oil tank will need filling every time you need to refuel, or more often.

If your saw has a manual oiler or manual override, test it again to be sure it's working. Check the chain tension again, and snap the chain a few times to be sure. If necessary, readjust for proper cold tension.

HOW TO HANDLE A CHAIN SAW

Now practice holding your chain saw and simulate a working stance. Space your feet far enough apart to permit a firm but comfortable balance. Grab the handles as if you mean it. Hold the saw firmly with both hands, with your thumbs curled around the handles. When you're bucking a log or working on the woodpile, you should keep your left elbow locked, or your left arm as straight as possible. Then, if the saw does kick back, you have more strength behind it to protect you. The saw will throw your arm up, on a pivot from your shoulder, instead of collapsing your arm backward, with the saw coming straight at you.

It is not a contradiction to say that you should work close to your saw. Don't be afraid of it. If your right arm is stretched, you will tire quickly and increase the chances of kickback. Hold the saw firmly and work close to it. When it's possible or convenient, as in limbing, keep the work between you and the cutting attachment of your saw.

Practice holding and moving with your saw until you are comfortable doing so. Also, become very familiar with the location of all controls, especially the ignition switch, or kill switch, and the oiler control. If your saw has no ignition switch, or OFF–ON switch, you must kill it by fully choking it. Become very aware of this and get used to reaching that choke control. There will be a lot of times when you'll want to turn that thing off without looking at it. When you're watching a tree fall unexpectedly, for example.

HOW TO START A GASOLINE CHAIN SAW

The fuel tank is full of the proper mixture of regular gasoline and two-cycle engine oil. The oil tank is full of bar and chain lubricant and the oiler is working properly. If it's a new saw or a new chain, you've drenched the chain with additional oil—either with clean 10-weight nondetergent, nonadditive oil or with the same chain and bar lubricant that you put in the tank. The bar and chain are "cold-tensioned." All nuts, bolts, and screws are tight. Your eyes, ears, hands, and head are protected with safety gear. You've moved at least ten feet from the fueling area and further from all fuel containers. No one else is near you and you are on the ground, standing in a safe area free of underbrush, boulders, or stray logs.

Place your saw on a clean piece of ground. Close the choke all the way. That means you pull the choke control button or lever all the way out, or in the direction of the arrow, or toward the word CHOKE. We say, "close the choke" because as you move the choke control, a plate closes off the top of the carburetor. Anyway, close the choke. Usually, this means pulling it.

If your saw has an OFF–ON switch, or ignition switch, or "short-circuit switch" as the Europeans call it, flip it to ON, to START, or away from the word STOP —whatever applies to your saw.

If your saw has a decompression valve, or a DSP valve, or a compression release, move it to the ON or START or OPEN position. In other words, push it in. This control relieves the pressure against the piston and makes it much easier to start larger chain saws.

Almost all modern chain saws are

equipped with a throttle latch. This is a button or lever near the trigger, usually on the right side of the rear handle. On some saws, this latch will automatically half-open the throttle when you push it in. You have to squeeze the throttle control or trigger and then push in the throttle latch button. This locks the trigger at the half-throttle position. If your saw has a trigger inter-lock system, you will have to use your grip to simultaneously depress both the safety catch on the top of the handle, and the trigger. Then you can set the throttle with the throttle latch.

If you have a standard, full-size chain saw with a rear handle, put the toe of your right work boot in the handle and press down, stepping on the handle. If you just kicked loose the throttle latch, reset it again. If yours is a mini-saw, steady the rear of the saw with your right knee. Keep all other parts of the body away from the saw.

Now look around carefully. Be sure the kids or your husband or somebody didn't sneak up on you. Be sure that the cutting attachment of your saw isn't touching any-thing, anyplace.

Take hold of the starter rope handle with your left hand. Get a firm grip with a re-laxed arm. Pull the starter rope out until you feel resistance. Without stopping, use more strength as you meet the resistance and *briskly* pull the rope to give the en-gine a swift, cranking spin. Don't pull the rope *all* the way out and don't let go. Hold onto the rope and it will rewind smoothly. Don't let it snap back.

Proper stance for starting the chain saw after all preliminary steps are taken

Figure 6.5

Repeat this procedure until the engine starts. After the engine has fired, move the choke control to half-choke whether or not the engine kept running after firing. If the engine stalled, repeat the starting pro-cedure with the choke control at half-choke. If the engine continued to run, let it run at half-choke for half a minute and then move the choke to the OPEN position, or all the way in or down. Let the saw warm at half-throttle and half-choke for a few minutes. Do not race the engine.

Normally, a chain saw that has just been fueled will need three to five cranks of the starter rope to prime the engine. In cold weather it might take longer. A chain saw that has run recently will often start with one crank. A warm chain saw, recently operated, will also usually start with the choke open, or OFF, and the throttle trigger at rest, undepressed.

After half a minute or so, be sure the choke is open, or OFF, or away from the words START or CHOKE, or pushed all the way back in. Keep your left hand firmly gripping the front handle. With your right hand, press the trigger a little, just enough to disengage the throttle latch. Release the trigger. Your chain saw is now idling.

If it stalled, try again. If it still won't idle, read ahead to adjust your carburetor according to Parp's instructions, or according to your owner's manual. Then repeat the starting procedure until your chain saw idles properly, without the chain moving.

"Hey! This thing is shaking me to death and it's about to blow up." Yeah. Wait till you see what it does to wood.

FIRST CUT

After your saw is warmed and idling smoothly, turn it off. Prepare a log for some practice cuts to help break in your saw and you. Get a good-sized log, at least 12 inches in diameter, and plan on cutting only part way into it, say a third or so. Don't cut more than half way through the log until you know what you're doing.

Have the log firmly supported on the ground. Let there be no part of the log that is not fully supported. Stand on the uphill side of the log. If your saw or chain is new, add extra oil by hand at this time. Use the same kind of oil that's in your saw's oil tank. Start your saw on the ground, not on the log. Be sure the cutting attachment isn't touching anything. Never start a chain saw with the chain touching wood or resting on a log.

Hold the saw firmly in both hands, with the engine at idle. Bring the cutting attachment up above the log, with the nose of the bar pointing up slightly. Bring the body of the saw down slowly, still at idle, so that the bumper spike engages the wood. The chain should still not be touching the wood.

If you have a manual oiler or manual override, pump it like crazy. At the same time, squeeze the trigger as you pivot the saw on the bumper spike. The engine and the chain must be going full speed when the chain touches the wood. The idea is to coordinate the downward pivot of the cutting attachment with the increasing engine speed so that you hit full speed and power a split second before you hit the wood. That will save the saw from racing "in the air," and will also save you from having the saw pulled violently forward by a slow-running chain.

As you cut, let the saw do most of the work. Don't force the saw into the wood. Pivot the saw on the bumper spike. Keep your left elbow straight but hold the saw firmly, while standing close to it. Use *plenty* of oil. Pump the oiler every ten seconds to break in a new saw. Keep your body just slightly to the left of the plane of chain rotation. Don't be afraid. You are in charge.

As the saw cuts down into the log, the nose of the bar will drop. When the cutting attachment has pivoted below horizontal, so that the nose is lower than the tail of the bar, move the saw so that the bumper spike grips lower on the log. About now you should be a third of the way through the log. Bring the bar up out of the cut very carefully, gradually decreasing engine speed as the bar comes out of the cut. If you accepted Parp's suggestions verbatim, your cutting attachment is not stuck in the log. If your bar is pinched because you cut too far, use a wedge or crowbar to widen the kerf enough to remove the saw. Don't use the bar to pry the saw loose, and don't try to cut your way out. Turn your saw off first so the moving chain isn't damaged by the wedge or bar.

If you didn't pinch the bar, your saw is still running at an idle and is removed from the cut. Without touching it, glance at the chain. If it's sagging, stop now, kill the saw and go on to the next section. If it isn't sagging, repeat the cutting procedure as above at another place on the log. Do this two or three times to heat the saw and the cutting attachment thoroughly. Be sure to use plenty of oil. If you have a manual oiler, pump it every 10 seconds while the chain is cutting. If you have an automatic oiler with a manual override, pump it every 20 seconds. Be sure to keep the saw going full speed. If you cut at less than full speed, the clutch will wear out incredibly quickly. When you remove the saw from the last cut, turn it off.

READJUSTING THE BAR AND CHAIN

Examine your chain while it's still hot.

A hot chain stretches and there should be a slight sag, so that the side straps in the bottom middle are not quite touching the bar. The drive link tangs should be just visible, and riding well up in the groove of the bar.

The best advice is never to adjust the chain while it's still hot. You should let it completely cool. But we can't always take the time we should to do things right.

To tension a warm chain, turn your saw OFF. Pull the chain around the bar and snap it a few times while pumping the manual oiler. Then lay the palm of your glove flat on top of the chain and give it as fast a spin around the bar as you can. If the sag is very slight, side straps almost touching along the bottom rails of the bar, the tension is satisfactory. If it's too tight or too loose, you must set the tension.

Loosen the nuts on the bar bolts just enough to be able to move the bar. Hold the nose of the bar up while you turn the chain-tensioning screw. When the side straps are almost touching at the bottom middle of the bar, the tension is approximately correct. It's difficult accurately to adjust a warm chain. Keep holding the nose of the bar up while you tighten the nuts on the bar bolts.

Instead of adjusting while the chain is hot, take a few minutes to let it cool, if you can. Then simply follow the instructions for cold-tensioning.

There is one rule that no experienced chain saw operator ever breaks. Never touch the chain or attempt to adjust tension while the engine is running.

HOW TO ADJUST THE CARBURETOR

You will need to adjust your chain saw's carburetor in any of the following situations:

1. While breaking in a new chain saw.

2. After breaking in a chain saw. (After about an hour of actual cutting time with a new chain saw.)

3. If the chain rotates when the saw is at idle.

4. If the saw stalls easily or fails to idle smoothly.

5. If the saw runs rough at high speed.

6. At an altitude different from the saw's place of manufacture, or after a change in altitude.

If your chain saw is new, it certainly should have had proper preliminary carburetor adjustment on delivery. If it didn't, let your dealer do it for you, if possible. Otherwise, follow your owner's manual or the steps below.

If your new saw bears a notice that the carburetor is altered for high-altitude operation, and you are going to a low-altitude area, arrange for your dealer to change the carburetor's circuit plate or jet size. A high-altitude saw will overheat at low altitudes.

If your saw was manufactured for low-altitude operation and you will be operating it at high altitude, have your dealer or mechanic determine the necessary carburetor changes. You may need to replace the standard circuit plate with a high-altitude circuit plate.

Chain saw carburetors are all very much alike. There can be some differences, especially between U.S. and European caburetors. However, almost all European chain saws imported to the United States have U.S.-make carburetors.

All chain saw carburetors are adjustable in different ways, from the outside, and any chain saw owner can and must occasionally perform these adjustments. You make the adjustments by altering two or three screws, depending on the saw.

The three screws are universally labeled as below:

• H is the high-speed mixture needle adjustment. (This is the screw that may be "missing" on some saws.)

• L is the low-speed mixture needle adjustment.

• I or T is the idle or throttle speed adjustment.

The H or high-speed mixture needle is the main adjustment screw and affects the mixture of fuel at speeds faster than idle. The L, or low-speed mixture needle, adjusts the fuel mixture at idle and is also called the idle *mixture* screw. Do not confuse it with the I or T which is always a large and predominant screw. The I or T alters the idle speed of the engine but does not affect the fuel mixture itself. It is the screw you will adjust most often. It is less delicate and crucial than either of the *mixture* adjustments.

The normal preliminary setting for these

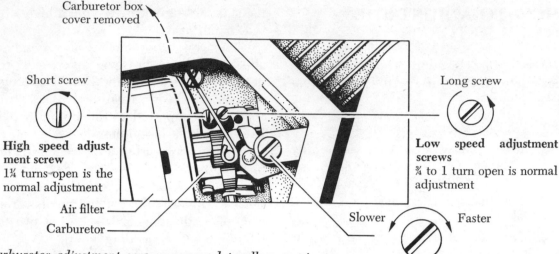

Carburetor box cover removed

Short screw

High speed adjust-ment screw
1¼ turns open is the normal adjustment

Air filter

Carburetor

Long screw

Low speed adjustment screws
¾ to 1 turn open is normal adjustment

Slower   Faster

Idle speed adjustment screw
The engine should idle without stopping and without moving the chain.

Carburetor adjustment screws are used to allow maximum performance and lowest fuel consumption. Check adjustments only on a warm engine and with a clean air filter. Remember, the air filter easily becomes clogged with sawdust, resulting in a loss in power, so clean it daily.

Figure 6.6

adjustments on U.S. and Canadian saws, and most European saws, is as follows. Make all of these adjustments with extreme caution. It's easy to damage a carburetor by turning the mixture adjustment screws too far. Use a fine screwdriver that fits. Make these adjustments with the engine warm and the air filter clean.

1. Gently turn the low-speed mixture needle (L) all the way in, until it just barely touches the seat. Then turn it back one full turn.

2. Do the same with the high-speed mixture needle (H).

3. Start the engine and allow it to idle.

4. Carefully turn the idle speed adjustment screw (I or T) until the saw idles smoothly. If the chain rotates at idle,

turn the idle speed adjustment screw counterclockwise until the engine idles smoothly with the chain motionless. If the saw stalls and fails to idle, turn the idle-speed screw clockwise half a turn at a time and each time restart the engine until it idles properly.

5. If the engine tends to stall when you increase the speed, open the low-speed needle (L) slightly.

6. If the engine tends to race and adjusting the idle-speed screw (Step 4) does not correct the situation, open the high-speed needle (H) slightly. If that makes the exhaust smoky under acceleration, you've gone too far. Start all over with Step 1.

After all these adjustments, the high-speed needle (H) must be at least ¾ of a turn out from the bottom, and the low-speed needle (L) must be at least one full turn out from the bottom. If these needles are adjusted closer than this, the engine will race and damage may occur.

In the event that all attempts fail and the above steps don't result in proper operation at idle and acceleration, you may have one of the carburetors that require different preliminary settings. If your saw is a European-make mini-saw, *decrease* the initial settings of the high-speed and low-speed needles (H and L) by ⅛ to ¼ turn.

If your saw is a U.S.-make mini-saw, *increase* the initial setting of the idle *mixture* adjusting screw by ¼ turn. This applies only if your U.S. mini-saw has only one screw for adjusting idle mixture and has a fixed high-speed needle that cannot be adjusted by the operator.

Chain saw carburetors are quite universal and repair or rebuilding kits are readily available. When your carburetor needs it, you'll be able to rebuild it yourself. The job is tedious but not difficult provided you obtain a high-quality kit from the carburetor's manufacturer and carefully follow all instructions.

Your carburetor should perform perfectly, with minor adjustments, as long as you keep dirt from falling into it and keep the air filter clean. Change the filter frequently. If you move from one altitude to another, simply follow the adjustment procedure as above, from the beginning, unless your saw bears a notice that your carburetor was especially built for certain altitude conditions.

MAKE A SAWBUCK AND CUT SOME FIREWOOD

After you've practiced cutting for a while, and still haven't cut any wood for your stoves, you will want to make a sawbuck to help make your wood cutting easier. It will also lead you into the best kind of wood cutting for a beginner so that you learn one or two of the basic principles of the most common cutting techniques. You can only learn to cut wood by experience.

It's best to have a helper for this project. When you're finished, the helper will be replaced by the completed project. A sawbuck is all the help you really need for working on your woodpile or for doing easy cutting jobs.

Parp assumes you'll be using your chain saw primarily for firewood and that you already have some wood around.

Find some logs about four inches in diameter and several feet long. Until your sawbuck is finished, you'll need some way to hold one end of each log while you cut the other. That's where the helper comes in. If no helper is available, you can use heavier logs to hold one end of the work.

Place the first log so that most of its weight is resting on a flat surface and one end is extending, unsupported, at about the level of your knees or a little higher. Get the log level with the ground. Have your helper hold the supported end of the log firmly, or brace it with heavier logs. Be sure it's braced sufficiently to prevent that end of the log from moving when you apply your chain saw to the other end.

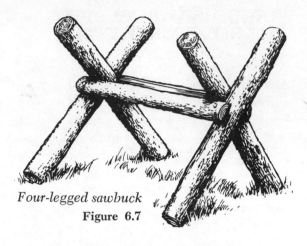

Four-legged sawbuck
Figure 6.7

Working in this manner and observing all safety precautions, cut two pieces of log, each three feet long. Since the logs are only four inches in diameter, you should be able to cut straight through from the top of the log without the log splitting. Be careful of the cut pieces as they fall. Don't try to catch them. If you move or stop work a few minutes, or pause to adjust the work, turn your saw OFF.

If you wish, you can notch the logs for assembly. See Chapter Eleven for the best notching techniques. Leave about a foot of log above the notches.

Now assemble the two three-foot pieces into an X, crossed at about a foot from the top. You can lash them together with rawhide or heavy cord or you can fasten them together with two long spikes or lag screws. This is the simplest and best sawbuck to use for cutting firewood on your woodpile. It can also be easily transported or stored.

You can make the same kind of sawbuck using 2 x 6 lumber cut to three-foot lengths and fastened together with one bolt and a wing nut. That makes it easy to fold it up for storage. If you do this, however, be very careful when you apply your chain saw to the lumber. If you're inexperienced, the chain can catch in the edges of the lumber and give you a bad pull.

To use your sawbuck, just stand it up and let the work form its third leg. It will look like an elongated tripod. Cut on the free side of the sawbuck, of course, and avoid hitting it with any part of your saw. As you cut logs into splitting lengths, set your saw down and lift the end of the log to move the sawbuck back. Work on smaller logs while you're gaining experi-

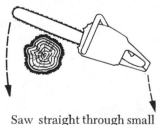

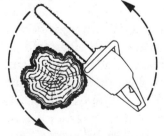

When cutting firewood-length pieces from a raised end, there is no stress, so undercutting isn't necessary.

Figure 6.8

Saw straight through small logs.

Pivot saw at bumper for thicker logs.

ence. Logs that are about eight inches in diameter are easy to handle and will provide good firewood. Work on the uphill side of the wood, watch out for falling pieces, and don't move with a running chain saw. Follow all safety rules and use plenty of oil.

Just when you start to realize that you're really having fun, you'll discover that you already have a large pile of cut firewood. When your arms get tired, take a long break or stop for the day.

WORKING WITH A GASOLINE CHAIN SAW

Lots of people say that a chain saw is only as safe as its operator. Parp hates other people's clichés as much as he does his own and that particular one is false, anyway. A chain saw is somewhat more dangerous than its operator.

You can take all the precautions and follow all the rules and you can have accidents. The risk is minimized, but it's still there. That's why it's a good idea always to work with a partner, or have someone nearby who will hear you scream if something horrible happens. Any sensible woodsperson will recognize that as a good idea.

But a good woodsperson, even though sensible, is primarily a woodsperson, and part of the reason you have a gasoline chain saw is the need for solitude and self-reliance. When the saw is turned off and it's time for a break, you want to look up at the blue sky and the gray rock, or you want to feel the closeness of silent snow falling, or you want to drowse on the warm grass. You don't want to talk to anyone, or to be distracted from contemplation by the proximity of another, no matter how quiet or compatible he or she may be.

So chances are you'll be alone with your chain saw often. Carry a whistle, a good loud one. If you get pinned by a tree, or cut yourself, or break a leg, you can blast on the whistle. Chances are someone will hear you, almost wherever you are. If you're further away than that, you probably know what you're doing and, in any case, you knew the chance you were taking and figured it was worth it. Parp certainly understands. Anyway, you have your first-aid kit, and your whistle or your gun, and you are as careful as you can reasonably be. After that, it's up to everything else.

When you're actually in the woods and working with your chain saw, the hardest thing to manage is your footing. Try to shut off the saw whenever you move, and try to clear any area where you're going to work. It is impossible to maintain a difficult balance and use a chain saw at the same time.

If you drive off to the woods with your pickup truck to get a load of logs, take along all the tools you're likely to need. Take extra fuel and all the extra maintenance parts, such as air filters, spark plugs, and an extra chain and sprocket. Start with a sharp chain and a clean saw. After every hour of work, stop and service your saw. That means you fill the fuel and oil tanks, clean or change the air filter, touch up the chain, and wipe off the saw. If you discover or suspect any problem with your chain saw, stop working until the problem is diagnosed and corrected.

Take frequent breaks. Listen to the living trees around you and don't cut them off for firewood. They are sentient creatures. They are also the tongues of the wind and the earth.

WORKING WITH AN ELECTRIC CHAIN SAW

Everything Parp has said about safety applies to electric chain saws as well. In addition, don't use more than one extension cord and don't stand in or on anything wet. Don't work in wet weather. Disconnect the saw before making any adjustments or performing any maintenance. Sell it to a neighbor or trade it in on a gasoline chain saw while it's still new —unless you can afford to keep it for those special cutting sessions indoors or in the backyard. It is quiet, anyway.

WOODCARVING, HOLE DIGGING, BRUSH CUTTING, AND AIR BROOMING

The potential uses for a chain saw and for its power unit are literally endless. New attachments appear every year, and very few disappear. Not all chain saws are capable of driving all of the possible attachments but even some of the smallest minisaws can be fitted to a hedge-trimmer and most saws can be adapted to a cut-off attachment.

A two-person earth auger is available for several saws. Stihl offers a two-person earth auger in sizes ranging from 3½ inches to 14 inches in diameter by 27½ inches long plus 20-inch or 39-inch extensions. This tool is used mainly for digging post holes and planting trees. If you live in a rural area where septic tanks are used, you can make $100 per day, or more, doing soil percolation tests with one of these augers. You can even dig wells. You can certainly earn some cash digging fence post holes for your neighbors.

Other augers are available to fit almost all chain saws. Atom Industries offers a wide choice of reversible augers for wood, steel, and masonry in many sizes.

Many chain saw power heads can be used to drive earth, ice, or wood drills. A large variety of long-reach brush cutters are available that make extensive clearing jobs easy. Cut-off attachments have circular blades that can cut concrete, stone, asphalt, tile, steel, and cast iron. They're often used by rescue crews and fire departments, but they can have more homey applications, too.

The Fred A. Lewis Company of Medford, Oregon, offers an incredibly tough winch that can be attached to an old reconditioned chain saw that may be too heavy for cutting wood by present standards.

There are so many different lumber-making attachments and mills for use with chain saws that we'd leave our main subject if we tried to review them all. The

MAKING IT GO   93

largest and most elaborate are from Granberg Industries. The least expensive is from Haddon Tools.

Wood carving with a chain saw requires no special attachment and has become very popular. Loggers first developed chain saw wood carving as a diversion, but it quickly became a featured aspect of logging carnivals all over the world. Some of the things carved by loggers rival the totem poles of the northwestern Indians in design and intricacy. If you ever have a chance to visit a logging carnival, don't pass it up.

Parp's spies tell him that a new and useful-sounding chain saw attachment will soon appear from one of the large manufacturers. It's called an air broom. The idea is that you'll be able to use it quickly to remove all those leaves and sticks that pack themselves under porches and in hedges and fences where you could spend a week picking them out by hand.

The fact that all these useful and dependable attachments are available and can be powered by a chain saw power head makes a good, strong saw even more desirable. It's a lot easier to spend $200 on a great tool that does a lot of different jobs than to spend $90 on a piece of discount junk that will collapse in three months without doing anything.

We're a long way from the trees now.

SELLING FIREWOOD

It occurs to most folks as soon as they get a chain saw. If you have a chain saw and if you have a National Forest nearby, and if you can get a firewood dealer's permit from the Forest Service, and if you can find a good large amount of dead wood, standing or down, and if you have a truck, and if you split the wood with an ax before you sell it, and if you hav a city nearby where you can sell it for top money, you'll make about $1.50 per hour or so. Parp mumbles something about letting them freeze in the dark.

If you add a partner that you share everything with anyway, or can pay off with wood and home cooking, you can up the income a little. To really show a fair profit, you have to increase your production. That can be done by adding more tools to your process.

The tool that makes the most difference is a wood splitter. There are many different kinds of wood splitters * and just about everything has been tried. The standard and traditional machine is the hydraulic wood splitter. A complete description would be off the subject, but these machines are operated by an engine that uses hydraulics to drive a plunger toward a steel wedge. You place a section of log on the track and release the plunger. It drives the wood against the wedge with a constant pressure sufficient to split the log.

There are many variations on the hydraulic wood splitter. Some are driven by connecting them to a tractor engine. Some come with the hydraulics set-up but with-

* See "A Review of Log Splitting Devices" by David Kimball in the fall, 1976, issue of *Wood Burning Quarterly*. An informative and amusing article.

*Hydraulic log
splitter*

Figure 6.9

out an engine. Most come complete with a special engine designed for the application and complete hydraulic rigging. A hydraulic splitter is the fastest method of splitting wood so far, but these machines are incredibly expensive. The general price range, currently, is from about $600 to about $3,000 and going up fast. A practical and dependable hydraulic wood splitter runs right around $1,000. You'd have to have a pretty brisk firewood business, especially considering the maintenance and service a hydraulic splitter requires, to justify that price.

A few years ago, a couple of people were trying to get started making hydraulic splitters in a garage near Taos, New Mexico. They were making the splitters one at a time, by hand. Amazing? What happened next is more amazing.

One of the partners met a man in Colorado who had an idea for a new kind of splitter. He was not in a position to develop fully or to market the idea himself so he made a deal with the folks from Taos. It was a good deal for everybody concerned.

In a short time, Taos Equipment Company (same two folks) were producing the now famous Stickler. The Stickler is a log splitter that presently costs less than $200, is totally maintenance free, has no moving parts, improves with age, and is a permanent tool that never wears out and never needs to be replaced. Now that's amazing. It's even safe to use, with reasonable care.

The Stickler is a long, pointed, screw-like device that bolts to the rear wheel of a motor vehicle. You jack up the vehicle and bolt the Stickler to the left rear wheel. With the engine running and the transmission in forward, you push a log onto the point of the Stickler. It splits it with a screwlike motion that sharpens the threads on the Stickler automatically. That's why it's maintenance free.

The Stickler comes with an emergency cut-off switch that has a magnet to hold it within reach on the vehicle. It makes you feel better, but the folks from Taos do demonstrations in which they run their gloves and jackets all around the Stickler to show how hard it is to get stickled. If you end up between the wedge and the plunger of a hydraulic splitter, there's no question about what happens.

To end this rave review, let's mention that the Stickler is just a little slower than a hydraulic splitter, depending on the operators, but is capable of splitting a cord of wood per hour. That means you can maybe make $75 a day, or so. And there are millions of cords of unused dead firewood left in the National Forests every year.

The Stickler can split any North American wood except southern sweet gum, black gum, and the rare Florida ironwood. It does not damage or wear out or overheat the vehicle used. The price of a running but unroadworthy vehicle, combined with the price of the Stickler, is far less than the price of any hydraulic splitter Parp has ever heard about.

It was invented by Mr. Arthur Stickler of Gunnison, Colorado.

Stickler

Figure 6.10

CHAIN SAW FOR HIRE

There are a lot of other ways to add to your income with your chain saw. Many towns don't have an established tree-trimming service and it's easier to get into this field than you may think. Sometimes it's not so easy to stay in, and other times it's real hard to get out.

Most areas require that you have a tree surgeon's license from either the county or the state but these requirements are often not enforced in small or medium-sized towns. And often it's easy to get a license, although some areas require a knowledge of forestry, which indeed you should have.

In areas that are hit by frequent wind storms, the official county chain saw will often be overworked. If you're on emergency call, you may get to go out before dawn and use your chain saw to remove downed trees or trim storm-damaged branches.

If you find yourself doing this very often, or if you want to try trimming trees for pay, you'll soon need some special equipment, safety clothing, and liability insurance. There are only a few areas of the country where you'll find forestry supply stores, but you can mail-order anything no matter where you live. Zip Penn and Bailey's both carry some of this professional equipment, but Bailey's is the real specialty house and they have everything.

Some of the things you might need someday are a tree jack ($300 to $1,500); a winch; logger's first-aid kit (Welsh, from Bailey's); face mask, respirator, or particle mask; chain saw chaps; climbing gear including belt ($70), spurs ($30), leg pads ($25), and climber's rope ($1 per foot).

The best safety clothing is from Scandinavia and isn't too easy to find. The Raket safety suit, however, is becoming available in nonlogging areas and will probably soon be carried by the mail-order houses. The Raket suit has four interwoven layers of glass fiber spaced by wadded polyester and covered on both sides with Enstex, a very tough, thin, and flexible sheeting. These Finnish suits are very flexible and comfortable and they're even trim-fitting. Not something you'd want to wear in the backyard, but tough, professional protection—even, to some degree, from serious chain saw wounds.

Raket also makes those incredible logger's safety helmets with ear protectors and bulletproof face masks.

Standard's logger's leggings or aprons are less elaborate and expensive and nearly as good. They are also more available. You can order either for about $40 from Zip Penn. These garments are designed to absorb the first shock of a chain saw blow and even to stop the chain, somewhat, until you have time to react.

Where the hell are those trees, anyway?

Keeping It Sharp • 7

A few months ago, Barnacle Parp enjoyed a three-day visit from his old friend, Three-Legged Muskrat. Muskrat, as you may have guessed, has spent a little too much time around chain saws. Anyway, Parp and Muskrat spent most of the hours of that three-day visit discussing various aspects and theories of correct chain-sharpening procedures, exceptions, possibilities, and discoveries. There wasn't nearly enough time and the discussion was soon interrupted by a thousand miles of Interstate 80, to be continued when this book is finished.

But Muskrat's murmurings of cold steel and fine filing linger in Parp's mind as a reminder that not everyone shares his attitudes toward chain maintenance.

Muskrat likes to put his whole saw in a vise, clamped at the bar. Then he carefully and expertly hand files each cutter and each depth gauge with a perfect coordination between the steel, his hand, and his eye. And he does get it pretty close. He takes off just enough steel to sharpen each tooth. He watches for burrs and removes them with a touch like breath. He can see exactly what he's doing, he knows exactly what he wants, and he is very patient.

Muskrat is a real old-fashioned expert who has worked with sharp steel all his life. When he is finished sharpening a chain by hand, it's almost as perfect as a chain that was machine-sharpened by an average person.

And the machine doesn't have to plug into anything in order to be precise. Several companies now produce variations on the basic clamp-on, hand-powered chain file guide that Parp recommends. Certainly the best-known and most widely available clamp-on sharpener is the Granberg FILE-N-JOINT.

A LIST OF TOOLS

In order to sharpen and service saw chain, you need these tools and supplies:

1. Spare chain loops or chain in reels.
2. File guide or chain grinder.
3. Depth gauge or jointer.
4. Chain file or grinding wheel to fit your chain.
5. Flat safety edge file for depth gauges.
6. Solvent or kerosene.
7. Clean oil for chain bath.
8. Measuring rule or inexpensive set of calipers.
9. Chain breaker.

10. Chain rivet spinner.
11. Flat eight-inch file for bar.
12. Grease.
13. Grease gun for roller nose or sprocket nose bars.
14. Toothbrush.
15. Rags.
16. Gloves.
17. Hand tools.

TYPES OF SAW CHAIN

There are several types of saw chain available from many manufacturers. No manufacturer produces all of the different kinds of chain there are, but any particular chain generally can be replaced with a chain made by a different company. No matter what kind or size of chain saw you have, a variety of chains are available to fit it. You do not always have to use the brand or type of chain that comes with your saw, but generally you do have to use the same size in a replacement chain unless you change the bar and sprocket as well.

Chipper cutter   Chisel cutter

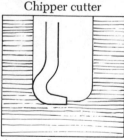 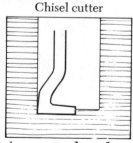

A round or chipper-type cutter must sever the same wood fiber several times as it passes through the wood.

A square-shaped or chisel cutter severs the wood fiber with a single pass. This cutter means faster cutting action and less work for both engine and operator.

Figure 7.1

There are four basic shapes of saw chain cutter. The first and most common is the *rounded chipper* shape that helped facilitate the development of the modern, lightweight chain saw. The round chipper tooth is traditional and became the standard before industry engineers realized that a squared cutter is more efficient. A rounded cutter has advantages: it's easy to maintain and may be sharpened with a round file. Most consumer saws are supplied with chipper chain as standard equipment.

When the engineers realized the advantages of squared cutters, a compromise design appeared. Commonly called *semichisel*, this cutter has a semisquare cutting edge. It may be sharpened with a round file.

The most efficient shape for a cutter is the *squared chisel* shape that is common on professional saws. This shape removes more wood with each cut and never cuts the same cross grain twice. It is more difficult to maintain since the filing must be done very precisely with a flat, bevel-edge chisel file. However, if you use a clamp-on file guide, this chain is as easy to sharpen as chipper chain.

The fourth cutter shape is used only on saws that have a built-in automatic sharpening system (such as the Oregon 80 type). This cutter has a distinctive clawlike shape that sticks up to allow the stone in the automatic sharpener to reach the cutting edges. It is difficult to maintain properly and cuts less efficiently than the manufacturers claim. It is also more expensive.

Although Parp recommends a clamp-on file guide for all saw chains, the rounded chipper and semi-chisel types may be sharpened with the common hand-held file guide. All authorities agree that a clamp-on sharpener is mandatory for true chisel chains. One of the best recent developments in chain is the Stihl Oilomatic Injected saw chain. This chain features oil channels built into the drive links. The channels carry oil directly to the rivets and other chain parts. The cutters are a semi-chisel design that cut as efficiently as chisel cutters but can be easily sharpened with a round file according to chipper chain sharpening methods. Also, the chain arrives prestretched and very sharp, eliminating many break-in problems.

Any of the various types of saw chain may be linked in different ways for special purposes. These differences are usually created by increasing or decreasing the space between the cutters, or by changing the shape of the side strap or drive link as in most safety chains. Sometimes the shape of the depth gauge is altered, also.

Standard chain in any type consists of cutters separated by one set of side straps sandwiching the drive links. The side straps are nearly flat across the top, and the distance between any two cutters is only slightly more than the length of a side strap. This configuration is by far the most practical and all others are for special uses only.

Skip chain is a special-purpose chain with greater distance between the cutters. This is achieved by adding extra side straps. This allows for maximum chip clearance and less engine strain when using very long guide bars in soft woods.

Ripping chain is designed for speed in ripping logs into boards and is ideal for use with a lumber-making attachment or mill.

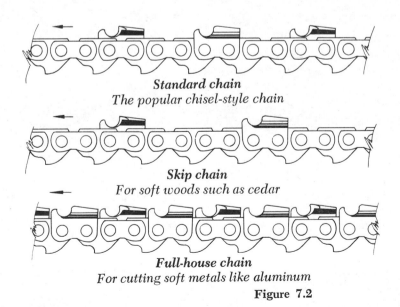

Standard chain
The popular chisel-style chain

Skip chain
For soft woods such as cedar

Full-house chain
For cutting soft metals like aluminum

Figure 7.2

For this chain, chipper-style cutters are reground to make narrow cuts. The design is based on the first chains developed for the early chain saws. They were called scratcher chains and they worked more like pionted slicers than like the chip-cutting teeth of today's chain. Ripping chain should not be used for cross cuts, as in bucking or felling.

Full house chain is a very limited special-purpose chain designed for cutting soft metals like aluminum. As the name implies, there is no spacing between the cutters. Full house chain should not be used on wood.

Safety chain came about when the chain manufacturers themselves tried to do something about kickback. This chain utilizes specially designed side straps or drive links. Depending on the manufacturer, either the drive link or the side strap has a high curve or rise that is supposed to keep the chain from catching in the wood. These chains are considerably less efficient than other designs and greatly increase the amount of time it takes to cut a log. They do somewhat decrease the effect of kickback, but not its frequency. Parp believes that a combination of caution and a chain brake are the operator's best protection against kickback.

PARTS OF A SAW CHAIN

Let's take a closer look at the parts of a chain and how those parts work so we can have a better idea how to keep them working properly.

The cutter is the most obvious part of any saw chain. It's the sharp part, of course, and it's the part that sticks up above the rest of the chain.

But the cutter itself has "parts," even though it is all of one piece. The depth gauge is the little tooth right in front of the cutting edge. As the chain moves through the wood, the depth gauge guides the wood up into the cutter at exactly the right height. If the depth gauge is too high, the chain won't cut. If it's too low, the cutter will be choked by the wood and will catch. The relationship between the cutter and the depth gauge may vary somewhat under certain circumstances, but the relationship must remain fairly close to the original factory design or the chain won't cut properly. Notice that if you make a change in either the cutter or the depth gauge, you change their relationship. As a cutter is sharpened, it becomes lower. A cutter can be sharpened only two or three times, lightly, before the depth gauge must be lowered. If you tend to file the cutters more than lightly, the depth gauges must be filed down and reshaped every time you sharpen the chain. The depth gauges must, of course, always be lower than the cutting edge.

Between the depth gauge and the cutting edge is the gullet of the cutter. As the name implies, this gullet affects the chain's ability to eat wood. When the cutting edge chips or chisels a bite of wood, the bite is forced out of the cutter between the cutting edge and the back of the gullet. Gullets should be cleaned with a round

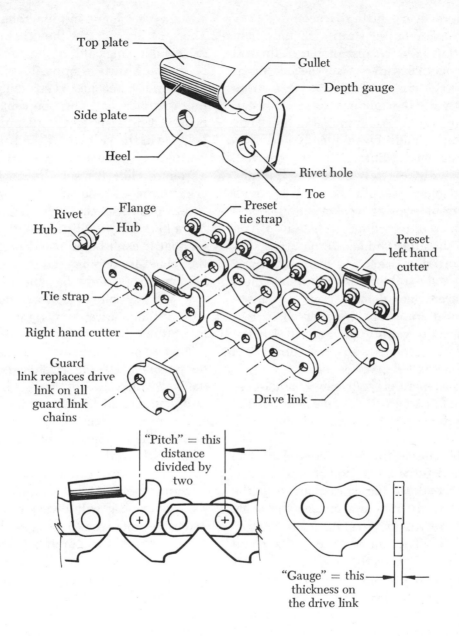

Parts of the chain.
Figure 7.3

file before every fifth sharpening.

Side straps or tie straps are the chain pieces that link the rest of the chain and hold it together with rivets. The side straps endure the most friction and wear from contact with the guide bar. As a result, they are subject to burrs and breakage. Side straps should be frequently and carefully examined. Burrs can be removed, lightly, with a safety-edge file but any other damage should be viewed as a symptom of error or weakness and should be diagnosed according to the Saw Chain Troubleshooting Guide. If tie straps become burred or peened to the point where they are tight and inflexible, the chain must be replaced. Such damage is always caused by a worn sprocket, improper chain tension, or badly worn guide bar rails. If the cause isn't corrected, any new chain will quickly be ruined in operation.

The last part of your saw chain is the drive link. Again, the name tells us the primary function of this part—it drives the chain.

As the engine turns the crankshaft, the crankshaft turns a sprocket or gear assembly attached to the crankshaft. As the sprocket turns, its parts engage the drive links of the chain to rotate it around the guide bar. The sprocket and the chain must match perfectly and as soon as sprocket wear becomes serious, symptoms will appear on the drive links. Always replace your sprocket before that happens.

At first glance, anyone might think that the hook at the front of the drive links is the part engaged by the sprocket. But,

of course, it's going in the wrong direction. The sprocket engages the other side of the drive link tang, and pushes against most of the tang surface opposite the hook. If that surface becomes damaged, the drive link is ruined and must be replaced. The hook is a different story. Its only job is to help clean the grooves of the bar. Once in a while you'll have to clean the hook with a round file. Be sure to maintain the original shape of the hook.

As a chain wears, it stretches. If a chain has a long life, it will frequently stretch so far that it can't be adjusted properly with the chain-tensioning screw. Before this happens, you might be able to remove a link in the chain to correct the problem. At that time, however, you must check the fit of the chain with the sprocket. If it doesn't match correctly, the chain should be replaced. If the stretched chain has damaged the sprocket, it must be replaced also, and should be in any case.

The entire cutting attachment is a precise assembly and all of its parts must meet and work together perfectly. No damage or wear can be isolated without affecting the rest of the attachment. Any damage or wear will always result in more extensive and worse damage that affects other, seemingly unrelated parts. Any noticeable damage or wear must be thoroughly diagnosed and corrected from effect to cause before continuing to use the saw. Never operate a chain saw that is working less than perfectly or shows any signs of mechanical damage whatsoever. It is dangerous.

CHAIN MAINTENANCE TOOLS

It is possible to sharpen a chain with a hand-held file and no file guide at all. It is also possible to lower the depth gauges without a jointer. It is even possible to do so reasonably accurately, but most of us are not that expert. In any case, it's faster and easier to use the proper tools.

There are three basic kinds of file guide. The first is a hand-held device usually called a *file holder*. Really, it looks as if all it does is hold the file, but it does have etched guide lines. As you file, you keep the guide lines parallel with the bar. This helps you maintain the correct filing angle. File holders are the cheapest and most commonly available tools for sharpening chain.

Clamp-on file guides are actually designed as guides, not holders. These tools, or jigs, are available in many sizes, styles, and price ranges. The better designs clamp on to the guide bar and include a small vise that locks a portion of the chain. The filing angle is set with a dial and then locked in place. The file is held by a swing that you move away from the chain on the backstroke. These tools are extremely accurate, versatile, and durable. Get one, says Parp.

If you want to be professional about it, you can get an *electric chain grinder*. These, of course, are more expensive, but they are still among the real bargains in our high-octane economy. If you use chain saws almost constantly, or if you sell fire-

wood, or if you want to service chain saws in your shop, you'll want an electric chain grinder. There are many different models available, ranging from about $60 to about $1,500, and more. VIP Industries has developed a "portable" model that operates off your vehicle's generator. It can also be set up in a shop and is designed to sharpen the chain while it is still on the saw.

Bell Industries, formerly Nielson, offers one grinder in the mid-price range, the K245, that will sharpen any chipper or chisel chain that requires a round file, and is capable of sharpening an unbroken loop chain as small as six inches. Most other shop grinders are more limited, and shorter

Bell saw chain grinder
Figure 7.4

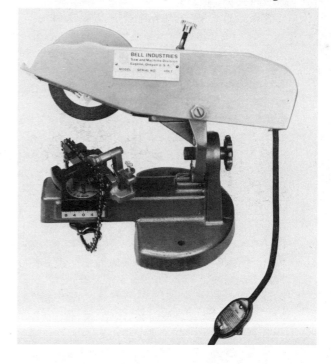

chains must be broken in order to fit them onto the filing vise. Bell's K245 is a very high-quality, dependable machine.

A professional-quality chain grinder does the most accurate sharpening and is much easier and faster than any other sharpener. It is a good investment for a small business.

The only electric shop grinder that will accurately sharpen true chisel chain is the Silvey SDM4. It is the most precise chain grinder in the world and it will outlive almost any other machine. Understandably, it costs about $1,400. You can lease one from Bailey's, however, for a small monthly fee. Silvey also makes a chipper chain shop grinder that allows you to leave your chain on the bar. Silvey's are definitely professional models and the round chain grinder costs about $330.

Since you must lower the depth gauges as you file back the cutters, you need a jointer to measure the relative heights of the depth gauges and the cutters. There are many simple devices available for this crucial measurement, and none of them is very expensive. The most common ones are called filemates or gaugits. These are usually fixed tools for specific chains and you need a different one for each size chain. Zip Penn sells a more versatile model, simply called Depth Gauge (part number Z-570), that has five different settings controlled with a dial. This particular tool has the advantage of allowing you to adjust the depth for different cutting operations and conditions, as well as for available chains. Priced at less than two six-packs, it's the most expensive saw

chain jointer Parp knows of. The Depth Gauge is pocket-size and accurate.

Sometimes a chain stretches so far that it cannot be adjusted to the proper tension. Sometimes a chain breaks. Sometimes a single link is damaged by abrasion, or cracks due to an unusual weakness. In these and other cases, you need chain repair tools. Adequate tools to do each of the required jobs come in both shop models and hand or toolbox models.

The cheapest combination of chain repair tools is a ball-peen hammer and a punch for removing rivets. The job can be done with these simple tools, but more specialized tools make the work easier and more accurate.

For breaking chain, all sorts of pocket *chain breakers* are commonly available at very low cost. These consist of a small anvil with channels to fit various chain sizes. You still use a hammer and punch to remove the rivets but the anvil holds the chain part steady and the channel forms a slot for the punched-out rivet. After the old part is removed, you put the replacement in position on the chain breaker and form the rivet heads with your hammer.

A somewhat more expensive but far superior hand tool is the Granberg BREAK-N-MEND. This tool, as its name implies, both removes the rivets and replaces them. It even restores old rivets so they may be reused. It forms perfect rivet heads without hammering and includes an adjustable anvil for all chain sizes, as well as a rivet spinner. Parp suggests it is the best all-around chain repair tool for most chain saw users.

If you use a chain saw professionally, or if you have a shop to work in, or if you want to make a profit on sharpening, selling, and repairing chain, you will want the shop tools designed to repair chains professionally. Many companies manufacture specialized bench tools for this purpose. *Bench spinners* and *bench breakers* are a one-time investment and they are tools that anyone can use with ease and accuracy. These tools have cost about $30 each for many years. They'll probably go up soon. They are hand-powered precision tools that can be set up anywhere by bolting them to a bench and they are exactly what the biggest professional shops use. Nothing better has appeared as yet, and probably never will. Again, Granberg's chain shop tools are among the best and most available.

We have reviewed, briefly, the main types of tools available for sharpening, jointing, breaking, and mending saw chain. Since damaged sprockets cannot be repaired, the only remaining component of the cutting attachment is the bar itself. For almost all chain saw users, it's far easier and cheaper to replace a badly worn or damaged bar than to repair it. In almost all cases, that's Parp's advice. But there are machines available to renew or rebuild guide bars. In some cases, one of these machines can be a good addition to a large professional chain saw shop. Specialty Motors manufactures the best of these, called Barshop. It is capable of turning large, old guide bars into small, new ones. It can also regroove worn bars, square rails, close grooves to standard size, and polish like new. It costs about $1,000. With new guide bar prices as low as $20, this machine would have to work long and hard to pay for itself. It is, of course, a very high-quality product.

It's a lot of fun to do things professionally. Many companies sell saw chain in reels of 25, 50, or 100 feet. With a bench grinder, a bench breaker, and a bench spinner and a few reels of chain, anyone can easily set up a nice little chain sales and repair shop. You can produce custom chains to fit any saw, for any cutting purpose. Or you can buy one reel of chain to fit your own saw and have the comfortable feeling of being well stocked for a long time. And you can equip a truck with professional tools to do the same jobs on location. A chain-maintenance business is one of the easiest and least expensive to establish and maintain, and it's a fast route to prestige in any wood-oriented community.

Files and File Sizes

The cutters of a chain saw require special files made especially for sharpening saw chain. Most chains on most saws are still the chipper type and require a round file of the correct size. All hardwares carry these special round files and they are always called chain saw files. They are not tapered and they are not rat-tails. Before you do anything to a saw chain, find out exactly what kind and size file that chain requires and never attempt to use anything else. Using the wrong file will always ruin a chain.

The best source of information about your chain is your owner's manual. If you don't have an owner's manual, or if the chain on your saw is different from the original, you will be able to determine what file you need from the Filing Chart.

HOW TO SHARPEN A SAW CHAIN

Chipper Chain

The question Parp hears most is, "When should I sharpen my chain saw?" And you know the answer. "Anytime it needs it." Your chain needs sharpening whenever the chain cuts slowly, whenever you notice that cutting is becoming more difficult, and whenever fine sawdust is pulled from the cut, rather than a proper chip. And that can happen incredibly often, depending on a number of factors. The best method is to keep it sharp and never let it get dull.

So first of all you start with a sharp chain. If your chain is new, it might not need sharpening. Might not. Chain manufacturers often sharpen the cutters before assembling the chain. When individual chains are assembled, the cutters are usually dulled in the process. A few manufacturers avoid this problem in various ways but it's something to watch for.

If your chain is dull or used or doesn't seem quite as sharp as it should be, have it sharpened professionally before you use it. Then you'll start sharp and with proper

angles, and it'll be easier to keep it that way.

In use, a chain normally needs touching up after every hour of cutting. It needs complete sharpening after 8 hours of cutting. Any chain should be professionally sharpened, by you or by someone else, every 40 hours of cutting. That's why you should get the best sharpening equipment you can and learn how to use it expertly. It'll save you a lot of time and money.

To sharpen a chipper chain, first examine the chain carefully for damage. Any damaged links should be replaced before you sharpen the rest of the chain. If you're leaving the chain on the bar, adjust the chain to the correct tension. It's better to use a vise. If you have a clamp-on file guide, it should have a built-in vise to hold the chain steady. If not, remove the chain from the bar and put it in a vise for sharpening. No one can accurately sharpen a loose chain.

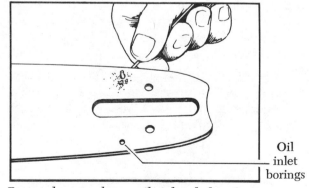

Oil inlet borings

Remember to keep oil inlet holes from clogging with sawdust by using a hooked wire.

Figure 7.5

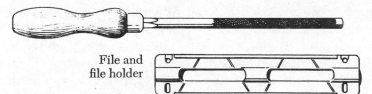

File and
file holder

Hold file level. Press against the cutter and make two or three light strokes forward.

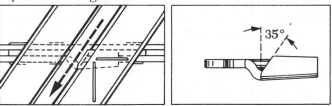

Always file from inside to outside of cutter.

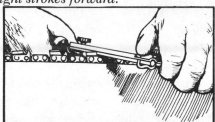

Keep angle index parallel with chain to keep top plates even.

35°

File your way around chain, doing one direction of filing before switching sides.

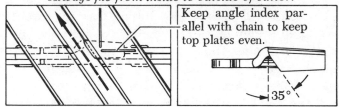

35°

Finish filing the other cutters from the other side.

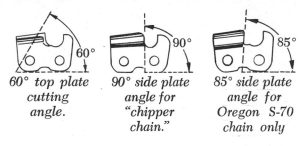

60° top plate
cutting
angle.

90° side plate
angle for
"chipper
chain."

85° side plate
angle for
Oregon S-70
chain only

Figure 7.6

Next, find the shortest cutter tooth on your chain. Use a ruler to measure them. In order to cut straight and to avoid excess wear and stretch, each cutter and depth gauge must be the same. Uniformity is the important factor in chain saw performance. The shortest or lowest or smallest cutter must be sharpened first and then all the others must be filed to match it exactly. The short cutter serves as a guide for filing all the other cutters.

When you've found the shortest cutter, attach or align your file guide so the file will move from the inside of the cutter to the outside. Set your file guide to the correct filing angle. In almost all cases, the correct angle is 35° and all file guides carry a 35° indicator for chipper chain. The 35° angle is best for chipper chain in all woods and adjustments for specific woods should involve the height of the depth gauge and not the top plate or cutter angle. The only exception applies to saws used only in frozen hardwood. If you cut only hardwoods that are always frozen, file your cutters at 30°. If you use one chain in the winter and another in the summer, sharpen your winter chain at 30° and your summer chain at 35°.

Hold the file level or with the handle no more than 5° lower than tip of the file. Do not change the angle of the file from horizontal. Keep it constantly level or maintain a constant 5° from horizontal. About ⅕ to ⅒ of the file's diameter should be above the cutter. File lightly with a steady hand. Only remove enough steel to sharpen the tooth or correct any problems.

Move the file away from the cutter on the backstroke. In other words, file only on the forward stroke, from the inside to the outside. Check your work carefully and proceed slowly until you are familiar with the entire operation. If the chain has previously been sharpened incorrectly or at the wrong angle, or if the cutter has been damaged by abrasion, file until all problems disappear.

When the shortest cutter is sharp, loosen your file guide or vise and move the chain to align the next cutter on the same side of the chain. Proceed in this way until all the cutters on one side are sharp and uniform. Then remove and reverse your file guide, or turn the saw around to sharpen the cutters on the other side. Again, use that first, shortest tooth as a guide to sharpen the others. All teeth on both sides must be uniform. If the cutters on one side are shorter than on the other side, the saw will cut crooked.

Note that you measure a cutter by measuring the *length* of its top plate. If all the top plates are the same length, they will also be the same height. That's what the ruler is for.

When you've sharpened all the cutters, examine them again for uniformity and for burrs. If you find slight burrs on the cutting edges, rub them with a piece of wood to smooth them out. If the burrs are more than slight, you held the file at too much of an angle. You should also compare your cutters with those pictured in this book or a new cutter. The angles should be the same.

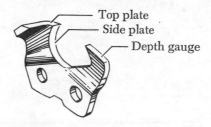

Preset left-hand cutter.

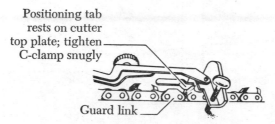

Top plate
Side plate
Depth gauge

Positioning tab
rests on cutter
top plate; tighten
C-clamp snugly

Guard link

Place top file cutter midway on bar.

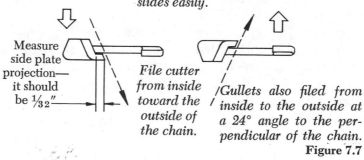

Support legs
fit over middle
of cutter to be
filed

Hold file
level at all
times

File depth gauge until file slides easily.

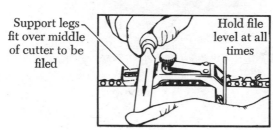

Measure
side plate
projection—
it should
be $\frac{1}{32}$"

*File cutter
from inside
toward the
outside of
the chain.*

*Gullets also filed from
inside to the outside at
a 24° angle to the per-
pendicular of the chain.*

Figure 7.7

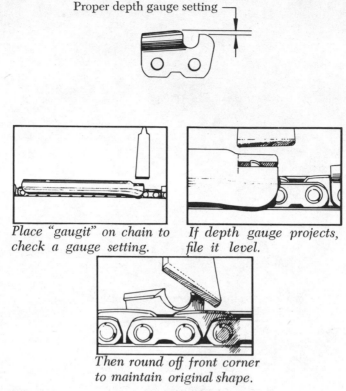

Place "gaugit" on chain to
check a gauge setting.

If depth gauge projects,
file it level.

Then round off front corner
to maintain original shape.

Figure 7.8

After you've finished all the cutters, check the height of the depth gauges with your jointer or filemate. If the depth gauges project up through the slot in your jointer, file them level. Use only a flat safety-edge file and leave the jointer in place as you file each depth gauge. Be careful not to hit the cutters or other chain parts. Even with a safety-edge file, you can damage a cutter if you hit it.

When all depth gauges are level and uniform, round off the front corners to restore the original shape. All depth gauges should be filed every second or third sharpening and they should be checked before cutting with a used chain. Do not "sharpen" depth gauges: they do no cutting themselves. Their sole purpose is to determine the depth at which the cutters cut the wood.

Finally, clean and lightly file the drive link tangs on the front face only to restore the cleaning hook. Be sure to maintain the exact original shape of the tangs. Their purpose is to clean the grooves of your guide bar.

Parp has repeatedly recommended Granberg's FILE-N-JOINT throughout this book. Granberg is the leader in research and development of chain saw tools and accessories. Their products are very high quality and are dependable, accurate, and reasonable. Although there are a number of clamp-on sharpeners available, Parp says this one is presently by far the best and is so much better that he suggests you carefully compare the quality and accuracy of any other clamp-on sharpener. The only guides that compare favorably are those made and sold by the European saw manufacturers and they're usually hard to find.

To use the FILE-N-JOINT, leave the chain on the bar and place the FILE-N-JOINT over the bar and chain. The sharpener clamps to the bar, but first you have to tighten the screw that adjusts and locks the chain clamp just above the tops of the rivets in the chain. The chain clamp acts as a vise. Then hold the FILE-N-JOINT parallel to the bar and tighten it with the inside knob.

Now loosen the chain vise screw slightly, so the chain is held snugly but still moves freely. Then move a cutter into position against the chain stop and set the angle dial to the correct top plate angle for your chain. Another dial adjusts the height so that $\frac{1}{5}$ to $\frac{1}{10}$ of the circumference of the file protrudes above the cutter. This is one of the reasons that a FILE-N-JOINT is so much better than hand filing, especially for

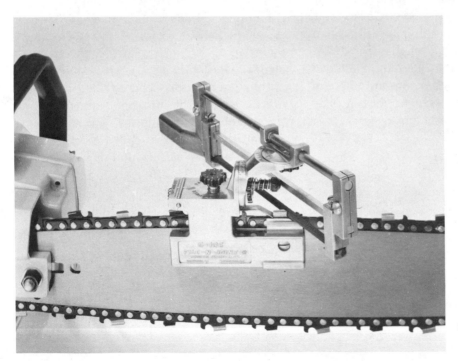

Granberg File-N-Joint
Figure 7.9

the beginner. It's very hard to hand-hold a file at the correct height and the correct angle at the same time.

You can then adjust the cutter length-stop to match your shortest cutter. Since you use the same setting to file all the cutters, all the cutters are precisely uniform in height and top plate angle.

Then you can use your FILE-N-JOINT to set your depth gauges with the same accuracy. Use the settings and angles recommended in your owner's manual or in this chapter. Be sure to make all settings with care, or this tool will consistently repeat your errors.

Micro Chisel, Super Chisel, and Semi-Chisel Types Requiring Round File

Most of the instructions for sharpening chipper chain apply to these chains as well. However, instead of holding or setting your file level, or with the handle 5° below horizontal, hold the handle of the file lower than the tip to maintain a constant angle of 10° from horizontal. The correct top plate angle for all semi-chisel chains of ¼" or

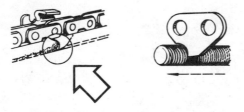

Keep drive link tangs sharp. Use a round file to sharpen the tang so it will clean the bar groove of sawdust.

Figure 7.10

.325" pitch is 30°. The correct angle for Stihl Supermatic chain is also 30°. The angle for all other chain sizes of these types is 35°, just as it was for chipper chain. Also lower the depth gauges in the same manner as chipper chain. Clean and lightly file drive link tangs, using a round file to restore the front hook section only.

Chisel Chain

A true chisel chain can be identified by a perfectly flat top plate and a squared cutting edge. If the edge looks round inside, it's either a chipper chain or a semi-chisel chain and should be sharpened with a round file, as above.

Before every fifth sharpening, clean the gullets of chisel chain with a round file that would fit a chisel cutter of the same pitch.

Chipper chains are sharpened with a beveled chisel-chain file. Use a file guide to maintain a 20° top plate angle on new chains. Gradually increase this angle as the cutters get shorter. The beveled corner of the file should fit into the front corner of the cutter and you file downward, against the cutting edge instead of toward it. The file moves from the front toward the rear of the cutter. Depth gauges are lowered just as they are for chipper chains. Clean and lightly file the drive link tangs with a round file to maintain original shape.

"Barracuda" Chain, Oregon 80 Chain and Power Sharp Chain

These are the chains installed on saws equipped with "automatic" or built-in self-sharpening devices. The cutters and depth

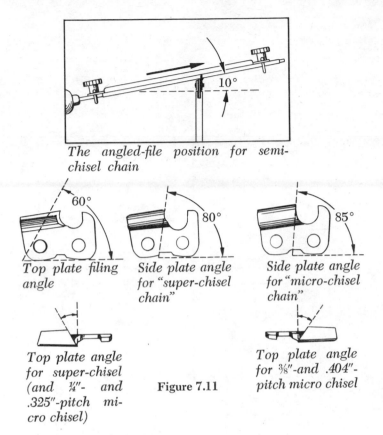

The angled-file position for semi-chisel chain

60°

Top plate filing angle

80°

Side plate angle for "super-chisel chain"

85°

Side plate angle for "micro-chisel chain"

Top plate angle for super-chisel (and ¼"- and .325"-pitch micro chisel)

Figure 7.11

Top plate angle for ⅜"-and .404"-pitch micro chisel

gauges are set at extreme angles to meet the sharpening stone in the system. The side plates of these chains must be hand sharpened since the built-in stone doesn't touch them. Manufacturers generally recommend that the side plates be hand sharpened about every fifth time the system is used. Parp says sharpen them every other time.

Be sure to keep your sharpening system clean and free of sawdust. You should always remove packed sawdust from the inside housing before using the system. Use a screwdriver or long wooden scraper.

To adjust the stone, turn the adjusting screw until sparks appear during sharpening. Be sure to retract the stone when not sharpening.

On all automatic sharpening systems there is a handle, knob, or some other device for oscillating the stone. You must use this control to oscillate the stone for the entire duration of the sharpening operation. This control moves the stone from side to side to fully sharpen both left and right cutters.

Whenever you replace your chain, always install a new sharpening stone and

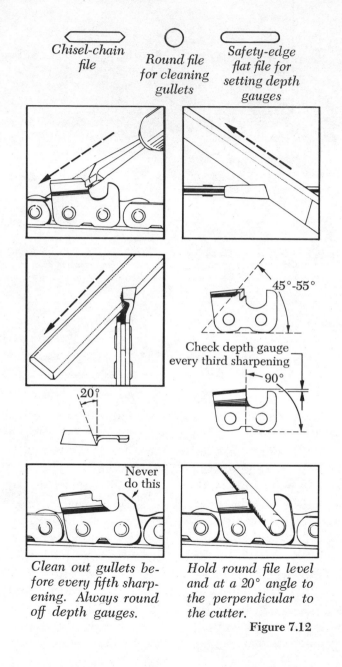

Chisel-chain file

Round file for cleaning gullets

Safety-edge flat file for setting depth gauges

45°-55°

Check depth gauge every third sharpening

90°

20°

Never do this

Clean out gullets be-fore every fifth sharp-ening. Always round off depth gauges.

Hold round file level and at a 20° angle to the perpendicular to the cutter.

Figure 7.12

tighten the locking nut securely.

When you hand-sharpen Oregon 80 chain, be sure to use an Oregon 80 Top File Guide on the top plates, and a FILE-N-JOINT, set at 24°, on the side plates. Use a flat file with the 80 Top File Guide and a 5 mm round chain saw file for the side plate. File top plates and depth gauges level with the 80 Top File Guide. The 80 Top File Guide automatically determines the correct filing angle and depth. Round off the front corners of the depth gauges to maintain the original shape.

SPECIAL FILING

You might decide to experiment with your depth gauges. If you do, you should have more than one chain and you should determine each chain's specific application. You should then avoid using a chain under conditions inconsistent with its special filing.

For example, if you live in an area of hardwood forests and long cold winters, you might want a winter, or frozen hardwood chain. To get efficient work from your chain under these conditions, leave your depth gauges higher than specified in the chart. If you want to change a ⅜-inch-pitch chipper chain into a hardwood winter chain, stop filing the depth gauges until they are somewhat higher than .020″. Try .017″ for a while, or gradually decrease the depth gauge distance until the cutting seems most efficient. A frozen hardwood chipper chain should also be filed at a top plate angle of 30°, rather than 35°.

For a summer softwood chain, lower your depth gauges .02″ or .03″ lower than the specified setting.

If you use your saw with a mill, or do a lot of ripping as when building a cabin, you should have a special chain just for ripping. The best way to get one is to special-order it, either from your dealer or from Zip Penn or Bailey's. You can also make your own ripping chain. Refile the cutters on any chain to a 15° top plate angle instead of the standard 35°. Do the filing with a round file no matter what type chain you use.

When a saw chain is used only for ripping, *change the filing angles as shown above.*

When a chisel chain is used for boring, *taper the tails of the cutters to increase boring efficiency.*

Figure 7.13

A very specialized chain is *boring* chain, a type seldom used by nonprofessionals. To make one, file the tails of the cutters of a chisel chain at a 45° angle. The little boring that most of us ever need to do can easily be done with a standard chain. For that matter, a standard chain will serve most of us very well most of the time. Parp has cut a lot of frozen wood and has never bothered to file a winter chain. It's always sunny where a Parp lives.

CHAIN REPAIRS

Once you have the tools, correct chain repair procedures are quite obvious. Again, though, uniformity is a major concern. When you replace any chain part, it must be filed to match all the other corresponding parts in your particular chain. The bottom edges of side straps and cutters ride on the guide bar rails and therefore wear down in use. New parts must be filed to match before they are installed. Drive link tangs must similarly be filed to match the rest of the chain.

Granberg's BREAK-N-MEND is a dependable and accurate combination hand tool that breaks chain, restores old rivets, and spins new rivet heads. To use it to remove rivets, place the side link between the movable anvils and adjust the knurled nut to fit lightly. The sides of the drive link (center link) rest on top of the anvils. You then adjust the tension of the punch by turning the knurled nut in the handle. Then squeeze the handle to punch out the rivet. That breaks the chain so you can replace the damaged parts.

The first anvil of the BREAK-N-MEND is a spinning anvil that allows you to re-shape a used rivet. Place the old rivet in the recess of the spinning anvil, head up, and squeeze the handle. The rivet comes out looking new.

To reassemble the chain, place the new pieces and the rivet into the recess of the spinning anvil, rivet head down. Adjust the pressure and close the handle to form a new rivet head. A little oil makes the spinning easier. File the new parts to match the corresponding worn parts of your chain.

If you use a pocket chain breaker or some other kind of anvil, place the damaged section of your chain over the channel that fits

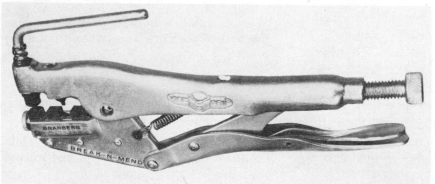

Granberg Break-N-Mend

Figure 7.14

Right	Wrong

Fit chain into the smallest slot of chain breaker so cutter is on top. Punch out rivets of damaged part.

Figure 7.15

your chain. Place the chain on the breaker so that the affected cutter is on top, not underneath (figure 7.15). Use a punch to knock out the rivet. Be sure not to use

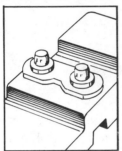 

Put preset part on flat surface.

Install chain on the new part.

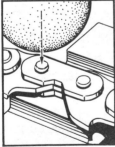 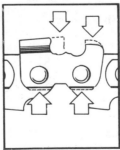

The dimple on the strap faces out. Form rivet head with round hammer.

Figure 7.16

File off bottom of new part to match worn parts. Then file new cutter back to match worn cutters.

excessive force. Drive from the cutter to the side strap underneath. File the new parts to match the corresponding worn parts of your chain. *Cutter top plates and depth gauges should be filed after assembling the chain, but the bottoms of cutters and tie straps must be filed first.* Put the new part in position on a flat part in your chain repair tool and install the chain over it. Form rivet heads with a ball-peen hammer, or a rock.

GUIDE BAR MAINTENANCE

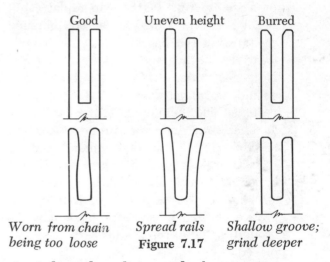

Worn from chain being too loose

Spread rails

Figure 7.17

Shallow groove; grind deeper

As indicated earlier, guide bar grooves should be thoroughly cleaned often. Use a toothbrush as much as possible but if the dirt or pitch is hard you can remove it with the end of a file, a wooden scraper, or the guide bar scraper on your filemate. Whenever you remove your bar, turn it over. Rotating a bar distributes the wear evenly and helps prevent the grooves from getting wider on one side. Guide bars should be separately oiled after cleaning.

As your bar gets older, check frequently to determine drive link tang clearance. The tangs must not touch the bottom of the grooves. The chain rides with the shoulders of the tie straps and cutters on the rails of the bar, not with the tangs scraping the bottoms of the grooves.

If a saw gets hung up or pinched in a cut, the rails can be pinched together and cracks or splits will sometimes occur on the guide rails. If they're small you can weld them if the bar doesn't have hardened rails or a stellite tip. It's best to replace, but slight bends or kinks can be straightened by pressing the bar or by laying it on a hard, flat surface and pounding it lightly. Note that the grooves at the tail of the bar should be funnel-shaped. If they become flattened, file them open with a flat file.

When your guide bar rails become rough or worn, lightly file them smooth with a flat file. Take care to file them evenly and be sure to check drive link tang clearance afterwards. If the tangs bottom in the groove, the bar must be professionally reground or else replaced. Parp says replaced.

Roller nose or sprocket nose bars must be greased daily. That's daily, every time you use the saw, even if it's for two hours. Clean the nose and the grease holes and pump the grease with a needle-nose grease gun. Keep pumping until grease comes out all around the roller. Watch the sides of your roller nose for burrs and remove them with a flat file. Disposable chain saw

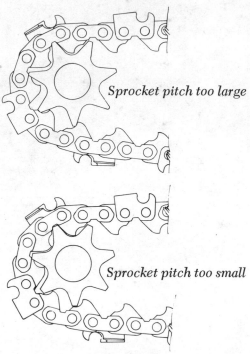

Sprocket pitch too large

Sprocket pitch too small

Figure 7.18

grease guns are available from your dealer or from the mail-order houses.

Whenever you work with your bar or chain, be sure to check and clean the oil holes carefully.

Sprockets

Never install a new chain on a worn sprocket. Sprockets are set to the same pitch as chain and must match perfectly for good performance. Gauges are available for measuring sprocket pitch. If you use plenty of lubrication in your cutting, if you keep all cutting attachment parts clean and properly filed, and if your chain, bar, and sprocket match correctly, and correct chain tension has been maintained, each sprocket should last through two chains. Any time you change chain sizes or types, you must also change the sprocket, even if the old one is still in good shape. Many companies sell sets that consist of bar, chain, and sprocket. Parp says that's the best way to renew your cutting attachment. See the Troubleshooting Guide in the Appendix for sprocket-related cutting problems. Grease the sprocket bearings every time you remove your sprocket.

Since both chains and sprockets change with wear, the most economical solution is to start with one new sprocket and two or three new chains. Alternate the chains to keep the wear equal. In this way, the sprocket and the chains will age together and the sprocket should last through as long as the chains do. When you replace the chains, replace the sprocket at the same time.

Touching Up on the Job

If you work steadily at cutting, even the best softwood will take the edge off a chain in an hour or two. To extend that time, as well as bar and chain life, use plenty of oil. Always watch for grit or sand in the bark, as abrasive material dulls a chain very quickly.

Whenever you take a break, check the edges of your cutters. You can easily and quickly restore them to near perfect with two or three light passes of a file in a file holder. Be careful to maintain the correct angles. Depth gauges rarely need lowering in the course of a day's work.

TROUBLESHOOTING

Occasionally, in one of your periodic examinations of your chain, you might find a problem with some part, such as a cutter. When you do, compare the problem part to the Saw Chain Troubleshooting Guide on pages 122-23. You should be able to identify the problem and thus discover its probable cause and remedy.

But not all cutting problems are immediately apparent, especially if chain saws are new to you. It's impossible completely to cover all the potential problems in a book, but if you experience a performance problem, try to identify it from the following paragraphs.

Chain cuts crooked, cuts at angle, engine drags: If your bar and sprocket are in good shape, these problems are caused by filing the cutters at different angles or by inconsistent filing pressure from tooth to tooth. A chain that is sharper or longer on one side will pull to that side. Refile to restore uniform cutters and reset the depth gauges. Check bar rails and tang clearance.

Chain dulls quickly: The most common cause of this problem is thin or feathered cutting edges caused by holding the file handle too low or by pressing down too hard on the file. A misaligned, worn, or wrong-pitch sprocket will also cause the chain to wear or dull quickly. Check sprocket for wear and correct size. Refile cutters using lighter strokes with file level or at a slighter angle, no more than $5°$ from horizontal. Also check and lower depth gauges, and check chain tension often.

Chain has been filed but won't cut; powders wood instead of chipping it: Blunt cutting edges produced by holding the file too high on the face of the tooth, or by holding handle too high. Refile with a clamp-on file guide.

Chain binds, requires pressure to cut: Incorrect top plate angle caused by holding the file at an incorrect angle (less than 35°) or height (producing backslope) or by letting it drift during filing stroke. Depth gauges left too high will also cause this condition. Refile with steady hand.

Chain overheats, scrapes wood instead of cutting: If you're using sufficient oil, this problem is usually caused by a back slope of the cutters. This happens when you hold the handle of the file too low, while simultaneously filing too high on the tooth. Have the chain reground professionally.

Chain grabs and jerks, cuts rough: This is caused by a forward hook on the cutters produced by excessive downward filing pressure with tip of file too high on the tooth. Have the chain reground professionally.

Cutters dig too far into wood, or take only thin slices: Both of these problems are caused by incorrectly set depth gauges. Check depth gauge setting. Refile and reshape depth gauges if they're too high; if depth gauges are too low, file back the cutters.

Chain slops in guide bar, overheats, cuts crooked: Bar rails are probably spread too far, or drive links are bottoming in the groove. If rails are spread, pound them back into shape using a bar groove gauge and try again. If problem persists, or if drive links are bottoming in the groove, bar must be replaced or regrooved on a bar-rebuilding machine. Parp says replace bar and sprocket, regrind chain.

Whenever these or any other cutting problems occur, you should remove your bar and chain from your saw and clean them in solvent. Then examine the chain carefully and compare its parts to the drawings in the Saw Chain Troubleshooting Guide at the end of this chapter. This chart should help you to identify the cause or causes of your troubles. When you know the cause, you'll also know the remedy.

ORDERING AND REPLACING SAW CHAIN, BAR, AND SPROCKET

Your dealer can order any replacement part for your chain saw if you can supply accurate information on the saw's brand, model number, type, and size. The size of a cutting attachment is usually stated as a measurement of the actual bar cutting length from the front of the saw's body to the tip of the bar. It's also often helpful to know the overall length of the bar itself, from tail to tip. It's best to make note of the drive link count of the original and scratch this number somewhere on the saw for reference.

Most chains carry a code number stamped on the drive link. This code indicates the gauge of the chain. In addition, the pitch of the chain is often stamped on the cutters or depth gauges. If you know this information and the number of links in your chain when it was new, you can easily order a replacement chain that is prefitted to your bar. Or you can order the chain, bar, and sprocket as a set.

Most dealers carry or can order more than one brand of chain. First, of course, they carry the brand of chain made by or for the saws they sell. They often sell a cheaper brand of chain as well, or chains they cut themselves from reels of chain.

You can also mail-order chain from Zip Penn or Bailey's, either in reels or in loops to fit your saw. Bailey's sells the higher-quality Oregon Saw Chain at a discount. If you place a large order, Bailey's will give you a special package deal. If you're way out in the woods, or if you're starting a chain saw business, this is the way to go.

To order chain for your saw, or to change brands, find your chain on the Saw Chain Conversion Chart, in the Appendix. The chart will tell you which other companies produce similar chains. You can also switch to another kind or type of chain, as long as it fits your bar and sprocket.

CHAIN MAINTENANCE CHECK LIST

1. Clean chain in solvent before and after sharpening.

2. File cutters at correct angle.

3. Check and lower depth gauges often.

4. Soak chain in oil between uses.

5. Use sufficient oil when cutting.

6. Check bar and sprocket condition frequently. Repair or replace immediately.

7. Avoid hitting dirt or abrasive material when cutting.

8. Check condition of chain parts frequently. Compare with Saw Chain Troubleshooting Guide.

9. Never force a dull chain to cut. Severe damage will result to chain, bar, sprocket, and clutch.

10. Check and set chain tension often. Allow no sag in any kind of chain on any kind of saw under any conditions. With standard bars, set tension so side straps just touch the rails along the entire bottom length of the bar. With roller nose or sprocket nose bars, set tension tighter. Also increase tension to sharpen chain on the bar.

11. Keep bar grooves clean and oil holes open.

12. Keep bar rails flat and uniform.

13. Check for drive link tang clearance in bar grooves.

14. Clean bar daily.

15. Grease roller nose and sprocket nose bars daily.

16. Check roller nose for burrs. Remove with file.

17. Sharpen front lower hook portion of drive link tangs.

18. Grease sprocket bearing whenever sprocket is removed.

SAW CHAIN TROUBLESHOOTING GUIDE

WEAR—CUTTERS AND TIE STRAPS

CONDITION: Cracks under rear rivet holes on cutters and opposing tie straps.
CAUSE: Excessive pressure on dull or misfiled cutters. Common during winter.
REMEDY: File chain correctly. Use oil freely.

CONDITION: Light damage on cutting edges of top and/or side plates.
CAUSE: Cutters hit sand or dirt, other foreign material.
REMEDY: File cutters to remove all damaged area.

CONDITION: Excessive wear on bottom of cutters and tie straps.
CAUSE: Depth gauges too high. Cutting edge cannot get into wood.
REMEDY: Lower depth gauges to proper setting. Keep cutters filed correctly.

CONDITION: Peening on front corner of cutters and intermediate tie straps. Causes tight joints.
CAUSE: Chain striking bar entry. Sprocket too small. Or loose chain tension.
REMEDY: Use proper bar and sprocket. Adjust chain tension correctly.

CONDITION: Peening on bottom of cutters and tie straps causes tight joints.
CAUSE: Loose chain tension. Result of dull cutters and forcing dull chain into wood.
REMEDY: Keep proper tension. Keep cutters sharp. Chain may need replacing.

CONDITION: Excessive heel wear on cutters and tie straps.
CAUSES: 1. Blunt top plate filing.   4. Low depth gauge settings.
        2. Forcing dull chain to cut.   5. Lack of lubrication.
        3. Forcing chain to cut frozen wood.
REMEDY: File cutters properly. Don't force dull chain to cut. Use oil freely.

CONDITION: Concave wear on bottom of cutters, connecting tie straps.
CAUSES: 1. Chain tension too tight.
        2. Normal wear from undercutting (cutting with top of bar).
REMEDY: Adjust chain tension. Reduce cutting with top of bar.

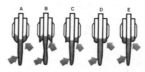

A. Open Bar Groove.
B. Severe abrasion and wobbly chain on thin bar rails. **C.** Rails not flat. **D.** Wobbly chain, rails too thick. **E.** One rail too thin or soft.

CONDITION: Excess wear on bottom of all chain parts.
CAUSES: 1. Uneven filing, worn bar rails cause chain to wobble.
        2. Excessive pressure, trying to make chain cut.
REMEDY: File chain properly. Recondition bar rails or replace bar. Replace chain if necessary.

CONDITION: Severe damage on either side of top and/or side plates.
CAUSE: Cutters hit abrasive material.
REMEDY: File cutters to remove all damage.

CONDITION: Edges burred and notch peened on tie straps.
CAUSE: Chain chatter due to loose chain tension and improper filing.
REMEDY: Correct chain tension. Refile chain properly. Replace sprocket if badly worn.

CONDITION: Peened notch in tie strap. Causes tight joints and broken drive links.
CAUSE: Chain run on badly worn spur sprocket or wrong pitch sprocket.
REMEDY: Replace worn sprocket. Chain may need replacing.

CONDITION: Broken tie straps opposite cutters.
CAUSE: Fatigue failure due to worn spur sprocket.
REMEDY: Replace sprocket. Replace broken tie straps. Chain may need replacement.

INCORRECT FILING

CONDITION: Backslope on side plate cutting edge. Cutter won't feed into wood.
CAUSE: File held too high.
REMEDY: Refile cutters to recommended angle.

CONDITION: Feathered top plate causes rapid dulling.
CAUSE: File handle held too low.
REMEDY: Refile properly at recommended angle.

CONDITION: Hook in side plate cutting edge. Cutters grab, cut rough.
CAUSE: File held too low, or file is too small.
REMEDY: Refile to recommended angle with right size file.

CONDITION: Blunt top plate cutting angle. Chain won't feed into wood, won't cut.
CAUSE: File handle held too high.
REMEDY: Refile properly, at recommended angle.

CONDITION: Top plate angle less than recommended. Causes slow cutting, excess wear on chain and bar.
CAUSE: File held at less than recommended angle.
REMEDY: Refile at correct angle.

CONDITION: Top plate angle more than recommended. Side plate cutting edge is thin and dulls rapidly.
CAUSE: File held at more than recommended angle.
REMEDY: Refile at correct angle.

DEPTH GAUGES

CONDITION: Uneven depth gauge height. Chain won't cut straight.
CAUSE: Uneven filing.
REMEDY: Use correct depth gauge jointer to lower gauges evenly.

CONDITION: Depth gauge is pointed, buries itself in wood.
CAUSE: Improperly filed depth gauge.
REMEDY: File cutters back so depth gauges can be set and reshaped properly.

CONDITION: Blunt depth gauge causes rough cutting.
CAUSE: Improperly filed depth gauge.
REMEDY: Round off front corner to maintain original shape.

DRIVE LINKS

CONDITION: Scars on sides.
CAUSE: Loose chain jumping off bar.
REMEDY: Adjust chain tension. Replace bent drive links.

CONDITION: Rounded concave bottom.
CAUSE: Shallow groove on bar tip.
REMEDY: Regroove bar tip. Bar may need replacing.

CONDITION: Battered and broken bottom.
CAUSE: Chain jumped bar. Spur sprocket hit drive links.
REMEDY: Replace damaged drive links, sharpen tangs with round file. Remove burrs.

CONDITION: Sides worn round at bottom.
CAUSE: Chain wobbled in bar groove. Caused by uneven cutters or worn bar rails.
REMEDY: Rework bar rails and groove. Correct chain filing.

CONDITION: Front or back peened.
CAUSE: Improper sprocket fit. Prolonged chain chatter.
REMEDY: Replace sprocket. Adjust chain tension. Chain may be damaged beyond repair.

CONDITION: Straight bottom.
CAUSE: Shallow bar groove.
REMEDY: Regroove bar or replace. Re-shape drive link tangs with round file to retain original shape.

CONDITION: Front point turned up.
CAUSE: Drive links bottoming in sprocket. Sprocket worn.
REMEDY: Replace sprocket. Sharpen tangs. Check for burrs.

CONDITION: Nicked bottom or back.
CAUSE: Cutting with loose chain. Or wrong pitch sprocket.
REMEDY: Adjust chain tension. Install correct sprocket. File off burrs. Replace damaged drive links.

Using Your Chain Saw • 8

The season is upon us. An old friend in the Forest Service has managed to get us a tree-removal permit for that huge stand of beetle-killed ponderosa pine. The trees have all been treated and are safe to use. It's still early and nobody else has even asked for a permit yet and now's the chance to put by as many cords of good wood as we have time and energy to harvest. We'll work together since it's safer and easier for two people to get two supplies of wood than for one person to get one supply of wood.

GETTING ORGANIZED

First, let's organize a system for the daily maintenance of our chain saws and other supplies and equipment. We'll plan on using the tailgates of our pickup trucks as work benches. The tools are in the cab; the fuel and rags are up on one side of the truck's box, where they won't be covered up with logs.

Last night, looking forward to a season's wood trip, we thoroughly cleaned and serviced and sharpened our chain saws and all our other tools. The fuel mix is fresh— we picked it up yesterday. Our saws passed our inspection and start easily and

run perfectly and cut straight. We've got extra spark plugs and air filters and chain loops and chain parts. I've got an extra bar and sprocket but you don't, so we'll be extra careful not to pinch your bar.

Speaking of pinching the bar, maybe we should review some of the theories of woodcutting and general chain saw use before we actually go out into the woods.

BUCKING

Lately we've been practicing with our saws out on the backyard woodpile and we have a real feel of the saws now, how they handle and cut. And we've gotten used to cutting easy logs, in easy situations, like propped up on our sawbuck with one end free, so all we have to do is cut.

But out there in the woods we're going to be cutting all sizes of wood, under all conditions. How do we avoid limbs that snap back and logs that roll? We'd better take time for a look at some different kinds of woodcutting situations.

Our plastic and aluminum wedges will be useful tools. In many cases, simply using a wedge will save a saw from being pinched in the cut. Let's remember that.

Out there on our woodpile, using our

sawbuck, we've cut a lot of logs with no trouble. They weren't huge logs, though. Suppose we have a really huge log that's supported on one end. How do we keep it from splitting or tearing when we cut through it?

The first thing to consider in any wood-cutting problem is the stress factor. What is the direction and nature of the stress? If we analyze the stress condition before we cut, we'll avoid some problems.

With this huge log supported on one end, and our cut coming just on the free side of the support, we need to minimize the amount of stress at the moment the cut becomes complete. A wedge won't do any good in this case. In fact, using a wedge would only increase the stress from above at the moment the cut is complete.

Let's start from the bottom of the log and cut upwards, with the top part of our guide bar. If we cut some of the diameter of the log from underneath, say about a third, then we can finish it from above with just one more cut and the stress will be considerably lessened. In other words, we'll start with a one-third underbuck and finish with an overbuck.

Remember always to work on the uphill side of the log and use a good stance.

When cross-cutting on a hill, *always* stand on the uphill side, because the logs will probably roll. Wedges are necessary to keep the cut open; use *only* soft plastic wedges.

Figure 8.1

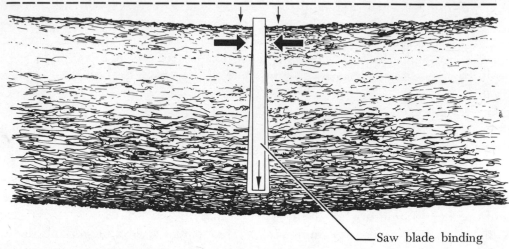

Saw blade binding

When a log is supported under both ends, *never* allow saw blade to get pinched in the saw cut by trying to cut through in one cut. Always cut on the compression side first and the tension side last.

Figure 8.2

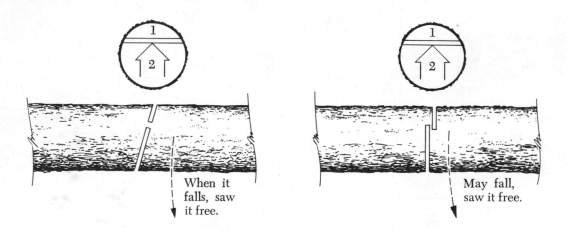

When it falls, saw it free.

May fall, saw it free.

Two hints for cross-cutting a felled tree with stem thinner than guide bar length, and supported at both ends.

Figure 8.3

Place feet far enough apart to allow a comfortable but firm and balanced center.

Now suppose our large log is supported on both ends. The weight is on the lower half of the log, below our cut. To avoid a splitting log and a pinched bar, begin the cutting in this situation with a one-third overbuck. Finish the cut with an underbuck and be careful to exercise firm control of the saw. Make both cuts at a slight angle so the bar isn't pinched in the kerf when the log settles. Another trick to avoid pinching the bar is to make the cuts so that they aren't directly opposite each other.

If you're going to buck a log that's lying fairly flat on the ground, so that the log is supported by the ground for almost its entire length, there's no way to underbuck it. In that case, use a wedge to keep the kerf open and avoid pinching the bar. Remember to stand uphill and don't let

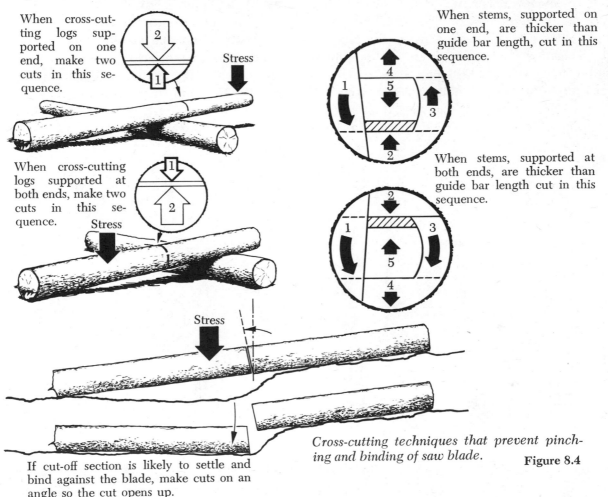

When cross-cutting logs supported on one end, make two cuts in this sequence.

When cross-cutting logs supported at both ends, make two cuts in this sequence.

When stems, supported on one end, are thicker than guide bar length, cut in this sequence.

When stems, supported at both ends, are thicker than guide bar length cut in this sequence.

If cut-off section is likely to settle and bind against the blade, make cuts on an angle so the cut opens up.

Cross-cutting techniques that prevent pinching and binding of saw blade.   **Figure 8.4**

your chain hit the ground.

Now let's say we have two logs that are larger in diameter than the length of our guide bar. In both of these cases we'll have to make a number of cuts in sequence. The idea is to leave a break-off hinge of uncut wood and the exact placement of that hinge depends upon the source and direction of stress.

Our first log is supported on both ends. To buck it, make one cut on the far side of the log. Then overbuck to leave a hinge in the upper third. The third cut on the close side of the log brings the saw into position for the fourth cut, an underbuck. Finish with a fifth cut, back up to the underside of the hinge. Watch your feet.

The second log is supported on one end, so we will want our hinge in the lower third of the log to prevent splitting. Begin

the first cut on the far side of the log, as above. Make the second cut an underbuck to form the hinge. The third, fourth, and fifth cuts reverse the previous operation. Watch the saw, this time.

Most of the time, any log you'll want to buck will be lying flat on the ground. The easiest method is to make a series of over-bucks on one side. Then simply roll the log over and finish the cuts by overbucking from the other side. Again, use wedges to avoid pinching the bar.

In all cutting situations let the saw do the work. If it's sharp and in good running condition you won't have to apply much force at all. Remember to begin any cut close to the bumper or bumper spikes and then allow the saw to pivot on that point. When you cut using this basic pivot motion you maintain maximum control and avoid

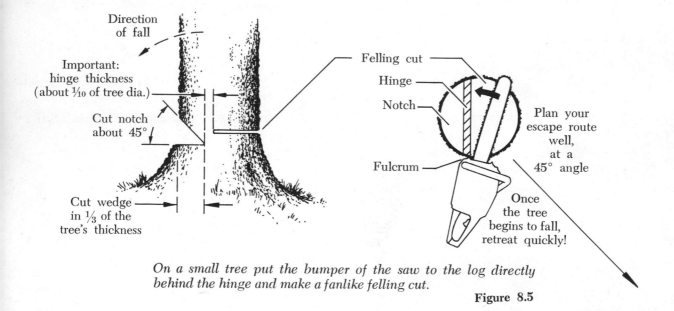

On a small tree put the bumper of the saw to the log directly behind the hinge and make a fanlike felling cut.

Figure 8.5

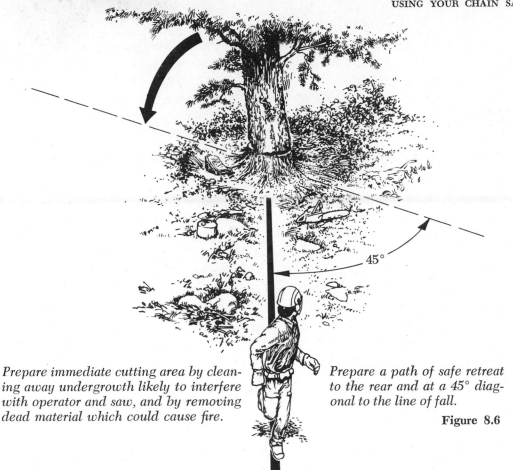

45°

Prepare immediate cutting area by cleaning away undergrowth likely to interfere with operator and saw, and by removing dead material which could cause fire.

Prepare a path of safe retreat to the rear and at a 45° diagonal to the line of fall.

Figure 8.6

most kickback and push-pull potential.

FELLING A SMALL TREE

Now let's practice cutting down one small tree. First, choose a tree that you're sure you want to cut down. Pick one that's fairly straight, so we can control the direction of its fall. It's very difficult to fell * a tree against the direction of its lean. Also, we want a tree that we're sure will fall in a safe direction, away from power lines,

buildings, parked cars, and other obstructions. Study the tree first, carefully, as you're walking toward it. Try to estimate its center of gravity. Now make sure that no one will come within the radius of the tree in any direction. Then clear a large

---

* The terms felling, felling lever, felling a tree, etc., are correct here, both grammatically and with regard to contemporary use. A person who fells trees professionally is called a faller, but that is an accepted solecism that loggers understandably insist upon. It does not affect the rest of the world, or the conjugation of the verb fall.

area all around the tree. Cut out all small brush and any limbs that you might fall over. Brush can also cause kickback if it comes in contact with the nose of the bar. Clear an escape route out from the tree. Your escape route must be back away from the planned direction of fall and at an angle from it. Don't plan on running directly opposite to the direction of fall since the tree may well fall exactly opposite from the plan. Make your escape route at a 45° angle back and away from the line of fall.

There are two basic cutting operations involved with felling any tree. These operations may be altered or complicated by the size of the tree, the lay of the land, and the required direction of fall. These two operations are the *notch,* or *directional cut,* and the *felling cut,* or *backcut.* The notch determines and controls the direction of the tree's fall. The felling cut or backcut removes most of the wood still holding the tree and causes it to break and fall. The notch and the backcut must always be made so as to form a hinge of uncut wood. As the tree falls, it pivots on this hinge, breaking it.

First, we make our notch. The basic notch for a small tree is made with two cuts. Make the upper of the two cuts first, to avoid pinching the bar. It's a drag to dig a saw out of a tree with the tree's full weight pressing down on it.

Move to one side of the tree, facing the planned direction of the fall. Aim across the top of your saw, along your front handle or falling sights (ribs cast into hous-ings or covers on the saw), at exactly the place where you want the tree to fall. This will correctly line up your guide bar with the trunk of the tree.

Now make the upper cut of your notch, cutting down at an angle. Cut at least a third of the way into the tree, but not as much as halfway. Then make the lower cut. With a small straight tree on level ground, make this second cut straight in to meet the first. Make the cut horizontal, and cut clear back to remove the whole notch. The hinge will be formed by uncut wood at least two inches thick between the back of the notch and the felling cut.

Now go behind the tree and make another horizontal cut, two inches or more *above the lower, or horizontal cut of the notch.* It is extremely important not to make this second cut so it will meet the horizontal notch cut. It must be a inch or two higher. It is also important not to cut through the hinge wood.

When enough of your felling cut is complete, stop your saw and leave it in the cut. Insert a wedge in the cut to prevent the cut from closing on your saw and to help control the direction of the fall toward the notch. Then start your saw again and continue until the cut is complete, leaving only the hinge. At this time the tree should fall. If not, give it a little push, or use a felling lever. As the tree starts to move, leave your saw on the ground and retreat quickly along your planned escape route. Remember that the butt end of the tree may kick backwards as the tree falls and that unseen dead branches may fall straight down, or in any direction, as the tree topples. Take no chances. Retreat quickly and without hesitation along your escape route.

That's how you cut down a tree when the diameter of the tree is less than the length of your guide bar. But we're also going to be cutting down trees equal to or larger than the length of our guide bars. These situations require a specific sequence of cuts.

FELLING LARGE TREES

To cut a tree with a diameter larger than the length of your guide bar but not twice its size, use the following method. Exercise great caution, because the technique in-

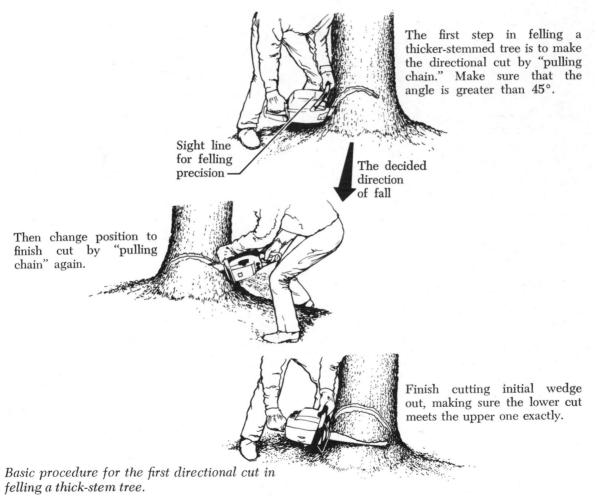

The first step in felling a thicker-stemmed tree is to make the directional cut by "pulling chain." Make sure that the angle is greater than 45°.

Sight line for felling precision

The decided direction of fall

Then change position to finish cut by "pulling chain" again.

Finish cutting initial wedge out, making sure the lower cut meets the upper one exactly.

Basic procedure for the first directional cut in felling a thick-stem tree.

Figure 8.7

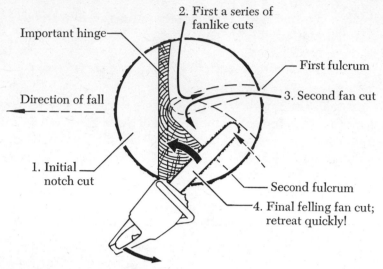

2. First a series of fanlike cuts

Important hinge

First fulcrum

3. Second fan cut

Direction of fall

1. Initial notch cut

Second fulcrum

4. Final felling fan cut; retreat quickly!

To fell trees with a diameter exceeding the bar length: start with the notch cut, in about ⅓ the tree diameter; finish with about three fanlike cuts, changing fulcrums as little as possible.

Figure 8.8

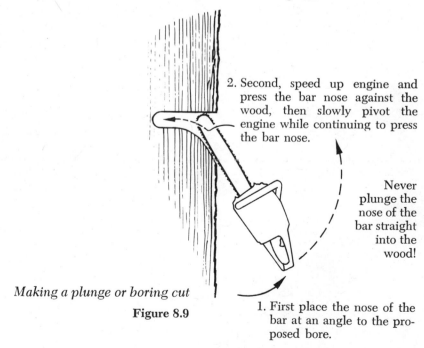

2. Second, speed up engine and press the bar nose against the wood, then slowly pivot the engine while continuing to press the bar nose.

Never plunge the nose of the bar straight into the wood!

Making a plunge or boring cut

Figure 8.9

1. First place the nose of the bar at an angle to the proposed bore.

volved is beyond the novice's reach. Make a notch, as before. Each cut of the notch may require as many as two cuts to complete. You can do this by making one half of the upper notch cut on one side and then moving to the other side of the tree to complete the upper notch cut. Do the same with the horizontal notch cut.

After the notch is formed, make a *plunge-cut* about an inch or two above the notch and on the opposite side of the wood that will form the hinge. Start the plunge-cut with the underside of the tip. When the bar has cut a few inches into the tree, straighten the saw to begin sawing straight inward from the tip of the bar.

When your plunge-cut is about halfway into the tree and about twice the width of your guide bar, proceed to make the felling cut by sawing around the tree. Make a pivot with the tip of the guide bar in the center of the tree. Be careful not to cut into the hinge wood and be sure to insert your wedge or felling lever in plenty of time to force the tree in the right direction. If you use a felling lever, be careful not to hit it with your saw. If you use wedges, be sure to use plastic ones, or make your own from hard wood.

To fell a tree with a diameter equal to or greater than twice the length of your guide bar, only one additional cut is necessary. This time the additional cut is in the notching operation and, in effect, cuts the hinge itself in half.

Make the notch, as before. Now make a plunge-cut at the back of the notch, right in the center of the tree. The plunge-cut should be at least twice the width of the guide bar.

Cutting a plunge at the back of the notch in this manner actually creates two hinges. Make another plunge-cut at one side of the trunk and on the felling-cut side of the hinge. The cut meets the plunge-cut that comes through the center of the notch. Continue the felling cut by sawing around the tree with the tip of the bar in the center of the trunk. Place your wedges or felling lever in plenty of time and be careful not to cut through the hinge.

Note that if you fell a large tree on a slope, you should make the bottom notch cut at an upward angle. This provides more control during a longer fall.

A *step notch* is often used by professionals or when the cutter wishes to leave a square end on the tree. For this notch, the upper cut is made almost horizontal and step notches are cut below it. Beginners shouldn't attempt this kind of notch since it's very difficult to avoid pinching the bar. For most of us wood gatherers, the step notch has no practical application.

ORGANIZED FELLING

We're going out into the woods to fell a good number of beetle-killed ponderosa pine trees. The trees are standing dead and are grouped pretty much together on the side of a slope facing the road but a good distance away.

We want to move the trees as little as possible and we want to fell them so they'll be easy to limb and buck into loading-sized

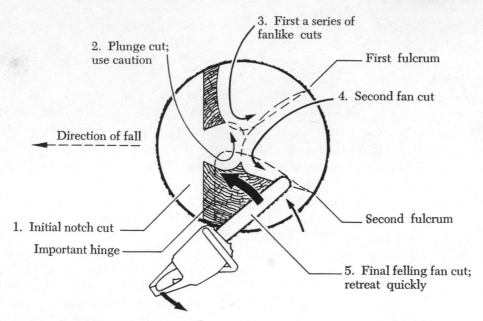

2. Plunge cut; use caution

3. First a series of fanlike cuts

First fulcrum

4. Second fan cut

Direction of fall

1. Initial notch cut

Important hinge

Second fulcrum

5. Final felling fan cut; retreat quickly

To fell big trees with a diameter exceeding twice the bar length, start by carefully making a plunge cut into the center of the tree, making sure to press nose of bar into the log until the guide bar is into the wood double its width before making the boring cut. Finish with about three fanlike cuts, changing fulcrums as little as possible.

Figure 8.10

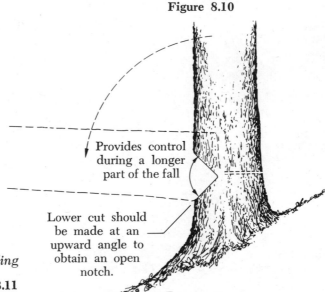

Provides control during a longer part of the fall

Lower cut should be made at an upward angle to obtain an open notch.

Preferable notching technique when felling on a slope

Figure 8.11

Felling organized for easy limbing

Figure 8.12

logs. We'll start out cutting at the edge of the trees closest to the road and we'll use one or more of the trees as a workbench for limbing all the trees that come later.

For a workbench, fell a tree diagonally across the center of your start of operation. Then fell tree number one so that it falls across the workbench. This lifts the trunk up off the ground and makes limbing and bucking easier. Limb the whole tree, from trunk to top. It helps to mark the tree for bucking while you're limbing it. With the tree limbed, it's easy to roll or see-saw the tree across the workbench to one side. Then you can buck it into lengths to be rolled downhill to the road. This method quickly leads to piles of bucked logs, ready for loading.

When you follow an organized felling procedure like this, save the side trees for last. You can use your accumulated piles of timber for workbenches for these trees. There's variation on this procedure, suit-

able for smaller groups of trees. Plan your felling so that each tree forms a workbench for the next. Buck each tree where it falls so that bucked sections form piles, ready for loading.

Still another variation works if you're felling on a slope. In this case you use several workbenches that will also form "roads" for rolling subsequent trees to the truck. In this case, no trees are bucked until they are all rolled down to the road.

Fell several thicker trees from those closest to the road. Fell them uphill, with their tops pointing into the trees to be cut. Note that this is dangerous, in that trees may slide back down hill. Cut the tops off the trees and limb them clean. Then simply fell the subsequent trees across your "road," limbing them, and roll them downhill where they can be bucked and loaded. Be careful to stay on the uphill side of any log you're limbing. Remember that a trunk may start to roll before you've finished

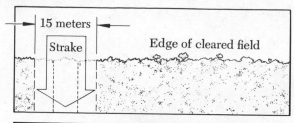

Choose a relatively thick "workbench" tree and fell it diagonally across the road approximately 5-10 meters in front of the group of trees to be felled. Try to have it be 50-70 cm above the ground. Limb this tree but don't cross-cut it.

Fell tree no. 1 across the bench tree. Cut off the top and slash in the road.

Figure 8.13

Limb tree no. 1 and mark cross-cut points. Pull, roll, or see-saw the stem into the timber zone. Cross-cut on your way back to the root and finish off lower limbing if necessary.

Fell the other trees in the group, following the same sequence of operations. Note how the diagonal bench helps you to balance the stems by varying the felling direction.

Figure 8.14

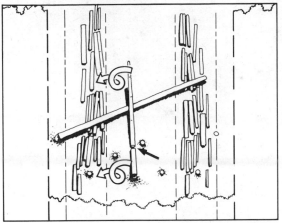

In certain cases it will be more advantageous to cross-cut the first log while on your way to the top, as this provides better balance of the rest of the stem.

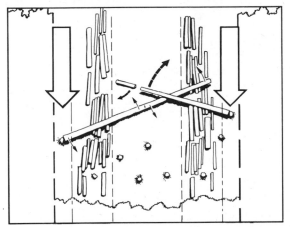

Save the side trees until last. Use the piles of timber as a bench and proceed as usual. Finally cut the original workbench in half and see-saw the two lengths to the timber zone.

Figure 8.15

The timber zone method is preferred for thicker stands with a comparatively small number of branches.

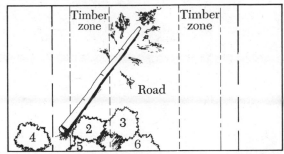

Plan and fell one group at a time. Place top and most of the slash in the road.

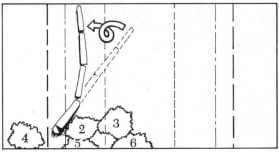

Cross-cut tree no. 1 and turn the first two top logs, leaving the others in position to use as a workbench.

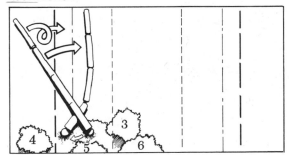

Fell tree no. 2, limb, and mark cross-cut points. Cross-cut a section to facilitate see-sawing or rolling the stem into the timber zone. Cross-cut the rest and finish lower limbing if necessary on the way back.

Figure 8.16

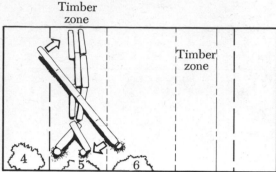

Timber zone

Timber zone

Continue felling the other trees in the group. Place the center of gravity somewhere on the woodpile.

Timber zone

Work evenly along both sides of the strake.

Figure 8.17

When felling trees on a slope, start by cutting 3 or 4 thickish "bench" trees perpendicular to the tractor road.

Tractor road

Fell the remaining trees straight across the bench trees; limb and mark cross-cut points; then roll the stems down to the road, but remember, never walk along the lower side of the stems because they may start to roll before you have finished.

Figure 8.18

limbing. Also note that "the root always wins" when rolling logs.

None of these operations should ever be attempted by a lone individual.

LIMBING

Of all the cutting operations, limbing is the one that holds the most unseen danger. The traditional North American method of limbing is to always keep your guide bar on the opposite side of the tree trunk and to limb only one side of the tree at a time. In other words, you keep the tree trunk between you and your guide bar: you remove all the limbs on one side of the tree, the side opposite you, and then you reverse your position and do the other side. If you're working for your own woodpile, limbing one side at a time is the easiest and safest approach.

In the woods, this method has several disadvantages. In the first place, one side of the log or the other is always downhill. It is very dangerous to limb from the downhill side of a tree. The limbs tend to fall your way and, of course, when the tree rolls, it rolls right into you. Also, limb-

Lever method of limbing
Figure 8.19

Limbing technique. Logger rests his saw on the log, and the saw does the work.
Figure 8.20

ing one side and then the other is the slowest and least efficient limbing method.

In these situations, Parp recommends the Swedish Forestry Method of limbing, as outlined in this chapter. Actually there are two of these methods, the lever method and the pendulum method. Of the two, the lever method is the easier and safer.

The *lever method* of limbing is so called because the saw's body is used as a lever for the necessary limbing movements. This method is most suitable on trees that have limbs of all sizes growing in a symmetrical pattern.

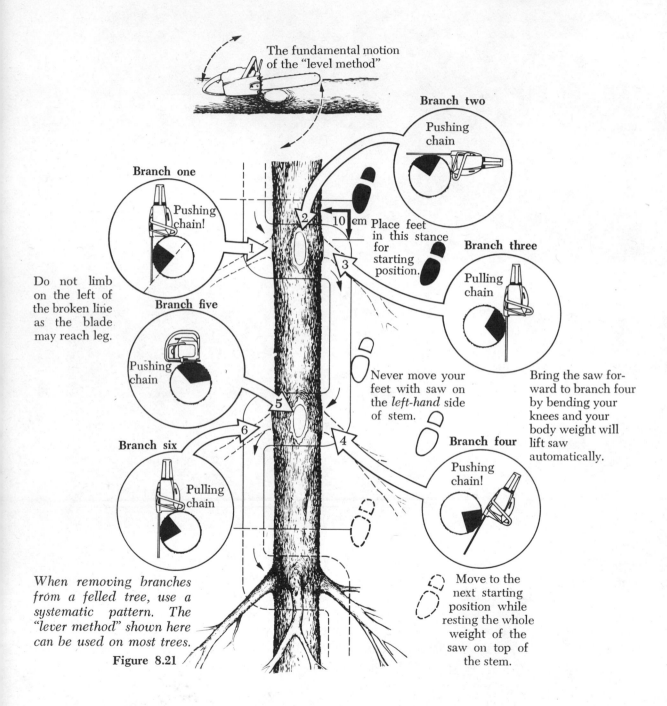

The fundamental motion of the "level method"

Branch two
Pushing chain

Branch one
Pushing chain!

2 10 cm Place feet in this stance for starting position.

Branch three
Pulling chain

Do not limb on the left of the broken line as the blade may reach leg.

Branch five
Pushing chain

Never move your feet with saw on the *left-hand* side of stem.

Bring the saw forward to branch four by bending your knees and your body weight will lift saw automatically.

Branch six
Pulling chain

Branch four
Pushing chain!

When removing branches from a felled tree, use a systematic pattern. The "lever method" shown here can be used on most trees.

Figure 8.21

Move to the next starting position while resting the whole weight of the saw on top of the stem.

Start limbing on the uphill side of the trunk end of the tree. Work toward the tree top so that the branches will be pointing away from you while you're working. Get a good stance with your feet wide apart. Stand close to the tree and get a good hold on your saw. Be especially alert for kickback and keep your thumb curled around the handle of your saw. In limbing, work close to your saw. You won't be able to keep your elbow locked anyway, and holding the saw close helps you maintain greater control. For all of these limbing methods you move your feet only at certain specific times, after certain cuts. The idea is to complete a sequence of cuts, move, do another sequence of cuts, move again, and so forth.

Suppose you have two groups or turns of three limbs each that are all safely in reach with your guide bar. Two are on your side of the trunk, two on the other side, and two straight up. The first one on the far side is number one. The closest straight-up limb is number two. The close limb on your side is number three. Number four is the second limb on your side, number five is the second straight up, and number six is the furthest limb on the far side of the trunk.

You will cut all six limbs from one position and you won't move your feet until after you've cut limb six.

To start the sequence, stand with your left leg out of reach of your guide bar and your right leg directly behind the rear handle of your saw.

Cut branch number one with the top of

your guide bar, and with your body weight on your right leg and your right leg leaning against the tree trunk for support. When branch number one falls, pull the saw toward you, using its body as a lever. Keep the weight of the saw on the tree. This will bring you into position to cut branch number two with the top of your guide bar.

With a slight swing and a shift of body weight to your left leg, during branch number two, you will automatically come into position to cut branch number three with the bottom of your guide bar.

When you move from that first group or "turn" of branches to the next, bring your body weight forward by bending your knees. At the same time, bring your saw across to your side of the trunk. Note that you do not change the position of your feet.

Branch number four actually begins the next turn of branches. For this, the saw is resting between the tree and your right leg. Hold the saw close with a firm grip. Most of the time, you cut branch number four with the top of your guide bar but if it's a thick branch, you may have to finish with an overcut.

When the saw comes up from branch number four, you roll it over so its weight rests on the tree trunk. This puts you in position to cut branch number five with the tip of your guide bar and allows your saw to continue its roll on the trunk to an upright position. This mean that you have to operate your throttle with your thumb while cutting branch number five. During

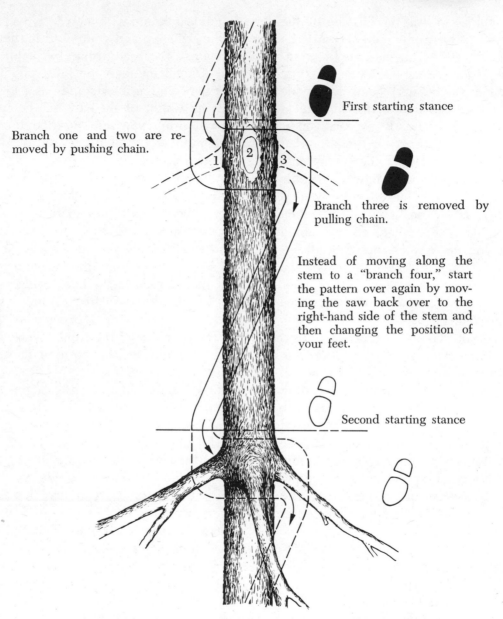

First starting stance

Branch one and two are re-moved by pushing chain.

Branch three is removed by pulling chain.

Instead of moving along the stem to a "branch four," start the pattern over again by moving the saw back over to the right-hand side of the stem and then changing the position of your feet.

Second starting stance

If the distance between branch turns is greater than 70 cm, the "lever method" pattern of movement must be changed.

Figure 8.22

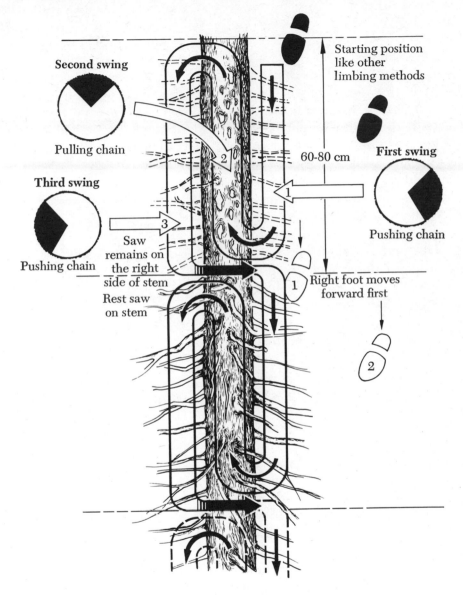

*The pendulum method of removing
numerous and irregular branches.*

Figure 8.23

this turn you bring your weight back evenly on both legs.

As the saw comes upright again, your finger once more moves to the throttle. You cut branch number six with the bottom of your guide bar, thus completing one entire sequence. You can now move to the next sequence with the entire weight of your saw resting on the tree trunk and the trunk between you and your guide bar.

This method is, Parp says, the easiest, safest, and fastest method of limbing yet devised. With just a little practice, anyone can master it and, in doing so, get to feel like a really expert woodsperson. And it's much easier than it might sound right now. The *pendulum method* of limbing is another sequential method in which the saw describes a pendulous movement through groups of branches. This method is most suitable on trees with smaller branches, especially if they're dry and small like the lower limbs of spruce trees, or on trees in dense stands. It's also useful on trees with numerous bunched branches, or branches that come in irregular turns.

Start by cutting a swath on your side of the tree. Cut to the extent of your comfortable reach. Then, with your saw resting on the tree, use the bottom of your guide bar to cut the second group of branches from the top of the trunk, back toward yourself. Swing the saw on its own weight so it comes into position for the last phase of the sequence. Shift your weight from your right leg onto your left leg. Use the top of your guide bar to complete the limbing sequence on the far side

of the tree. This leaves the trunk between you and your guide bar and allows you to move safely to the next position. The final step is to transfer the saw from the left side of the trunk to your side for the beginning of the next sequence.

There will be many times when you have to use the lever method and the pendulum method on one tree.

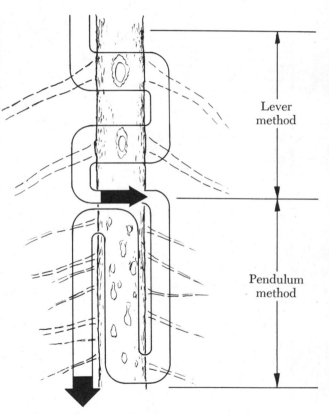

Lever method

Pendulum method

Which method should you use? Both lever and pendulum methods have their merits, even on the same tree. However, it should be observed that the lever method is the more labor-saving of the two.

Figure 8.24

A LOGICAL METHOD FOR FELLING, LIMBING, MEASURING, AND BUCKING

This is an easy and efficient method for accomplishing all the steps necessary for turning standing dead trees into bucked logs.

1. Select and aim your first tree and each successive tree so it will fall in a convenient work area in the direction of your truck.

2. When the tree is down and you are ready to limb it, fasten a logger's measuring tape to the butt end of the tree.

3. As you limb the tree, the measuring tape plays out behind you. Since you are using the lever and pendulum limbing methods, you are always on the safe, uphill side of the tree. You can use your saw to place bucking marks where you'll see them later. Make your bucking marks at multiples of whatever length logs you want. Jerk the measuring tape loose and reset it at each bucking mark.

4. When the entire tree is limbed, measured, and marked, cut off the top. Use a lifting hook to move the light end onto your log pile.

5. Buck the tree at the marks, working back toward the butt. At the same time, clean up your limbing job.

6. Roll the bucked sections, or use a tong and hook to stack them on your timber pile.

7. Roll the logs down to your truck or back your truck up to the timber pile for loading.

Limbing Thick Branches

You'll often run into thick or complex branches that will temporarily stop your finely developed and speedy limbing methods. These large or complex branches can result in a pinched bar or a split tree unless they are cut properly. When you run into one of these problems, first analyze the stress factor. Cut or remove any branches that may obstruct your work. Then cut the branches that induce the highest stress. After that you can safely cross-cut the main branch itself. If the main branch is very thick, undercut it first and finish it with a top cut to avoid splitting. If a branch is in a bind, start with a top cut and finish with an undercut. Be very careful of limbs that may spring out at you or grab your saw.

PRUNING

The only limbing procedure that isn't covered in these paragraphs is pruning. To remove a limb from a standing, living tree, always start with an undercut a few inches out from the trunk of the tree. Then finish with a top cut a little further out from the trunk. This way the limb won't split and break off near the trunk and tear the bark from the tree. When the limb is removed, cut the stump off flush with the trunk and paint over the wound with pruning paint.

When you're cutting small brush, or clearing the underbrush around a tree you're going to fell, be sure to keep your bar close to the ground and cut at the thickest parts of the branches. If you cut

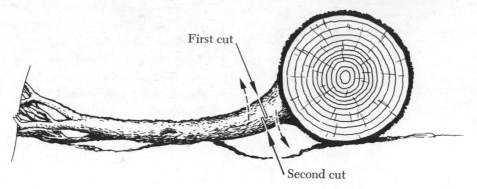

Branches in a bind should be top cut, then undercut, if the tree's weight is on the branch.

Figure 8.25

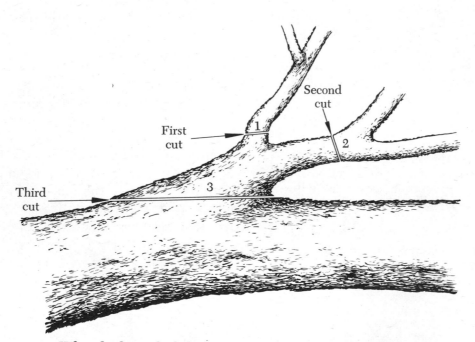

When limbing thick branches, avoid pinching and splitting by choosing the proper sequence of operations, paying extra attention to stresses and tension.

Figure 8.26

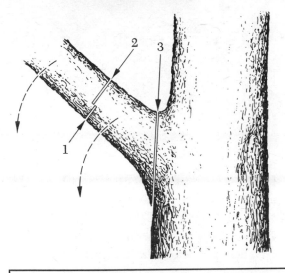

higher up on the branch, the branches will whip toward you and the chain will catch in the work, causing push or pull or kickback.

Now we're ready to go out into the woods and get those beetle-killed ponderosa pine. We really don't spend enough time in the woods.

When pruning, make an undercut near the trunk and finish with a top cut a little farther out from the trunk. This prevents the limb from splitting and breaking off near the trunk. Then flush out the stub near the trunk.

Figure 8.27

WORK-SEASON CHECKLIST OF SUPPLIES AND EQUIPMENT

1. Chain saw. Perform maintenance.
2. Owner's manual. Re-read.
3. Extra chain.
4. Chain repair parts.
5. Chain breaker.
6. Rivet spinner.
7. Small machinist's hammer.
8. File guide.
9. Depth gauge or jointer.
10. Chain file.
11. Flat safety-edge file.
12. Flat file for bar.
13. Extra spark plug.
14. Spark plug wrench.
15. Screwdrivers.
16. One or two extra air filters.
17. Extra starter rope.
18. Wrench for bar nuts.
19. Grease gun for roller nose or sprocket nose bars.
20. Solvent or kerosene.
21. Fuel—fresh and ready-mixed with two-cycle engine oil.
22. Clean chain lubrication oil.
23. Toothbrush.
24. Rags.
25. Gloves.
26. Hardhat.
27. Ear protection.
28. Eye protection.
29. Safe work clothing.
30. Ax.
31. Plastic wedges for felling and bucking.
32. Sledge or heavy hammer.
33. Hatchet.
34. Felling lever.
35. Cant hook.
36. Logging tape.
37. Whistle.

How It Works and Why It Doesn't • 9

THE ENGINE

All but one of the currently manufactured gasoline chain saws are powered by a small, one-cylinder engine known as a two-cycle or two-stroke engine. All of these engines are air-cooled and all are lubricated simply by mixing the lubricating oil with the fuel. At one time, Solo Manufacturing produced a chain saw that was powered by a two-cylinder engine. It was still an air-cooled, two-stroke engine and it is no longer in production. The only real exception to the two-stroke rule is the Sacks-Dolmar KMS4, which is powered by a Wankel rotary engine. It may be a great saw, but it's expensive and its engine is so unusual that Parp prefers to ignore it.

The words two-stroke or two-cycle do not mean that the engine has two cycles. Those words mean that all of the functions or phases of the engine's operation are completed during one upward and one downward stroke of the piston. If even one function or phase is impaired in any way, the engine will not perform properly and usually will not work at all. In order to understand why a particular chain saw engine isn't working, you need to be familiar with all the functions necessary

to the saw's operation. Once you are familiar with these functions, it becomes much easier to isolate and determine a cause of trouble. Such a procedure is universally known as troubleshooting.

When you learn the functions of a chain saw's engine, and when you learn to troubleshoot accurately, it becomes possible to decide whether your trouble is one that you can repair yourself, or whether you need to take your saw to a professional mechanic. If you can learn to troubleshoot your chain saw, you will save many trips to the mechanic, much "down-time," and a lot of money. Most mechanical difficulties with chain saws are elementary, easy to isolate, and easy to repair yourself—even without tools or spare parts.

The most common problem that prevents a chain saw from starting is a turned-off ignition switch. You may think that this is ridiculous. It isn't. When you know this basic truth, you know that the first thing you do when your chain saw won't start is to check the ignition switch. Then you turn it on. Then you start your chain saw. Many, many people take turned-off chain saws to mechanics. The point is, if you approach all mechanical difficulties logically, you will usually be able to discover and correct the problem yourself. Logically means "in order"; that is, you check the first thing first. The first thing to check when your engine won't start is the ignition switch. The second thing is the fuel supply. Before we go any further, let's look at the functions of a two-stroke chain saw engine.

HOW IT WORKS

It's a way of trapping fire. That's what an engine is. It's a way of trapping fire and then changing the energy of the fire, which is chemical energy, into mechanical or turning energy. The turning energy is then transferred to the chain in a very simple and direct manner.

We get our fire by burning a highly combustible vaporized mixture of gasoline and air, with a little oil thrown in to keep the moving parts lubricated. We burn this vaporized fuel mixture in a special kind of trap called a *combustion chamber*. This trap is solid all around to contain the energy from the fire. But the energy has to go someplace and, since we want to use that energy, we fit one side of the trap with a *plug*. The plug fits tight enough to hold the fuel vapor in, but loose enough to move when the vapor burns. Thus, when the vapor burns, the energy from the fire moves the plug to create the change from chemical energy to mechanical energy. The trap is cylinder-shaped and the plug that fits into it is called a *piston*. The piston has almost the same diameter as the *cylinder*. In order to make it fit as tight as

possible and still work, the piston has a ring fitted into a slot near its top. This ring, called a *piston ring*, fits very snugly against the walls of the cylinder. It helps seal the sides of the trap.

In order to burn vaporized fuel mixture in our trap, we need some way to force the vapors into the trap. We also need some way to vaporize the fuel and to hold it under pressure in a waiting room near the trap. We'll look more at the *carburetor* in a while, but for now it's sufficient to imagine it as a storage chamber or waiting room where the fuel is vaporized and held under pressure. Now we need a door that opens and closes when we want it to.

Many chain saws are designed so that the piston itself is the only door between the waiting room, or carburetor, and the trap, or combustion chamber. Others are designed with a small door made out of spring steel, called a *reed valve*. In either case, the door opens at exactly the right time and the pressurized fuel vapor rushes in to fill the combustion chamber. When that happens, the piston moves up in the cylinder to compress the fuel vapor. When the piston has squeezed the fuel vapor into a much smaller area, it's time to start the fire. We start the fire by making an electric spark that jumps from one electrode of a spark plug to another. Since the spark plug is screwed very tightly into the top of the combustion chamber, the spark starts a fire in the vaporized fuel. The fuel vapors burn very quickly and force the piston down again.

But now we need another door since we

have to get rid of the useless burned gases. Most of the energy from the fire is used to push the piston down but some of it remains as burned fuel vapors. These burned vapors are called *exhaust* and the door through which we expel them is called the *exhaust port*. If we don't get all the burned vapors out of the combustion chamber, there won't be room for the new fuel vapors. The pressure behind the fresh, incoming fuel vapors will help, since it will tend to chase out the exhaust vapors.

Once again, the piston itself can be used as a door. We'll just put a small hole or three in one side of the combustion chamber. We'll position it so that it becomes uncovered or opened when the piston moves down. But it also has to be positioned so that the fresh, incoming fuel vapors don't escape with the exhausted vapors. Many chain saw engines have a piston that is domed so that when the exhaust port is uncovered, the new fresh vapors are deflected upwards into the combustion chamber.

Now let's start over from the beginning. We have a supply of vaporized fuel mixture standing by under pressure. This mixture is forced or drawn into the cylinder when the piston opens the door or valve. When the piston moves up, it compresses the fuel mixture and reduces it in volume. Then the compressed mixture is ignited by a timed electric spark from our spark plug. The burning fuel vapors expand instantly, forcing the piston down. The piston is connected by a *connecting rod* to a crank assembly on a *crankshaft* (see figure 9.1).

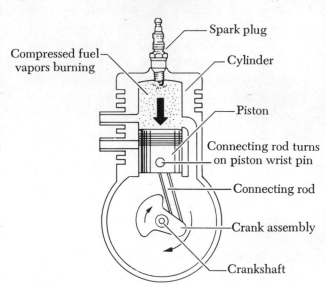

Crank assembly, connecting rod, and piston inside crankcase of chain saw engine.

Figure 9.1

When the piston goes down, the connecting rod turns the crank and the crank turns the crankshaft and so the power from the chemical energy of the burning fuel is transformed into the mechanical energy of the turning crankshaft. At this time the piston also uncovers the other door and the burned gases are exhausted from the cylinder so that a new cycle can begin. This sequence of events, in order, is *intake, compression, ignition, power,* and *exhaust*. Note that each of these events must occur in each cycle and at the proper time in order for the engine to work. Whenever a chain saw engine fails to work, the trouble can always be traced to one or more of these events.

In a chain saw engine, the full cycle of all five events must occur while the piston is moving from its bottom position to its top position and back again. The upward movement of the piston is said to be its *compression stroke* and its downward movement is called its *power stroke*. Thus we say that all five events occur within two strokes of the piston, the upward stroke and the downward stroke. That's why it's called a two-stroke or two-cycle engine. Actually, the more accurate term for this kind of engine is a two-stroke engine.

Compressed fuel vapors are burned each time the piston nears the top of its compression stroke. Each downward stroke is a power stroke and has behind it the force of the expansion caused by the burning fuel vapors.

In order to force the fresh fuel vapors into the combustion chamber, the pressure of the incoming fuel vapors has to be somewhat higher than the lowest pressure existing in the cylinder. Chain saw engines are designed so that the crankcase itself is the last storage area for the incoming fuel vapors. The piston and the cylinder act as a pump to increase the pressure of the fuel vapors in the crankcase so that they rush into the combustion chamber when the valve or port is opened. In this way the crankcase is used as a scavenging pump and most chain saw engines are referred to as two-stroke, crankcase-scavenged engines.

Figure 9.2 is a simplified drawing of a reed valve two-stroke engine in the intake

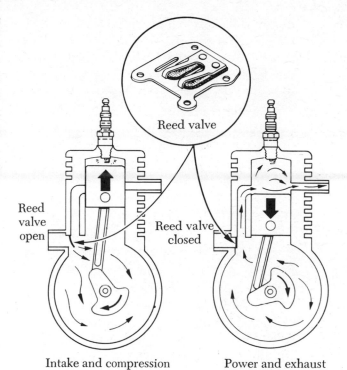

Intake and compression   Power and exhaust

Phases of reed valve chain saw engine.

Figure 9.2

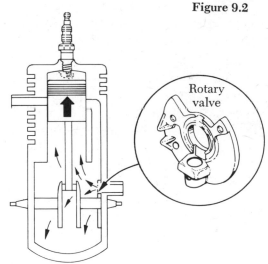

Rotary valve chain saw engine.

Figure 9.3

phase of its cycle. The piston is at its lowest point. It has passed the intake port to allow the vaporized fuel mixture to enter the combustion chamber. When the piston moved down, it slightly increased the pressure in the crankcase, helping to force the vaporized fuel from the crankcase up through the intake port. The burned gases from the last cycle have just finished escaping through the exhaust port. The piston has just finished delivering power to the crankshaft. The piston will now start upward on the compression stroke. While it travels upward, it will close off both the intake port and the exhaust port; it will also cause the pressure in the crankcase to drop considerably lower than the atmospheric pressure outside. That pressure drop will cause the reed valve to be pushed open by still another incoming charge of vaporized fuel from the carburetor. When the piston comes back down again, its return will again increase the pressure in the crankcase, close the reed valve, and force the new fuel vapor up through the intake port into the combustion chamber just after the exhaust leaves through the exhaust port. And so it goes, several thousand times per minute.

You can see why it's important to keep your exhaust ports open and free of carbon deposits. You can also see that the reed valve must open and close properly and that the carburetor must do its part by vaporizing the fuel mixture. And, of course, the spark plug has to work, and work when it's supposed to. You can also see how all those exterior things that you are familiar with—spark plugs, muffler, fuel tank—are related to less familiar parts and events that occur inside the engine. The process of troubleshooting always begins outside and goes inside until the trouble is identified.

Many chain saw engines use a three-port system instead of a reed valve. A piston-ported engine, as this type is called, utilizes the skirt of the piston itself as a slide valve. Figure 9.4 shows a piston-ported chain saw engine. Many of the most dependable chain saws incorporate this basic design.

In a piston-ported chain saw engine, there is no reed valve. Instead, there is a third port at one side of the cylinder, leading from the carburetor. When the piston goes up on its intake and compression stroke, it creates a low pressure area in the crankcase. It also uncovers the third port, allowing the vaporized fuel mixture to flow into the crankcase to fill the low pressure area. When the piston goes down on its power stroke, it blocks the fuel port and increases the pressure in the crankcase. The increased pressure in the crankcase forces the vaporized fuel mixture up into the cylinder. When the piston is down, the exhaust ports are uncovered to allow the exhausted gases from the last cycle to escape. When the piston goes up to compress the fresh charge of fuel, it closes off the exhaust ports and the intake ports, allowing no escape for the fresh fuel, which is then compressed until ignition occurs.

Now that we have a general overview of the principles of a two-stroke chain saw engine, let's take a look at how some of

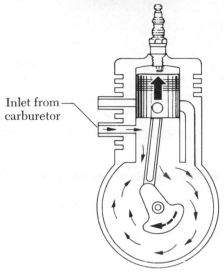

Inlet from
carburetor

Intake and compression

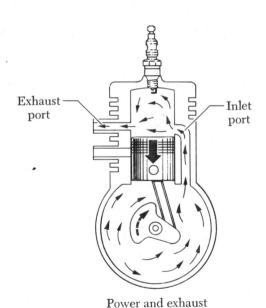

Exhaust
port

Inlet
port

Power and exhaust

Phases of piston-ported chain saw engine.

Figure 9.4

the particular needs of such an engine are met.

THE FUEL SYSTEM

In order for the engine to burn fuel, it must have a constant supply of fuel mixed with air in a vaporized form. The basic idea of a carburetor is a very simple concept. If you create a strong flow of air across the top of a container of liquid, the air flow will pull small amounts of the liquid up and into itself. If you make the opening to the container of liquid rather small, you can condense and control the amount of liquid that is mixed with the air. In the case of a gasoline chain saw engine, the liquid is gasoline and the container is the fuel tank. The place at which the fuel is mixed with air is the carburetor.

Carburetor design is based on the *venturi principle*. The principle is that if a gas flowing through a passage encounters a sudden decrease in the diameter of the passage, as in figure 9.5, it increases in speed and decreases in pressure as it passes through the narrower passage.

In a chain saw, the upward movement of the piston creates a low pressure area in the crankcase, as we have seen. This low pressure area then creates a flow of air into the crankcase. The flow of air is regulated by a *throttle* which consists, simply, of a plate that opens and closes and determines the effective size of the air passage and, therefore, the amount of airflow. Since the airflow is created by low pressure in the crankcase, there is no need

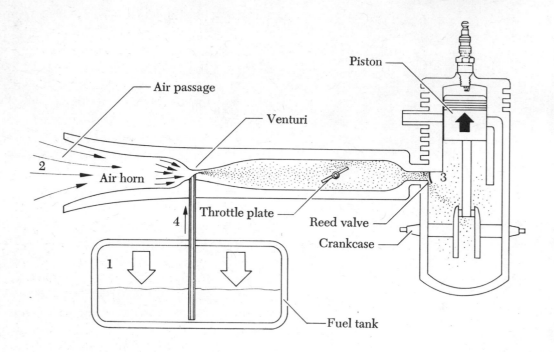

The venturi principle applied.

I. Atmosphere exerts pressure on fuel, at 1, and into air passage at 2.

II. Upward movement of piston creates low pressure area in crankcase at 3, opening reed valve and pulling air into air passage at 2.

III. At venturi, air speed increases while air pressure decreases. Air pressure at venturi is now less than air pressure on fuel, at 1.

IV. Low air pressure and high air speed in venturi pull droplets of fuel up through fuel line at 4. Droplets mix with air stream and become vaporized.

V. Continued low pressure in crankcase pulls vaporized air-fuel mixture past open throttle plate and into crankcase.

Figure 9.5

to mount the gas tank above the engine, as is the case with some small engines. Since the chain saw must operate in any position, a gravity-feed fuel system would not be suitable.

One of the most common fuel-system failures in chain saws is the result of a leak, or loss of vacuum pressure in either the carburetor, or the crankcase, or the point at which they meet. Another common failure occurs when dirt clogs the tiny passageways in the carburetor or the fuel line. Carburetors very seldom "break."

In figure 9.5 you see a representation of a fuel line from the fuel tank to the venturi in the air horn, where it ends in a fuel jet. As the airflow is sucked through the air horn by the vacuum in the crankcase, it passes through the venturi where it undergoes an increase in speed and a subsequent decrease in pressure. Since there is less atmospheric pressure at the jet, the airflow across it draws fuel from the jet in the form of little drops that are then carried into the crankcase with the air. Most of the mixture burned in a chain saw engine is air. Although the percentage of fuel mixed and burned with the air is very small, that amount is critical. If there is too much fuel, the engine will flood and fail to run. If there is too little fuel, the engine will either run lean and overheat, or it will be starved and not run at all. The exactly correct mixture of air and fuel for different engine speeds must be precisely controlled by metering mechanisms in the carburetor. The mixture that engines burn is actually about 11 pounds of air to each pound of fuel at idle.

In an automobile engine, a simple float is used to regulate the amount of fuel that is in the carburetor at a given time. The fuel level raises the float until the float moves a mechanism that cuts off the flow of fuel. Again, this design will not work on a chain saw because the engine must operate in all positions. All modern chain saws utilize an all-position carburetor. This kind of carburetor has no float.

In a chain saw's all-position carburetor, the flow of fuel into the carburetor is controlled by fitting the inlet valve to a spring-loaded diaphragm. The pressure of the spring is offset by the vacuum at the fuel jets in the venturi of the carburetor. Also, a pulsating diaphragm is operated by the changes in crankcase vacuum and acts as a fuel pump.

In a chain saw, this fuel pump is a part of the carburetor. It consists of a flexible diaphragm that moves up and down in response to the changes in pressure in the crankcase. As the diaphragm moves, it opens and closes passages between the fuel tank and the carburetor. Again, it is the engine's crankcase itself that provides the vacuum and the changes in pressure that are the basic source of mechanical energy for various aspects of the fuel system.

Figure 9.6 is a simplified drawing of a chain saw fuel pump. You can see that the changing pressure in the crankcase causes the diaphragm to move up and down. When the low pressure pulls the diaphragm up, a suction is created under the diaphragm. This suction opens the inlet

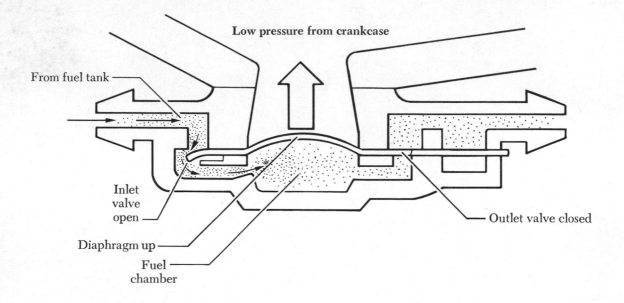

Low pressure from crankcase

From fuel tank

Inlet valve open

Diaphragm up

Fuel chamber

Outlet valve closed

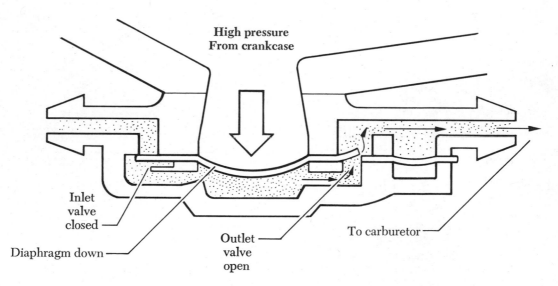

High pressure From crankcase

Inlet valve closed

Diaphragm down

Outlet valve open

To carburetor

Chain saw diaphragm fuel pump.

Figure 9.6

valve. Fuel then flows through the inlet valve and into the fuel chamber. At this time, the suction is also pulling on the outlet valve to keep it closed. When the pressure in the crankcase pushes the diaphragm down, the inlet valve will close and the pressure in the fuel chamber will push open the outlet valve.

An engine's fuel mixture requirements are different at different engine speeds. At low speeds, the vacuum in the crankcase is low and so the airflow doesn't do a thorough job of vaporizing the fuel droplets. At high speed, the air flowing in the venturi becomes stretched and thin but the fuel doesn't stretch accordingly. Thus the engine requires a richer mix of fuel and air at both idle speeds and at high speeds. That's why all chain saw carburetors have high speed and low speed mixture control *jets* and screws that adjust needles affecting these jets. Even if the high-speed mixture screw is "fixed," as it is on many smaller chain saws, it is still there to perform its function.

The high-speed screw controls a jet located in the venturi at the point of lowest pressure. The idle-speed screw controls three jets located in the air horn below the venturi, near the throttle valve.

Almost all currently produced chain saws are equipped with either a Walbro carburetor or a Tillotson carburetor. Figure 9.7 is a schematic drawing of a typical Walbro carburetor, at the time of starting, with all parts and functions labeled. Figures 9.8 through 9.10 show this same carburetor at each of the three principle operating phases. With these illustrations as a guide, you can see exactly how the external adjustments affect the carburetor at different phases of operation. Figure 9.11 is a schematic drawing of a typical Tillotson carburetor. Although constructed somewhat differently, the Tillotson performs very much like the Walbro at each of the different phases of operation.

Parp says that it's not so important that we understand exactly how each part of the inside of a carburetor works. As long as we understand the basic principle and function of the carburetor and how it fits into the whole picture of the fuel system and the engine, we'll be able to locate most problems related to the carburetor. Modern carburetors are so developed that with the proper rebuilding kit, attention to the instructions, and reasonable care, almost anyone can rebuild a carburetor. Almost any time that an internal malfunction occurs in a carburetor, the best solution is to rebuild the entire carburetor, step by step. Again, that is not very difficult and is usually easier and more practical for most chain saw users than attempting to isolate and repair a single carburetor problem. Besides, when one thing goes wrong inside a carburetor, you can usually assume that the whole thing needs to be cleaned or rebuilt. Nevertheless, specific individual carburetor service steps are covered in Chapter Ten.

Fuel Tank Vents

A deceptively small but essential part of any fuel or flow system is the vent. As

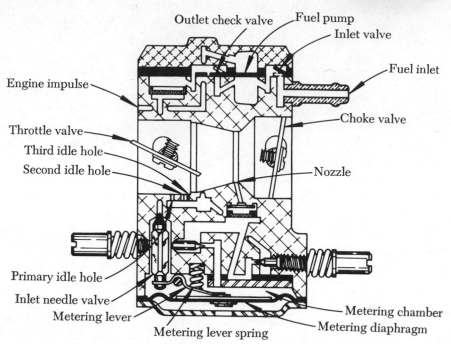

Starting phase of typical Walbro chain saw carburetor

Figure 9.7

Fuel inlet: fuel drawn from tank
Inlet valve: opens on demand from fuel pump
Fuel pump: responds to engine impulse force
Outlet check valve: forced open by pump pressure
Engine impulse: actuates fuel pump diaphragm no. 4
Throttle valve: regulates engine speed as it exposes primary, second
and third idle holes, then nozzle for dual delivery
Third idle hole: increases fuel flow at part throttle
Second idle hole: allows additional fuel flow on acceleration
Primary idle hole: only fuel source to engine at idle position
Inlet needle valve: lifts off seal to allow fuel entry
Metering lever: lifts inlet needle off seat
Metering lever spring: transmits force to metering lever
Metering diaphragm: drawn up by vacuum to activate metering lever
Metering chamber: fuel reservoir, feeds to idle and nozzle holes
Nozzle: increases fuel discharge for high speeds
Choke valve: Closes air passage at starting position

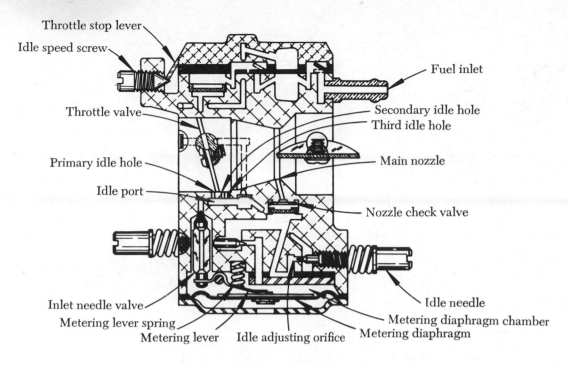

Walbro carburetor at idle phase

Figure 9.8

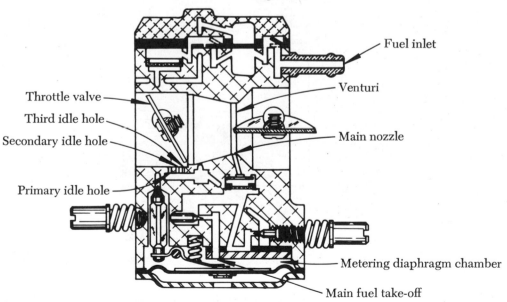

Walbro carburetor at part throttle phase

Figure 9.9

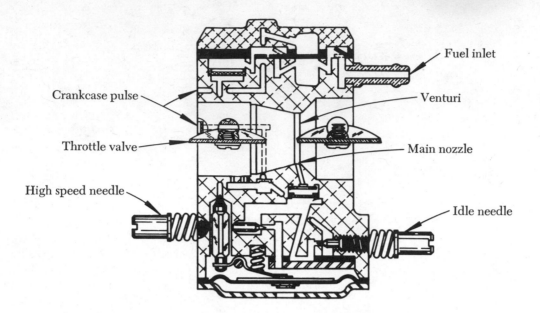

Crankcase pulse

Throttle valve

High speed needle

Fuel inlet

Venturi

Main nozzle

Idle needle

Walbro carburetor at high speed phase

Figure 9.10

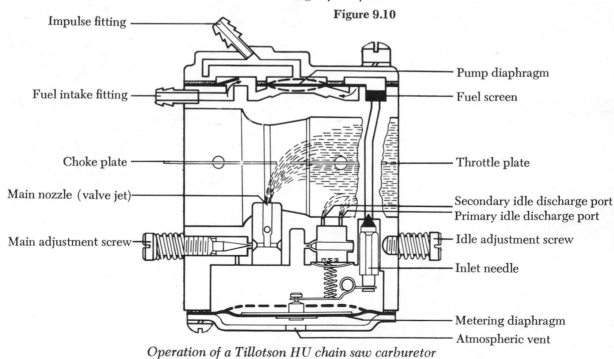

Impulse fitting

Fuel intake fitting

Choke plate

Main nozzle (valve jet)

Main adjustment screw

Pump diaphragm

Fuel screen

Throttle plate

Secondary idle discharge port
Primary idle discharge port

Idle adjustment screw

Inlet needle

Metering diaphragm

Atmospheric vent

Operation of a Tillotson HU chain saw carburetor

Figure 9.11

the fuel level in a fuel tank goes down, air must be allowed to enter the tank to replace the used fuel. Otherwise, a vacuum will develop and no fuel will flow. This is equally true of the chain oil tank.

Many chain saws have the simplest of all vent systems. It is essentially a hole in the tank cap. Since dirt could easily get through the hole and into the fuel, some method of filtering the incoming air is always employed. In the simpler systems, there is merely a filter screen or piece of fiber. These caps should be replaced often since they are more likely to become clogged and the filtering system is not sufficient to stop dirt from getting into the fuel.

Other cap-vent systems are more elaborate. A common design has a valve that is opened when a vacuum develops in the fuel tank. When the tank is tilted, the pressure of the fuel closes the valve.

All fuel tank vent systems should be checked and cleaned regularly. A clogged vent can silence a chain saw instantly, and a partly clogged vent can make it stammer.

Fuel Line Pick-up Filter

Fuel flows from the fuel tank to the carburetor. It flows through a fuel pick-up line that is weighted on one end so that it sits on the bottom of the fuel tank. The weight moves when you tilt your chain saw so that the end of the fuel pick-up line is always at the lowest part of the fuel tank.

Water is heavier than gasoline. Take Parp's word for it. That's why water sometimes collects at the bottom of the glass bowl in your vehicle's fuel pump. In a chain saw's fuel tank, any water—even the smallest amount—will sink to the bottom of the lowest part of the fuel tank, right where the end of your fuel pick-up sits. That's why water can clog your fuel filter and fuel pick-up line. Your fuel filter can look clean and be as clogged by water as if it were full of mud.

Parp is mumbling about how moisture condenses in partly filled fuel tanks while it is stored for long periods of time—more than two months. That's one of the many reasons that stale fuel is bad for your chain saw, whether it's stored in your chain saw's fuel tank or in a gasoline can. It turns into varnish.

IGNITION SYSTEM

Now we need a way to create that spark in the combustion chamber that will fire the vaporized fuel mixture after it's compressed by the piston.

All commonly available chain saws utilize a flywheel and magneto ignition system. The *flywheel* is a heavy wheel mounted on the crankshaft at the side of the engine opposite from the sprocket and drive mechanism. Part of the flywheel's purpose is to add its weight as momentum to the turning crankshaft to help keep the engine turning smoothly. The flywheel in a chain saw is also fitted with permanent magnets. This is true of both conventional magneto systems and electronic, or breakerless ignition systems.

The flywheel and the crankshaft are held

together by a small piece of relatively soft metal called a *half-moon key*. This key fits into a slot in the crankshaft that corresponds to a slot in the flywheel. Note that one very common problem with all small engine machines is a sheared, damaged, or partially sheared half-moon key.

When you pull the starter rope on your chain saw, you spin the flywheel. Because the flywheel is firmly attached to the crankshaft, you also turn the crankshaft. When the crankshaft turns, the crank moves the piston up and down. We have already seen how the piston, moving in the cylinder, creates pressure changes in the crankcase and how the pulsations of those pressure changes provide the impulses that activate the fuel system. Thus, spinning the flywheel with the starter rope causes the piston to move and the fuel mixture to flow. It also simultaneously creates the electric energy that causes the flow of electricity that results in the spark at the spark plug that burns the compressed fuel mixture. When you pull the starter rope on your chain saw, you are providing the initial energy that turns the engine, moves the fuel, and creates the fire. After the engine starts, it does all this for itself, and replaces your arm as the energy source with the expansion of the burning fuel mixture.

The other part of a flywheel and magneto ignition system is the *magneto*. A magneto is a coil of wires that are tightly wound and held by a cylinder-shaped container. It is also a generator of alternating current that converts magnetic energy from the magnets in the flywheel to electrical energy

that flows to the spark plug. The word magneto is short for magnetoelectric machine.

If you think back to your grade school days, you might remember doing a electromagnetic experiment in your science class. If you're like Parp, you didn't understand it then, and you won't now, and you don't give a damn and nobody knows anything about electricity anyway because it's clearly magic or else how could pictures come through the air? Right?

O.K. Say it's magic. It's nevertheless true that if you move a wire across the lines of a magnetic field you can produce electricity in the wire. If the wire is part of a complete circuit, you can make electrical current flow through the circuit. If you wind another wire into a coil around the wire in the circuit and then move the coiled wire through the magnetic field, the voltage of the current you produce is multiplied by the number of turns in the coiled wire.

And another thing about the relationship between magnetism and electricity. Just as you can use magnetism to induce an electrical current, a flow of electricity also creates magnetism. Whenever an electrical current is flowing in a conductor, a magnetic field exists around the conductor. If the conductor is a tightly wound coil of wires, the magnetic forces merge to create one magnetic field, stronger than that surrounding a single wire.

The strength and direction of the force of a magnetic field present around a conductor is determined by the strength and direction of the electrical current in the conductor. If you change the current, you also change the magnetic field. If you stop the current completely, the magnetic forces collapse. If you stop the current in a coil of wire, the magnetic forces collapse across the turns of the coil and induce a new current.

Electricity only flows in a complete circuit, and a current of electricity always takes the path of least resistance to complete its circuit. In other words, electricity is only alive when it can travel from one place to another and back again, by a different road, and it always takes the easiest road.

Now what we want to do is use the ideas we've just reviewed, and a few others, to produce the spark that starts the fire in our fire trap, the combustion chamber.

We have a flywheel with permanent magnets cast into it. If we move those magnets past a coil of wire, we'll create a potential electrical pressure, or voltage, in the coil. We can use the potential voltage thus produced to create the spark. Note that the flywheel and the coil must pass at exactly the correct distance from each other. Actually, the flywheel passes closest to a laminated core of soft iron plates called an armature core. Soft iron is an excellent conductor of magnetic forces, so it is used to transfer the magnetic forces from the flywheel magnets to the magneto coil. It also concentrates the strength of the magnets. The distance between the flywheel magnets and the armature core at their closest is known as the armature air

gap. Magneto edge gap is a different matter that we needn't bother our heads about now.

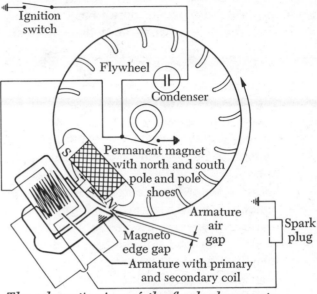

The schematic view of the flywheel magneto ignition system (breaker point system).

Figure 9.12

A magneto coil actually consists of two coils, or windings of wire. The inner winding is called the primary winding and the outer winding is called the secondary winding. The primary winding consists of about 200 turns of rather thick copper wire and the secondary winding consists of about 10,000 turns of very thin wire.

In a chain saw's magneto system, the primary winding is connected to an electric switch, called *breaker points*. The points open and close to break or complete the electrical circuit. They are caused to open and close by a simple mechanism, a lobe on the crankshaft. One of the points is fixed in a certain position and the other can be moved by the lobe on the crankshaft. Each time the crankshaft turns, the lobe pushes the movable point away from the fixed one. At that instant, the points are open and the circuit is broken. When the lobe passes its point of contact with the movable point, a steel spring brings it back into contact with the fixed point and the circuit is complete again.

The magneto's primary winding and the points are also connected to an overload device called a *condenser*. The condenser absorbs the flow of current at high voltage when the spark plug fires and prevents the current from arcing across the breaker points before it's supposed to. If that happened, it would short-out the circuit to the spark plug and prevent the spark.

When you pull the starter rope and spin the flywheel, its magnets pass the armature core and the magneto coil. The armature transfers the concentrated magnetic forces to the magneto coil. The magneto coil converts the magnetism to electrical energy. When the crankshaft lobe, also moved by the spinning flywheel, moves past the movable breaker point, the points close and the electricity flows through the points to ground.

Now this is the tricky part. When the points are opened, the flow of current in this primary circuit is interrupted. Since the flow of current caused a strong electromagnetic field to surround the primary winding of thick wire, the interruption causes this field to collapse across the sec-

ondary winding of thin wire. This compresses the current and tremendously increases the voltage. It increases it so much that, if it weren't for the condenser, it would leap across the breaker points even though they are open. The electrical pressure increases from about 300 or 400 volts to about 15,000 or 20,000 volts. This is caused by the far greater number of turns in the secondary winding. And, of course, the current always moves to the secondary winding when the primary circuit is interrupted because it is the path of least resistance.

Since this high-voltage current is blocked from jumping across the open points by the condenser, it travels along its secondary lead to the spark plug. Here there is no condenser to stop it and the gap is small and easy to jump. The current jumps across the gap and we have our spark. Since the spark plug is screwed into the cylinder head, the electrode that's connected to the threads forms an electrical ground and the circuit is complete.

We now have fuel to burn, a place to trap the fire, a way to use the energy from the trapped fire, and a spark to start the fire. We have an engine. If any of the systems of the engine hesitate or fail, the engine will run poorly or not at all.

ELECTRONIC (BREAKERLESS) IGNITIONS

Many new chain saws, and many more each year, are equipped with breakerless ignition systems. Until recently, these systems were considered too expensive for installation on relatively inexpensive machines such as chain saws. But the production of these systems so increased, and the production methods became so efficient that the considerable advantages of these systems quickly outweighed their higher costs. Of all gasoline-powered small engine machines, chain saws have the most to gain from the breakerless ignition.

Changing or adjusting the breaker points in chain saws has always been a job that the average owner was reluctant to attempt. The flywheel nut has to be removed, a formidable obstacle in itself, and the flywheel has to be separated from the crankshaft. Parp believes that anyone with a little confidence could successfully change

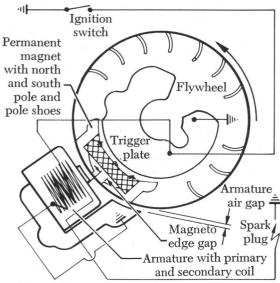

The schematic view of ignition system of 015 L Electronic

Figure 9.13

or adjust the points in any chain saw, but many users lack the confidence. And most manufacturers, dealers, and mechanics have contributed to the difficulties by making the job seem mysterious and specialized.

The breakerless ignition has no points to adjust and no moving parts to wear out. It can be permanently sealed against moisture and dirt, the two culprits most responsible for ignition failure. The breakerless ignition also greatly increases the efficiency of any engine at all speeds and significantly reduces its polluting emissions. A worthy advance. It is also virtually maintenance-free.

In the breakerless ignition, the points and condenser are replaced by various transistorized circuits that may include the use of a capacitor, a gate-controlled switch and trigger, and diodes, thyristors, or rectifiers. Most chain saw users have no need for a technical explanation of how electronic ignitions function but we'll go through some of these elements that may be involved as nontechnically as possible.

A *capacitor* is an electrical storage device and safety or overload control that is designed to discharge stored voltage through a coil to create the high voltage current that provides the spark. A capacitor is not always used in electronic ignitions. Essentially, it replaces the condenser, and then some.

A *gate-controlled switch* is an electronic switch with no moving or mechanical parts. It is opened and closed by changes in current direction. A positive current direction closes the gate, or turns it on. A negative current turns it off. The trigger is actually an electrical current that activates the gate-controlled switch.

Diodes, thyristors, and *rectifiers* are electronic devices that allow current to flow in only one direction. They the semiconductors. When current is traveling in one direction, they conduct and the current flows. When the current reverses, they refuse to do anything.

All of these devices are very small and may be incorporated into a single unit called the *trigger plate*. That's why these ignitions are often called solid state circuits. Solid state circuits employ semiconductors as control devices, or switches.

Magnetic induction still supplies the initial potential voltage for breakerless systems, just as it does for conventional systems. When the flywheel turns, magnetic forces cut across the windings of the magneto coil and produce a negative current in the primary windings. In a typical system, a diode then allows the current to flow. Remember that this diode is a one-way device. When it is conducting, the situation is similar to a conventional system at the moment when the breaker points are closed and a current is flowing in the primary windings of thick wire.

As the flywheel turns, it reverses the direction of the magnetic forces. This, of course, reverses the direction of the current in the primary windings and the diode sits down on the job. Again, a condenser or safety device prevents the current from proceeding before it is supposed to. At this time, the gate-controlled switch is turned on by a positive voltage and a current flows in the primary windings. The gate-controlled switch is then immediately opened, or turned off, by a negative current in the coil induced by the trigger. This interrupts the current at its maximum voltage and its electromagnetic field collapses across the secondary windings, creating the high voltage that provides the spark.

POWER

We don't want the chain on our chain saw always to move when the engine is running. We do want it to move when we increase the speed of the engine by depressing the throttle control that opens the throttle plate and allows more fuel to flow. To insure that the chain moves when we want it to and stops when it should, all chain saws utilize a *centrifugal clutch*.

Since the crankshaft is a turning mechanism, it possesses centrifugal force. Centrifugal force is another of those ideas you probably discussed and experimented with in your grade school science class. You also have experienced it, in considerable strength, anytime you've even ridden a ferris wheel or some other amusement park ride. As your body spins on the wheel, you feel a force pushing you out away from the center of the wheel. That force is centrifugal force. The word "centrifugal" is an adjective that describes moving or being directed away from a center or axis. Anything spinning on an axis has a tendency to move away from the axis. That's part

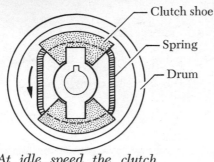

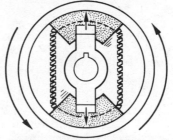

Clutch shoe

Spring

Drum

At idle speed the clutch shoes rotate freely in the drum.

Figure 9.14

When engine speed increases, the shoes are thrown outwards by centrifugal force and press so hard against the drum that it, and the chain, start to move.

of the reason why you tend to fall over when you're drunk.

A centrifugal clutch consists of a drum casing with a hub that fits over the drive side of the crankshaft. The hub fits over a bearing assembly and the crankshaft can turn in the hub without turning the drum. Inside the drum, clutch shoes are attached by springs and the entire friction assembly is held to the crankshaft by retaining washers or by a half-moon key similar to the flywheel key. At rest or at idle, the springs keep the clutch shoes from touching the inside walls of the clutch drum. When the engine idles, the drum stays still and the shoes turn within it and with the crankshaft. When you speed the engine, the crankshaft turns faster and the centrifugal force on the clutch shoes is increased. At speeds above idle, the centrifugal force pushes the shoes outward, against the inside of the clutch drum. This causes the drum to turn and, since the sprocket is attached to the clutch drum,

the sprocket turns also. The sprocket turns the chain.

Note that if the engine is operating at only a moderate speed, the shoes are not pushed very tightly against the walls of the drum. This results in friction between the shoes and the drum. That's why a clutch wears so rapidly if you cut wood at less than maximum engine speed.

Clutch bearings are another common cause of trouble. If water gets into these bearings they can become rusted. In that case, the bearing assembly must be replaced.

CHAIN LUBRICATION SYSTEMS

Now that we have our chain moving, we need some way to keep it lubricated and some kind of mechanism that will allow us to adjust the chain tension when necessary. A discussion of these matters will complete our brief overview of the general mechanics of a chain saw.

The most common chain lubrication system is still the *hand-operated oil pump.* These assemblies have very few parts and are quite simple in operation. A typical thumb-push oil pump consists of a push rod that moves a plunger inside a very small, cast-unit, simple pump. A pump plunger spring presses against the pump plunger and so exerts the pressure that moves the push button back out after you remove your thumb. When the spring pushes the plunger and the push button out, a vacuum is created inside the pump. This pulls the oil from the oil tank through an intake check valve. When you push on the button, the plunger forces the oil through a discharge check valve, into the oil line that leads to the oil discharge hole near the mounting area of the guide bar. The oil squirts through oil holes in the guide bar and onto the chain itself. A bent push rod is the most common problem occurring with manual oilers.

Automatic oiling systems are somewhat more complicated and there is quite a lot of variation in design. In general, there are two different kinds of drive mechanisms, and two methods of attaching the pump assembly to the chain drive mechanism.

If the pump is driven directly by the crankshaft, as it is with many chain saws, the pump is operating any time the engine is running. This means, often, that the pump is using oil even when the engine is at idle and the chain isn't turning. A small amount of oil may be wasted with this system.

Some chain saws (Stihl, some Homelite models, and others) have automatic oil pumps that are driven by the sprocket, the clutch drum, or the sprocket shaft. With this system, the pump delivers oil only when the clutch is engaged and the chain is turning. If the chain isn't moving, no oil is pumped.

Automatic chain lubrication pumps are driven either by a worm gear or by an eccentric. The worm gear may be part of either the crankshaft or the sprocket shaft. An eccentric, when used, is a part of the crankshaft. Let's look at the eccentric system first.

An *eccentric* is a disc or wheel that has its axis of revolution displaced from its center so that it is capable of imparting reciprocating motion. That is, it turns lopsided. That way it can push something away and then allow it to return toward itself. It is easy to produce a crankshaft that has an eccentric portion.

As the crankshaft turns, the large side of the eccentric pushes the plunger away. When the plunger is all the way back, it opens the inlet channel and the pump distribution cylinder fills with oil. When the eccentric turns away, a spring pushes the plunger forward and the oil in the pump cylinder is forced out through a check valve. When the plunger moves back, the check valve closes to prevent oil from being sucked backward into the pump.

Not all of the oil that enters the distribution cylinder is pumped to the chain. Some of it returns to be pumped again. At

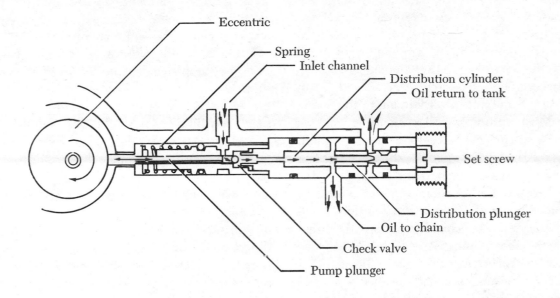

Eccentric

Spring

Inlet channel

Distribution cylinder

Oil return to tank

Set screw

Distribution plunger

Oil to chain

Check valve

Pump plunger

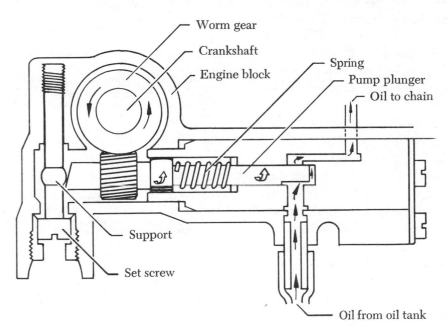

Worm gear

Crankshaft

Engine block

Spring

Pump plunger

Oil to chain

Support

Set screw

Oil from oil tank

Two different automatic chain oiling systems
Figure 9.15

one end of a typical eccentric oil pump system there is a set screw that moves the distribution plunger and changes the relationship between the amount of oil going to the chain and the amount being returned. This set screw can be used to adjust the amount of oil flowing to the chain.

Most automatic oil systems are driven by a worm gear, either on the crankshaft, or on the sprocket shaft. In a typical system, the worm gear turns and causes the pump plunger to rotate. A reduction system is used to reduce the rotation speed of the pump to considerably less than that of the crankshaft. As in the figure, one end of the pump plunger is beveled. A spring pushes this end against a curved support that is located eccentrically in relation to the pump plunger. The entire support assembly may be moved by changing the set screw that controls its position. This changes the eccentricity of the support and alters the amount of oil delivered to the chain.

As the plunger turns, the eccentric support pushes it back and forth. As the plunger moves back and forth, it opens and closes the inlet and outlet channels and so pumps oil to the chain.

Some oil pumps are located behind the flywheel of the chain saw. Others are located in a recess in the crankcase on the drive side of the saw. All are hidden and covered to protect them from dirt and impact and chain saw owners.

Most recent automatic oil pumps are adjustable but many are difficult to adjust. There's a reason for this. As you can see,

it is easy to damage an oil pump by putting too much pressure on the set screw or by turning the adjustment mechanism too far. Most oil systems are designed so that they only need to be adjusted if you dramatically change the size of the guide bar used. If you're only going to do some heavy cutting for a while, you shouldn't need to adjust your oiler. That's why Parp prefers to have a manual oiler in addition to an adjustable automatic oiling system. That way, the chain is always oiled by the automatic system and you can add more oil during heavy cutting sessions by using the manual oiler freely. For the average user, any of today's quality automatic systems will supply sufficient lubrication under almost all conditions, without additional manual oil.

CHAIN ADJUSTMENT MECHANISM

All chain adjustment mechanisms are very similar. They consist of a chain adjustment screw and a nut that moves on the screw. The screw is installed in a cast housing, usually on the bar mounting pad but sometimes built into the clutch cover.

When you turn the screw, the adjusting nut moves. The adjusting nut has a pin on one side, usually a square pin, that fits into a square hole at the tail of the bar. When you turn the screw, the nut moves and the pin moves the bar. If you exert excessive pressure on the adjusting screw, all of that pressure is concentrated by the adjusting nut. Since all of that pressure is on one small part of the screw, the screw can bend or the threads can strip if the adjusting nut is not in position in the hole in the guide bar. When you clamp down the guide bar mounting nuts you can bend the adjustment screw or even punch a hole in the crankcase or tank casting. That's about all that can happen to this mechanism, but it happens often enough.

TROUBLESHOOTING

Even if you never want to try any mechanical repairs on your own chain saw, learning to troubleshoot can save you a great deal of time and money. Parp believes that anyone can learn to perform most of the services and repairs that a chain saw usually needs. It is certainly true that anyone can learn to troubleshoot accurately enough to determine at least the likely cause of most problems. In any case, if you try to determine your own problems before you go to a mechanic, you'll discover many instances of insufficient fuel, turned-off switches, fouled spark plugs and loose nuts, bolts, and screws.

Troubleshooting is a logical process that always begins with the easiest tests and the most obvious functions and proceeds to the most complicated or difficult only after all others have been exhausted. In other words, as we said before, troubleshooting is a diagnostic process that begins outside, with the symptoms, and goes inside until the cause is discovered.

Parp is nudging me to suggest, before we go any further, that if your saw is under warranty when a problem develops, you should see your dealer before you do anything yourself. Unless you're out of fuel or forgot to turn the ignition switch on. Any other problems in a new saw should go straight to your dealer. All chain saw warranties become void if an unauthorized person, mechanic or not, attempts any repairs other than those called for by normal owner maintenance. And most chain saw manufacturers are extraordinarily generous about allowing repairs on their warranties. Parp has seen manufacturers accept saws on warranty that have been terribly abused, although he says no one should push their luck on this. If you added STP to your fuel tank, forget it.

A great majority of apparent chain saw engine failures are not true engine failures. Almost any time that a chain saw fails to start or fails to continue to run, the failure is caused by a problem or problems in either the ignition system or the fuel system. If your year-old chain saw suddenly refuses to operate at high speeds, or runs poorly at any speed, you should not assume that your piston rings are worn or that the crankshaft is bent. These are relatively uncommon troubles that should only occur after many, many hours of hard use, if at all. It is much more likely, for example, that your carburetor needs adjustment or repair or that your fuel line is split. Before you tear into the heart of your engine, exhaust all the easier and more external possibilities.

The first thing you should do, always, is to take a good look all over the entire exterior of your saw. It's a detective process: you don't know, often, what you are looking for but you do have a pretty good idea how things should look. Many times you'll discover that your high-tension wire (spark plug cable) is loose, or that your carburetor is loose (though this problem may not always be visible), or that fuel is leaking from a defective gasket. Troubleshooting always starts with a visual inspection.

By the way, the only reliable check of chain saw engine compression is to pull the starter rope or spin the flywheel by hand to determine if the resistance to engine turning is normal, as caused by the compression in the combustion chamber. Chain saws often continue to run, and run well, even after a considerable loss of compression, depending on the cause. Any other compression test on a chain saw can be very misleading and is usually a complete waste of time. Manufacturer's shop manuals sometimes specify a compression test and a compression range, but even these should be viewed as arbitrary and inconclusive.

In the Appendix you will find a group of troubleshooting charts. Before you follow these very far, you should become familiar with a typical and logical process of troubleshooting. We'll begin where the first simple chart left off.

If your chain saw refuses to start and you are certain that the problem is not covered by the previous chart, proceed as follows.

First, you pull the starter rope several times. Does the engine turn over when you pull the starter rope? If the engine does not turn over, the problem is your starter and there's no question about it. If it does, your simple chain saw starter is probably working and you should go on.

Next, remove the spark plug. If your fuel system is delivering fuel to the cylinder and compression chamber, and if your spark plug is cold, you will be able to smell gasoline on the spark plug. If the plug is quite dry but still smells rather strongly of gasoline, the problem is probably not in your fuel system. If the spark plug is dry and odorless, your fuel system is probably not delivering fuel. If the spark plug is wet or fouled or oily, it's most likely that you have a problem in either your fuel system or your ignition system.

You still don't know whether your problem is in the fuel system or in your ignition system. If the spark plug is wet, it's either because your fuel system is delivering too much fuel to the cylinder or because your ignition system is failing to provide the spark necessary to burn the fuel.

The easiest next step, and the most logical, is to determine whether or not your ignition system is delivering a spark. This was covered for other reasons in Chapter Five, but we'll repeat it here for the sake of convenience and some minor differences.

Find a heavily shaded place. Disconnect your spark plug cable and leave the spark plug screwed in. If your cable has a boot or cap that fits over the spark plug terminal, insert a metal rod or nail or paper clip in the boot so that it projects from the boot. Hold the metal piece or the spark plug wire so that the end of it is about ⅛ inch from the top of the spark plug. Be sure to hold the cable by the rubber insulation and keep your hand back from the end of the metal. Pull your starter rope briskly. Each time you pull the rope, a spark should jump from the cable end to the spark plug terminal several times. You may not be able to see the spark if you're outside in broad daylight, but you will be able to hear it. In moderate shade, you should be able to see the spark as it jumps.

If you see several strong blue or white sparks each time you pull the starter rope, your ignition system is good at least as far as the spark plug, and if the spark plug is good then the ignition system is probably good all the way through. In that case, your problem is most likely to be in the fuel system.

If you get no spark at all or if the spark seems very weak, you have a problem in the ignition system. More than likely it's the magneto.

If your spark plug was dry when you removed it for the first test, leave the plug screwed in and the cable disconnected while you pull the starter rope several more times. Then immediately remove the spark plug. If it still isn't wet with gasoline, your problem is probably in the fuel system. To make sure, pour a very small amount, about ½ teaspoon, of fresh, correctly mixed fuel straight down into the spark plug hole. This will fill the cylinder with fuel. Then immediately replace the spark plug, connect the cable, and pull the

starter rope. If the engine starts and runs briefly, you can be certain that your problem is in your fuel system.

Now if you determined that your problem is in your ignition system, you should replace the spark plug first of all—unless it's quite new and you know for certain that it has been firing up until the time of failure. And even still it's worth trying another one. You should always keep new plugs around for exactly this reason. You may have a defective spark plug, or the plug may be fouled in such a way that you can't visibly detect the fouling. If you replace the plug and the engine runs, your problem is solved. If you replace the plug and the saw still doesn't run, you know that your ignition failure is probably someplace between the magnets in your flywheel and the end of the spark plug cable. The culprit is probably that magneto.

If you determined that your problem is in the fuel system, you should now double-check the fuel in the fuel tank. If you have any doubts, discard the fuel and replace it with a fresh, correct mixture. While you're at it, check the vent in the fuel tank cap. A clogged fuel cap vent can prevent fuel from reaching the cylinder. If that doesn't do it, check the air filter. Even if it looks spotless, clean it thoroughly with gasoline, blow it out, and allow it to air dry. Do the same with the fuel line filter. Even a small amount of water in the fuel filter will block the line and no fuel will reach the cylinder.

While your air filter and fuel filter are drying, smell the carburetor. If you detect a heavy gasoline smell, your problem is probably there. Unless you find a disconnected or broken fuel line, you will probably have to remove, clean, and rebuild the carburetor. That is not difficult and you really should be able to do it yourself. See Chapter Ten.

If your ignition failure was not the fault of a turned-off ignition switch, fouled spark plug, or loose spark plug cable connection, carefully examine as much of the spark plug cable as you can see. If you find any breaks or cracks in the insulation, that may well be your problem. If not, as Parp said before, it's probably your magneto. It could be that a simple servicing of gaps, timing, and so forth will correct the problem or it could be that you'll have to replace the magneto. Of course, it could possibly be the points, if you've let your maintenance slip, or it could be the ignition switch. See the next troubleshooting chart, the next chapter, *The Chain Saw Service Manual* (Intertec Publishing Corporation), and your favorite good luck charm.

If you have cleaned or replaced the air filter and fuel filter and your saw still doesn't start, readjust the carburetor from step one as in Chapter Six and try again. If that doesn't do it, squirt a small amount of fuel into either the crankcase or the combustion chamber, through the spark plug hole. If you have a spark and fuel, and if all of the parts are together, the saw should run. And if that doesn't do it, you've at least eliminated a lot of possibilities.

Parp cautions that much of the material in this chapter and many of the suggested procedures assume that you have treated your saw properly and performed all the maintenance and service procedures recommended in your owner's manual and in Chapters Five and Six. If you have not done these things, you may miss some very obvious problems (such as excessive carboning of exhaust ports) and erroneously conclude that your fuel system has a major malfunction. You cannot follow a logical process by leaving out Step One. Step One is to follow all the steps of a sound maintenance and service schedule.

Most of the Appendix, p. 224, consists of troubleshooting charts. These charts cannot be a cure-all for every chain saw difficulty, or anywhere near it. In fact, many of the repairs or procedures referred to are only within the capabilities of a well-trained mechanic, whether professional or not. But these charts should nevertheless help you to decide what your problems are likely to be and whether you should try to fix your saw yourself or take it to a mechanic or junk it.

We'll start with the cutting attachment but we'll concentrate on the mechanical aspects of the drive, clutch, and adjustment mechanism. Parp has detailed the saw chain itself in Chapter Seven and in the Saw Chain Troubleshooting Guide. There is, of course, some unavoidable repetition. In the charts in the Appendix, Parp has tried to list the troubles and causes in the order of their likelihood. Some exceptions were necessary.

Some Repairs • 10

This chapter intends to bridge a part of the gap between your owner's manual and the more advanced repair guides such as shop service manuals and Intertec's *Chain Saw Service Manual*.

Parp thinks back to his first experiences with chain saw mechanics and remembers that gap clearly. *The Chain Saw Service Manual*, like its companion volume, *Small Engines Service Manual*, is chiefly for professional mechanics, professional users, or others who are already reasonably familiar with service and repair procedures. As such, *The Chain Saw Service Manual* is an extraordinary contribution and a great service aid for which Intertec deserves high credit.

The Chain Saw Service Manual offers detailed information on virtually every recent chain saw and some that aren't so recent. Included are extremely detailed drawings, diagrams, and specifications of every engine, part, and function of the saws covered. A mechanic can refer to these drawings and specifications to discover the exact order of assembly and disassembly. But it doesn't tell you, for example, that you'll probably need a spanner wrench in order to remove the clutch, or that you need some way to protect the piston head and limit the turning of the crankshaft when you remove a clutch nut or flywheel nut.

There are several excellent and specialized books on the subject of small engine repair. The best of these, says Parp, is Paul Weissler's *Small Gas Engines*, a *Popular Science* book from Harper and Row. Parp differs considerably regarding some of Mr. Weissler's comments on chain saws, but not regarding repair procedures for the engines themselves. Parp suggests that a combination of your owner's manual, a shop manual for your saw, *The Chain Saw Service Manual*, this book, and Mr. Weissler's *Small Gas Engines* would be an excellent library of resource material with which to begin a study of chain saw mechanics. Begin, Parp says, because books and mechanics don't mix readily. What you really need is some gumption, a collection of tools, a chain saw that doesn't work, and a diminishing wood supply with winter coming on about fifty miles west of Nowhere. That will make a mechanic out of you.

In other words, hands-on experience is the only real teacher. There are, however, many easy repairs you can make now with a minimum of tools. Once you get started,

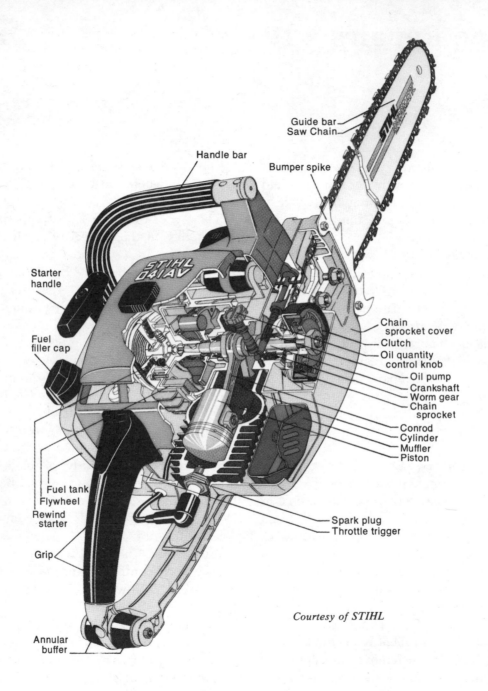

Handle bar

Bumper spike

Guide bar
Saw Chain

Starter
handle

Fuel
filler cap

Chain
sprocket cover
Clutch
Oil quantity
control knob
Oil pump
Crankshaft
Worm gear
Chain
sprocket
Conrod
Cylinder
Muffler
Piston

Fuel tank
Flywheel

Rewind
starter

Spark plug
Throttle trigger

Grip

Courtesy of STIHL

Annular
buffer

you'll be reluctant to surrender your saw to that guy in town who calls himself a mechanic.

THREE TIPS

Here are three tips worth mentioning. First, always keep your work in order. Lay down your parts exactly as they come off. Draw pictures to remind yourself of particular assemblies. If you remove bolts and screws that are different sizes, be sure you put them back where they belong. If necessary, draw a picture of the assembly and label the parts or punch the bolts and screws through the picture in the correct places.

The second tip is never to use a tool that doesn't fit the job and to be exceedingly cautious about substituting for recommended tools or procedures.

The third tip is that one tragedy is common to all beginning mechanics, especially if they begin on chain saws. Many chain saw parts are made of soft metals such as aluminum, brass, and magnesium. Threads cut into these metals are exceedingly easy to damage. Be cautious about applying force or pressure to a wrench or screwdriver. Damaged threads can be repaired with a Heli-Coil thread repair kit (address in Appendix).

ANOTHER LIST OF TOOLS

To begin basic maintenance, service, and repair operations on your chain saw, you should have a fairly good collection of hand tools. Here is a list of the most basic tools you'll need. Some special tools will be mentioned in the course of discussing repair procedures. If you will read each section before attempting the procedure, you will know which tools you'll need.

- Small machine hammer
- Slip-joint pliers
- Set of ignition or small low-profile combination wrenches
- Set of combination wrenches through 1 inch
- ¼″ and ⅜″ drive socket sets with extensions
- Set of deep-well sockets
- Spark plug socket
- Set of long allen-head wrenches (professional quality)
- Small and large vise grips
- Assorted slot-type screwdrivers
- Small, medium, and large Phillips screwdrivers
- Plastic feeler gauge set
- Test light (this you can make)
- Small, medium, and large needle-nose pliers
- Center punches
- Offset screwdriver
- Wooden mallet
- Tap and die set, or Heli-Coil thread repair kits
- Impact driver set and bits (same drive size as your socket set)

Other than noted exceptions, the repair instructions in this chapter apply specifically to the Stihl 031 AV, a popular mid-range lightweight chain saw. This allows Parp to be more particular than if he were discussing several saws at once. Most of these instructions can be readily applied to any other chain saw, especially if you have a shop manual for that particular saw, or the *Chain Saw Service Manual* as a guide.

The first and most important and most basic maintenance procedures for chain saws are those covered in Chapters Five, Six, and Seven. If you follow those procedures conscientiously, as well as any others recommended in your owner's manual, you'll avoid or postpone many of the repairs mentioned in this chapter.

CLUTCH AND SPROCKET

The entire drive mechanism is a relatively simple assembly. As long as you keep your parts in order and take precautions to protect the piston head, you should have no trouble.

Because of the turning direction of the crankshaft, chain saw clutch assemblies have left-handed threads to keep them from loosening when the chain is turning. That means you have to turn them clockwise to get them off. Since this is the direction in which the crankshaft turns, you need some way to stop it. When you turn the clutch, and hence the crankshaft, you move the piston up and down. Therefore, one way to stop the crankshaft from turning is to stop the piston from going up and down. We're already up against two of

those specialized shop tools that Parp mentioned earlier.

The first is a crankshaft locking nut. This tool is supplied with all Stihl chain saws and so isn't really just for the pros. But most chain saw manufacturers do not supply a crankshaft locking nut or screw, or a reasonable substitute. Check your owner's manual to be sure. You can make a passable substitute with a clean lightweight rag or towel. This is risky since you may well leave bits of thread in the cylinder but it will do in an emergency. Another method is to use a short length of starter rope with a knot that will slip through the spark plug hole.

The second special tool is a clutch wrench. Again, Stihl and a few other manufacturers supply a clutch wrench with every chain saw, but most do not. There is no very satisfactory substitute. The problem is that the face of the clutch is flat and the disassembly points differ widely in size and shape from saw to saw. You can and should obtain a clutch wrench from your dealer or the distributor of your chain saw. There are adjustable spanner wrenches available that are designed to fit many small engine clutches. These are inexpensive tools and have other uses as well.

If the clutch shoes are just dirty or oily, you won't need to replace them. Just remove them and wash them in gasoline. When dry, roughen the clutch shoes with emery cloth.

If the clutch shoes are worn, replace the complete set. Likewise, if your springs or spring hooks are stretched or fatigued, replace all springs and hooks. Otherwise you'll be doing the whole job over again immediately.

Whenever you remove your clutch, check the bearings. Most bearings consist of needles in a needle cage. If they are rusted they will need to be replaced. Always grease new or old bearings with a high-quality waterproof grease before re-installing. Also put a small amount of oil onto the crankshaft behind the clutch drum.

First, remove the guide bar nuts, sprocket cover, guide bar, and saw chain. Then remove the starter assembly from the other side of the chain saw. Otherwise you might damage the starter when you re-assemble the clutch and tighten the clutch retaining nut. Do not disassemble the starter, but simply remove the entire housing and assembly from the saw.

After the starter assembly is removed, remove the spark plug. Then screw in the crankshaft locking nut by hand. Insert a clutch wrench between the clutch shoes and turn the clutch clockwise, gently, until the piston stops against the crankshaft locking nut. Then use a socket and breaker bar or combination wrench to loosen the clutch retaining nut. Remember that this nut has left-hand threads and so is removed by turning it clockwise. Use a spanner wrench or clutch wrench to hold the clutch still while removing the nut.

On both sides of the clutch of a Stihl 031 you will find clutch retaining washers. These details differ with other saws. In this case, the washers hold the clutch shoes in position on the clutch assembly. These washers are slightly arched and each has a rim on one side. They must be replaced exactly as you found them.

Remove the first washer and note its correct position. Then insert the clutch wrench and unscrew the clutch assembly by turning it clockwise. Remove the second retaining washer. Remove the chain sprocket, needle cage, or bearing, and the clutch cover plate. On this model, a drive pin extends from the cover plate to a hole in the chain sprocket. This pin drives the automatic oil pump when the clutch is engaged.

Before you disassemble your clutch any further, take a good look at the clutch shoes and other parts of the assembly. If you decide that your problem is here for sure, remove the damaged parts of the clutch. Remember that springs and shoes must be replaced as a set. If the clutch drum is scored or burned, you'll have to replace it. Be sure to examine the sprocket, now that you can see it easily, but Parp assumes that you've already eliminated the sprocket as the cause of your trouble. If you do see signs of moderate to excessive wear, you should replace the sprocket as well. Replace the needle bearings if they are burned, rusted, or damaged.

The cover plate should be in good condition and you should be able to reuse it. If it's bent, however, you must replace it.

There are very few parts to worry about in a chain saw clutch and these clutches are usually stronger than you can imagine.

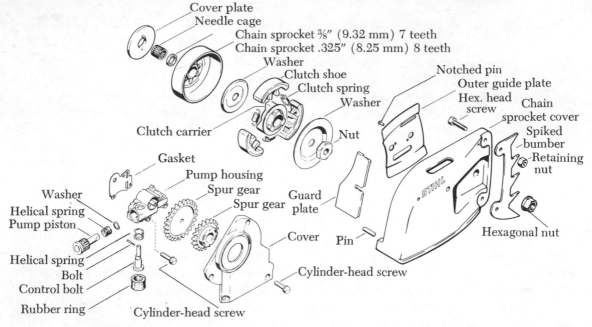

Cover plate
Needle cage
Chain sprocket ⅜″ (9.32 mm) 7 teeth
Chain sprocket .325″ (8.25 mm) 8 teeth
Washer
Clutch shoe
Clutch spring
Washer
Clutch carrier
Nut

Notched pin
Outer guide plate
Hex. head screw
Chain sprocket cover
Spiked bumber
Retaining nut

Gasket
Pump housing
Spur gear
Spur gear
Guard plate
Washer
Helical spring
Pump piston
Cover
Pin
Helical spring
Bolt
Control bolt
Rubber ring
Cylinder-head screw
Cylinder-head screw
Hexagonal nut

Oil pump, chain sprocket, clutch, and chain-sprocket cover (Stihl 031 AV).

Figure 10.2

Most clutches outlive the chain saws they come with. If you replace clutch parts more than once in a chain saw's life, something is very wrong. Most likely you're not cutting at full engine speed.

To reassemble the clutch, place the clutch cover plate so that the oiler drive pin extends into the hole in the small spur gear of the oil pump. Then replace the greased needle cage or bearing, the chain sprocket, and the inside clutch retaining washer. On other saws, a half-moon key may be used to attach the friction assembly to the crankshaft. Be sure this key goes back in its exact original position. Half-moon keys frequently have nearly invisible differences from end to end that make

them work in one position only. A retaining washer must be replaced so that it is pressed against the clutch assembly under tension.

Now screw the clutch back onto the crankshaft so that the countersunk side of the clutch carrier thread goes toward the chain sprocket. Then use your clutch wrench to turn the clutch until the piston is again resting against the crankshaft locking nut. Tighten the clutch to about 25 ft./lbs. Then replace the outside retaining washer and the clutch retaining nut. If possible, use a torque wrench to tighten the clutch retaining nut to the torque recommended by your manufacturer. In the case of our example, it is 28.94 ft./lb.

A dirty or improperly operating clutch must be disassembled as follows:

Figure 10.3

Remove starter cover with rewind starter. Unscrew spark plug, and screw crankshaft locking screw into spark plug hole by hand. Then remove chain sprocket cover.

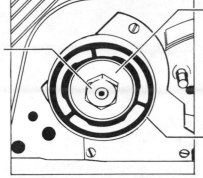

Clutch carrier

Hexagonal nut

Chain sprocket drum

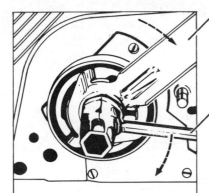

Place clutch wrench between clutch shoes and turn clockwise until piston bottoms at the crankshaft locking nut.

While holding clutch with wrench, loosen and unscrew hexagonal nut with combination wrench.

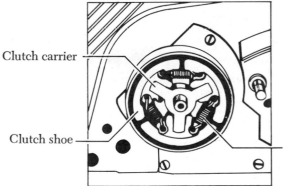

Clutch carrier

Clutch shoe

Spring

Replace damaged parts of the clutch; only the *whole set* of clutch shoes and springs should be replaced if damaged. If only very dirty, wash all parts in clean gasoline and then with compressed air. Roughen surfaces of clutch liners with emery cloth.

Remove the front washer and unscrew clutch with clutch wrench by turning it *clockwise*.

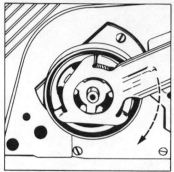

Then remove the second retaining washer from the crankshaft, then the chain sprocket, the needle cage, and the cover plate.

Crankshaft
locking nut

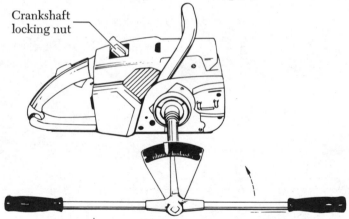

Tighten the new clutch with torque wrench to 3.5 kpm (25.32 ft./lbf.)

Then put the second retaining washer onto crankshaft and screw in hexagonal nut. Tighten nut to 4 kpm (28.94 ft./lbf.)

Replacing clutch.

Figure 10.4

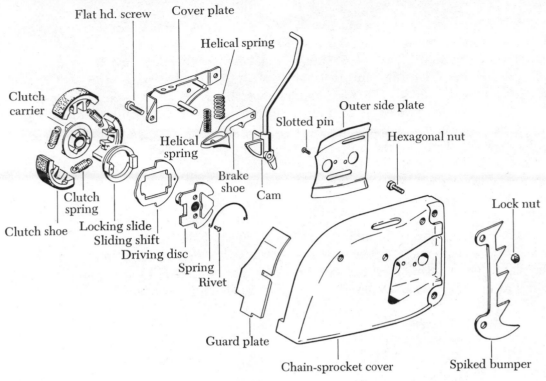

Chain-sprocket cover, brake shoe, and driving disc (Stihl 031 AV).

Figure 10.5

Now remove the cylinder plug or crankshaft locking screw and replace the spark plug. Put the starter in place, but before you tighten it, pull the starter rope until the starter pawls engage the rope rotor. You'll have to remember to do this every time you remove the starter housing from your saw. Now you can replace your guide bar, chain, and sprocket cover.

AUTOMATIC OIL PUMP

Again, we'll stick with the Stihl 031 as an example. The 031 has an automatic oil pump that is driven by a worm gear driven by the chain sprocket. The worm gear is driven by the chain sprocket via a drive pin and two spur gears.

You have determined that your problem is in the oil pump. You have already cleaned the guide bar oil outlet holes and the guide bar groove. You have also already cleaned the oil pick-up body and checked the oil pick-up hose. When you check the hose, by the way, don't bend, twist, or pull it; to replace it, you often have to disassemble the crankcase.

Every automatic oil pump is designed

with close limits between the maximum and the minimum oil flow. On our example, the maximum oil flow is 0.61 cubic inches per minute. The minimum is 0.244 cubic inches per minute. The minimum setting is used for guide bars of 14 inches or 15 inches, and higher settings are used with larger bars. To make this adjustment on this saw, use a screwdriver to turn the set screw on the control bolt. It will travel only ¼ turn at the most. Do not exert force.

Our sample oil pump is located in a recess in the crankcase and is protected by a cover plate. To remove it, first remove the clutch and chain sprocket as described in

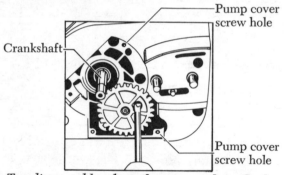

To disassemble the oil pump take off the clutch and chain sprocket. Remove the four screws of the pump cover and pull the small spur gear off the crankshaft. Then unscrew the three cylinder head screws, one of which is accessible only through the bore in the big spur gear.

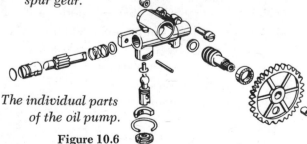

The individual parts of the oil pump.

Figure 10.6

the previous section. If the pump drive pin on the clutch cover plate is broken or sheared, you must install a new cover plate. Like most parts, this will only be available from your dealer, your manufacturer, or the manufacturer's distributor in your area.

The pump cover is secured to the crankcase by four screws. Remove the screws, take off the cover, and pull the small spur gear off the crankshaft. You are now looking at the large spur gear on the oil pump. It has a hole in it. When you turn it, you will see (one at a time) two or three screws. These hold the pump in place. Turn the spur gear so that you can insert your screwdriver through the hole and remove each of the screws. You can now remove the pump.

You will probably not need to replace any pump parts. If your pump is not delivering oil, you can bet that the problem is dirt and clogging. To clean it and inspect its parts, pry off the retaining ring that holds the two segments of the pump together. On many saws, a round pin holds the pump control bolt. Simply pull the pin from the pump housing with pliers. Then remove the control bolt with its 'O' ring and bushing. Remove the pump plunger with its spring and washer. Then carefully remove the worm gear, spur gear, and ring washer.

Clean all pump parts thoroughly and blow out the pump passages. If you find any defective or worn parts, replace them. If you find a handful of shavings, replace the pump. If you replace only the pump plunger, install the washer and spring in the pump before inserting the pump plunger and bushing. Reassemble the pump and reinstall it in the exact reverse order of disassembly. Be sure to replace all ring gaskets and washers.

CARBURETOR

Parp suspects that the day of the nonrebuildable, throwaway carburetor isn't far away. Now everything in Parp revolts at the idea of another conquest for the throwaway culture, but he can also understand how and why it may happen—he just hopes he's wrong. And there is hope that the present kit system of repair is so efficient and well established that it will prevail.

These kits are so good and so well developed that it's now an understatement to say that you don't have to understand your carburetor in order to rebuild it. All you need is the kit, a small screwdriver, a small needle-nosed pliers, a ¼-inch drive socket set, a set of low-profile combination wrenches, some solvent, a soft toothbrush, and, possibly, some nonhardening sealant such as Permatex Number Two or Form-a-Gasket. A source of compressed air can be a great help in cleaning out the carburetor passages.

There is no point at all in reviewing the directions for rebuilding a chain saw carburetor. All the directions you'll ever need come with the kit. Just be sure you get the

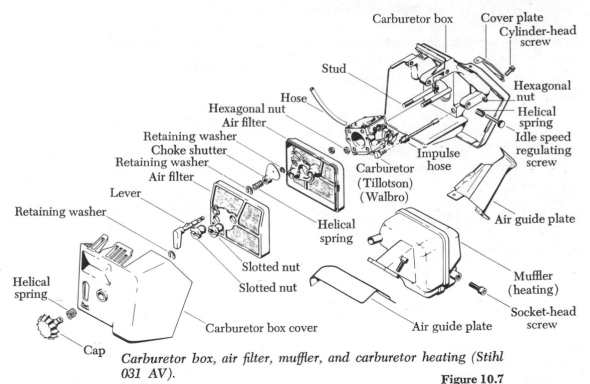

Carburetor box, air filter, muffler, and carburetor heating (Stihl 031 AV).

Figure 10.7

correct kit, and only buy one that was made for your carburetor by the original manufacturer of your carburetor. Parp says that all substitute kits made by other companies are grossly inferior.

In almost all cases, the best approach to any genuine carburetor problem is to buy a rebuilding kit and rebuild the entire carburetor following the easy instructions, step-by-step. Just a few tips are in order.

Never touch a carburetor with slip-joint pliers. Never tighten any "screws" on a carburetor unless you know what you're doing. You may damage the needles. Handle your carburetor carefully. Keep all the parts in order, laid out on a flat surface as you remove them. Lay out the new replacement pieces from your kit with the old parts that they replace. That way you'll get it back together in order. Take note that every single mistake that Parp has seen made by carburetor rebuilders was the result of mixed-up parts or replacing a part upside down or backwards.

With linkage, fuel line connections, and throttle connections, look very closely at the correct assembly before you take it apart. If anything sticks or seems stubborn, don't force it. Look carefully to see if anything is blocking the approach you're taking. Many parts can be removed or loosened only when in a certain position. Again, disassembly problems of the carburetor itself will be covered in your kit instructions but your kit won't mention the linkage of your particular saw, or the fuel line fittings. Most fittings simply pull off, but be careful not to twist or split

lines or bend linkage.

Identifying the jet screws and throttle screw is not difficult. The throttle screw, or idle-speed screw, is the one that doesn't go into the body of the carburetor. It rests against a mechanism that moves the linkage that moves your throttle plate. It is usually a large screw and the saw housing above it is usually labeled T or I. The jet screws are near each other. The larger one is the high-speed adjustment and the smaller one is the low-speed adjustment. If you remove your carburetor only to replace the gasket between the carburetor and the crankcase, don't touch the jet screws. If you're rebuilding your carburetor, pay particular attention to your kit's instructions regarding these needle screws.

Since you've got the kit, Parp suggests that you remove all parts that you can replace with new ones. It's the only way to thoroughly clean the carburetor and it's the only way to be sure you've done a complete job by replacing all the worn or damaged parts. Clogging, wear, and damage, for example, are often hard to detect in filter screens, and a leaking welsh plug is nearly always impossible to detect. A welsh plug leak usually makes the carburetor difficult or impossible to adjust, or causes it to lose adjustment quickly.

Our Stihl 031 AV is equipped with a Tillotson HU carburetor, a model that is used on a great many other saws and is very similar to most other contemporary chain saw carburetors. Its main difference from the Tillotson HS carburetor is its

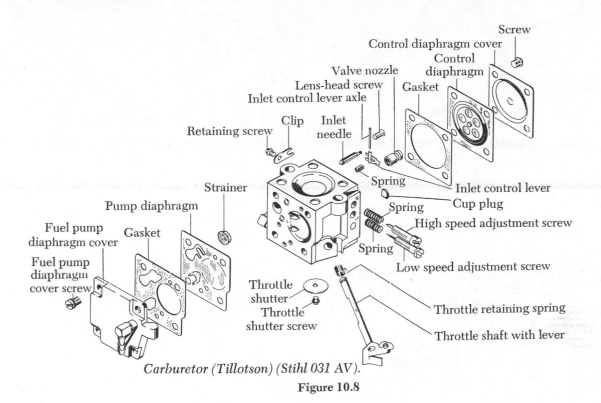

Carburetor (Tillotson) (Stihl 031 AV).

Figure 10.8

smaller size. Also, the HU is choked by a choke plate in the air box near the air filter rather than by a choke plate in the air horn of the carburetor itself. It is sometimes pictured in the air horn only for convenience.

The fuel pump is an integral diaphragm fuel pump, as discussed in Chapter Nine. The fuel pump is a unit that operates independently from the rest of the carburetor.

An impulse hose connects the impulse chamber of the fuel pump with the crankcase. The impulse operation of a diaphragm fuel pump is discussed in Chapter

Nine. When pumping, the diaphragm pulls fuel from the fuel pick-up in the fuel tank, through the fuel line, and through the inlet and outlet valves of the fuel pump to the needle valve of the carburetor. The inlet needle of the needle valve is linked with the metering diaphragm by an inlet control lever. Under the metering diaphragm is a chamber that is vented to atmospheric pressure by a hole in the metering diaphragm cover. The metering diaphragm is activated by alternating pressure pulsations from the crankcase. When the diaphragm moves upward, it unseats the inlet needle and allows fuel to flow into the diaphragm

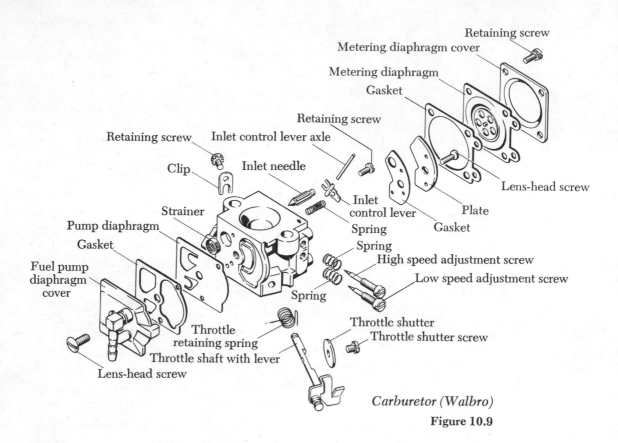

Retaining screw
Metering diaphragm cover
Metering diaphragm
Gasket
Retaining screw
Retaining screw
Inlet control lever axle
Clip
Inlet needle
Lens-head screw
Strainer
Inlet control lever
Plate
Pump diaphragm
Spring
Gasket
Gasket
Spring
Spring
Fuel pump diaphragm cover
High speed adjustment screw
Low speed adjustment screw
Spring
Throttle shutter
Throttle retaining spring
Throttle shutter screw
Throttle shaft with lever
Lens-head screw

Carburetor (Walbro)

Figure 10.9

chamber. The carburetor and the crank-case are connected by an elbow connector.

To remove the carburetor, take off the air box cover, the oil filter retainers, and the air filter. Remove the retaining washers from the throttle shaft and unhook the throttle rod. Then disconnect the fuel line from the tank vent fitting and unscrew the nuts from the carburetor studs. Now you can carefully pull the carburetor away from the saw.

To disassemble the elbow connector, loosen the two screws at the top of the handle bar. Remove the collar screws at the handle frame and the three screws that hold the carburetor box to the handle frame. Push back the handle frame and pull the impulse hose from the fitting at the bottom of the cylinder. Then you can push the elbow connector out of the car-buretor box and remove the hose clip and the elbow. All of these details will differ on other saws but the basic procedure is very similar. Remember to keep all your parts in order and draw pictures or write yourself notes to help remember how and when you did what. Reassembly is usually done in exactly the reverse order of disassembly.

If you have a carburetor kit, you are now ready to rebuild your carburetor. Just be sure you clean it thoroughly and use your toothbrush to scrub the air horn with solvent. Don't soak the entire carburetor in solvent if it has unremoved plastic or nylon parts, as most carburetors do; instead, you should use a canned carburetor cleaner such as Gumout. Squirt the Gumout into all openings and passages and use your toothbrush to clean whatever you can reach. This is a passable but incomplete approach.

INDIVIDUAL CURBURETOR REPAIRS

This section is included primarily as emergency reference material. If you're fifty miles west of Nowhere and can't wait for the dogsled to bring a carburetor kit, you might need to try one or more individual repairs. To do that, you will at least need gasket material from which to cut gaskets. Good luck. If you have an old carburetor around for spare parts, that may sometimes help but most carburetor troubles are caused by dirt. If you can clean the culprit and replace the gasket between the carburetor and the crankcase, you may be back to cutting wood soon. Obviously, anyone fifty miles west of Nowhere should have a couple of axes and a large bow saw with an extra blade.

If your problem is corrosion caused by stale fuel or improper storage, you should be able to get away with cleaning your carburetor and replacing it as is, without disassembling it further than is necessary for cleaning.

If corrosion is your problem, pay special attention to your choke and throttle plates and shafts. Move the shafts to see if the plates move freely. Clean the shafts with solvent or Gumout as far as you can. If they come clean this way, leave them on the saw. If not, remove the lockscrew in the center of the plate and then remove the plate and the shaft. You can then clean them thoroughly and reinstall them.

To disassemble the carburetor, remove the four screws that hold the pump diaphragm cover to the carburetor body. You'll find that the diaphragm is stuck to a gasket that must be peeled off. Separate these parts very carefully.

When you remove the diaphragm and gasket, you will find a filter screen. Clean the screen and the diaphragm carefully. The diaphragm has valve flaps—the inlet and the outlet valves. If these valve flaps are damaged you'll have to replace the diaphragm even if it means waiting for the dogsled. Lay out these parts in order as you remove them.

Four screws hold the metering diaphragm cover. Remove these screws and remove the metering diaphragm and gasket. Again, the diaphragm and gasket will stick together so separate them carefully. It is possible, in an emergency, to replace these gaskets with Form-a-Gasket or some other nonhardening sealer, but be very careful not to use too much sealant or get it on the diaphragms. You may also cut new gaskets from any suitable gasket material. Since blown gaskets are, other than dirt, the most common carburetor failure, you may be able to correct all your problems by cleaning the carburetor without taking it all the way apart, and then replacing the gaskets with homemade ones. A rebuilding kit is, again, a better approach when one is available.

The pivoting device of the inlet control lever is fastened to the carburetor body. The inlet needle is linked to the dovetailed guide of the inlet control lever. To remove the inlet needle, remove the screw and take out the inlet control lever together with the inlet needle. Be sure to remove the small spring, also. Note that there is a rubber tip on the inlet needle, or a rubber fitting that the needle presses into. You can now replace any defective parts, if you have replacements, and you can completely clean the metering sections and inlet control parts.

Check the tapered ends of the adjustment screws. If they're bent or damaged, they'll have to be replaced. You can pry out filter screens with the awl blade of a Swiss Army knife, which is also a fine tool for removing welsh plugs. If you don't have a carburetor kit, don't remove any welsh plugs. Just paint over them with the nail hardener some people use on their fingernails. Don't remove any jets unless you have to. These will come clean while still in the carburetor.

When we reassemble the Tillotson HU

carburetor, we must be sure that the inlet needle is correctly linked to the guide in the inlet control lever. The dovetailed end of the inlet control lever must not be bent. Install the inlet control lever so that the longer end of the lever is flush with the floor of the diaphragm chamber. The rest of the reassembly process is straightforward, or straightbackward, actually, and you should have no trouble as long as you kept your parts in order, or can visualize the reassembly process from this section or from drawings. For carburetor adjustment procedures see Chapter Six. The normal settings for a Tillotson HU are: H or high-speed screw: out 1 turn from light bottom. L or low-speed screw: out 1⅛ to 1¼ turns from light bottom. In reassembly, note that the H screw is shorter than the L screw.

If you tore the gasket between the carburetor and the crankcase, don't reach for your ax. Just apply a thin but adequate coat of Form-a-Gasket to the area and tighten firmly to set the seal. Happens to everybody.

FUEL LINE

The fuel is drawn from the tank through the fuel line pick-up in the tank, through the fuel line and into the carburetor. All of these parts have to be cleaned now and then, as Parp said before. You should certainly do this anytime you clean or rebuild your carburetor.

On the Stihl 031, you disconnect the fuel line from the fuel tank vent and pull the whole thing out of the vent. Then you clean it all in gasoline, including the tank and cap. When you reassemble the parts, just be sure to put the pick-up back together and get the fuel line straight.

To install a new fuel line, in this case, just cut it to match the old line and fit it to the pick-up assembly with the insert. Installing a new fuel line on most other chain saws involves a few more problems so let's go back to the Poulan 4200.

To remove this fuel line, you just pull it out through the fuel tank filler hole. The new line must be 7¾ inches long, including a section on one end cut at a 45° angle for purposes of installation only.

Remove the fuel filter from the old fuel line and install it on the square end of the new fuel line. Then insert a stiff wire through the hole in the bottom of the air box so that it comes out through the fuel filler hole. Slide the new fuel line onto the wire, angled end first, and use the wire as a guide to push the point of the angle out through the air box hole. Use your needle-nose pliers with one tip inserted into the fuel line, the other grasping from the outside. Pull about two inches of the fuel line into the air box. Remove the wire. Then carefully cut off the angled end of the line just below the angle. Cut it square. At this time somewhat less than two inches of line are showing in the air box. Again use your needle-nose pliers to pull more fuel line into the box to a total length of 3⅝ inches. Route the fuel line to the carburetor over the choke control rod.

Obviously the details will vary, but these examples demonstrate correct procedures that will apply to all other chain saws, as well as solutions to most of the problems that you'll ever run into with fuel lines. If you watch for the problems mentioned here, you'll have no trouble seeing how Parp's suggestions apply to your saw. You might have to route your fuel line under the choke rod instead of over it, but you'll know which it is because you'll notice how the original was installed.

REED VALVE

A reed valve job is fairly easy with the better chain saws so we'll use a good one for our example. Our model this time is the Poulan 4200; the Stihl 031 has a piston-ported engine and so does not incorporate a reed valve. Poulan builds an excellent and very popular chain saw. They also build many saws for other companies who affix their own brand names, so it seems likely that this simple procedure will apply to many chain saws owned by readers of this book.

A reed valve job is actually an item of fuel system service, rather than a true engine problem. Therefore, we start with the carburetor once again.

The Poulan 4200 has a single nut right on top of its top cover. When you remove the nut and the top cover, you have access to the air cleaner, carburetor, insulator block, reed valve assembly, and cylinder.

Remove the two nuts holding the air filter and lift it off. Disconnect the fuel line and remove the cotter pin that holds the choke rod to the choke shaft. Then remove the carburetor studs and the carburetor. Disconnect the spark plug wire and lift out the air baffle that sits against the cylinder fins behind the carburetor. If the spring clips on this baffle are fatigued or broken, the baffle should be replaced with a new one. Be sure to replace this baffle when you reassemble your saw: it's an essential part of the Poulan cooling system.

Now lift up the insulator block that the carburetor was sitting on. The reed valve assembly is immediately under the insulator block. Remove the two screws holding the reed valve assembly.

When you have the reed valve assembly removed, check the reed tip gap. If the gap is larger than .010, replace the reed. Also replace any bent, broken, warped, or cracked reeds. If the assembly is cracked elsewhere, which is not likely, it will have to be replaced.

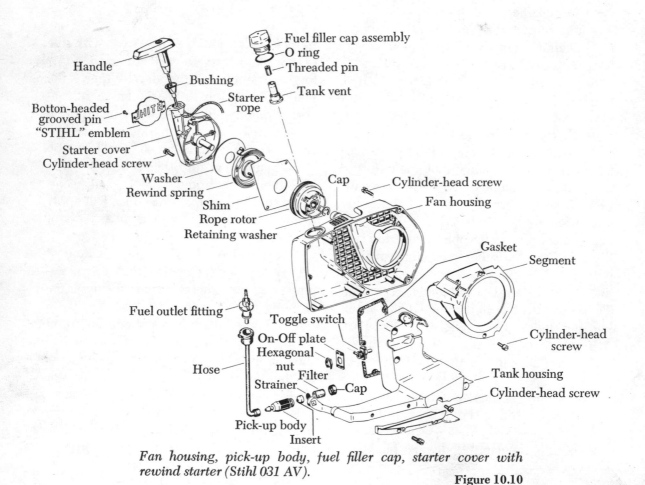

Fan housing, pick-up body, fuel filler cap, starter cover with rewind starter (Stihl 031 AV).

Figure 10.10

Reassemble in the reverse order of disassembly. For other saws, the entire process is very similar. The reed valve, when used, is always between the carburetor and the crankcase. The only complication you might encounter is a torn gasket, which you can replace or repair with Form-a-Gasket. If you find that you must disassemble the two halves of an engine block in order to replace a gasket, forget it. Use the Form-a-Gasket.

REWIND STARTER

We discussed starter rope and spring replacement in Chapter Five and that's most of what can happen to a starter. There are just a few other things we should mention now.

If your spring and rope are in good condition but the rope is hard to pull and then goes back only part way or very slowly, the mechanism is probably clogged with dirt or the spring may be frozen.

The spring, of course, doesn't really freeze but at very low temperatures the oil on the spring can thicken enough to stick the coils together. Remove the screws in the starter housing and move the starter assembly away from the saw. Then apply kerosene to the spring coils. Don't slop the kerosene in through the sawdust guard.

If the starter is clogged with dirt or tree resin, as often happens, you should remove the spring (in one piece) and wash all parts in kerosene. Then oil the spring and reassemble.

If you find that the starter pawls on the flywheel are damaged, they must be replaced. This is extremely rare. Note that you must use identical replacement pawls. If you can see a problem with the pawls, you can also see how they come off. These screws may be held in place with Loctite and you'll have to use your impact tool. Be very careful not to break the flywheel. Use the hammer very lightly. Draw a picture of the correct assembly of the pawls.

When you replace the pawls, use Loctite (see Appendix for address) and be sure the new pawls can move freely and don't pinch.

IGNITION SERVICE

Why didn't Parp call it a tune-up? Because, in a chain saw, a tune-up amounts to a complete overhaul of all systems. Or, for many people, it consists of replacing the spark plug and breaker points. The first approach is too much for most of us, and is beyond this book in any case. The second notion of a tune-up is often a little worse than doing nothing at all.

Complete ignition service consists of a thorough cleaning, a check for damaged, worn, or frayed parts or wires, a renewal of nonpermanent ignition parts whether they appear worn or not, and a check of all adjustments and required gaps. The adjustments include spark plug gap, armature air gap, ignition timing, and magneto edge gap. The parts to replace are the breaker points and condenser for sure, the magneto coil if necessary, and probably the spark plug. The parts to check are all leads, wires, cables and connections, the flywheel magnets, and the coil.

If you do all of these jobs plus clean and adjust or rebuild the carburetor, remove carbon and clean all cooling and exhaust system parts, lubricate moving parts and service the cutting attachment, you could call it a tune-up. But only if your engine is mechanically in good condition. You can't tune a chain saw that has worn piston rings. That's why Parp didn't call it a tune-up and that's why we're only going to discuss ignition service in this section.

Although Parp believes that the fuel system causes most chain saw problems, he also knows that professional mechanics see more ignition problems than anything else. That's because the owner is more likely to be intimidated by the ignition system than by the fuel system, and so the owner is more likely to correct fuel system problems at home. When the ignition fails, most owners head straight for the mechanic.

Parp does not wish to discourage you from that approach to ignition problems. It is very often the best approach. Ignition work is more likely to be fussy and to require special tools than most other aspects of chain saw repair.

Chain saw manufacturers supply their authorized repair people with special shop

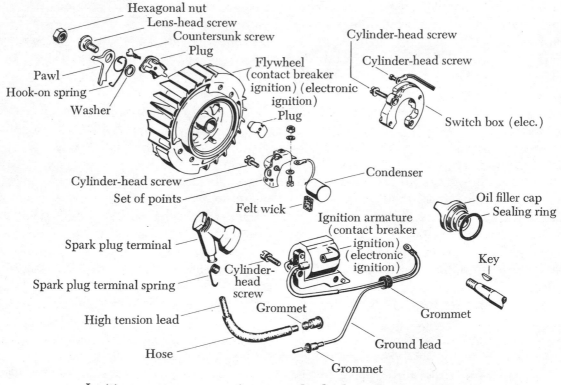

Ignition armature, set of points, flywheel, and oil filter cap (Stihl 031 AV).

Figure 10.11

service tool kits. Many of the tools in these kits are related to ignition service. At the very least they include a flywheel puller and an ignition timing device. They also often include an ohmmeter and other testing devices and tools. Few chain saw owners have these tools or have access to them, but we can get around this in most cases. For that reason, Parp will be deviating from recommended procedures occasionally.

The Spark Plug

Always begin any ignition system service with the spark plug. If necessary, use the combination tool that came with your saw to remove the spark plug. If possible, use a spark plug socket and breaker bar. Avoid those cheap spark plug "wrenches" with the rod handle, the kind sold in discount department stores. They can damage your hand and anything else that gets in the way. If you have any doubt about your spark plug, replace it. Always try to replace your spark plug with exactly the same kind of spark plug, preferably from the same manufacturer. In all cases use a quality, name-brand spark plug. And Parp says that those charts that tell you that plug 901 from Brand Z is the same as, or is replaceable with, plug 817 from Our Brand X, are often stretching it a bit in commercial interest. Stick with the plug your manufacturer put in the saw, or be very sure that it's identical from the hex nut down.

Good spark plugs are so well made and so inexpensive that a complete discussion

of them would be a waste of paper, even if it were possible. Just remember that you will not always be able visually to detect a spark plug problem. A slight film of oil on the insulator can short out the spark plug and take the high-tension current straight to ground, or weaken it considerably. But before you throw it away, that old spark plug can tell you quite a lot.

Since chain saw engines are lubricated by mixing oil with the fuel, moderate oil fouling of the plug, after a time, is normal. This fouling will cause a used chain saw plug to be somewhat darker than a normal automobile spark plug after normal use. Most automobile spark plugs have light tan or gray electrode deposits after service in a clean engine. Normal electrode deposits on a chain saw spark plug are thin and dark gray to black but flaky and not thick. If the deposits seem thick and oily you may be using too much oil in your fuel mix, or the wrong kind of oil. If the deposits are thick sooty carbon you may have an exhaust problem, probably caused by carbon-clogged exhaust ports or a dirty muffler. If the deposits are thick flaky carbon, something like graphite, your fuel mixture is too rich. A rich mixture can be caused by an incorrect carburetor adjustment, worn carburetor parts, a choke that sticks, or a dirty air filter. If the deposits are light-colored and flaky, your engine is running too lean. A carburetor problem or an air leak may be the culprit. If the deposits are light and the electrodes appear blistered, melted, or burned, your engine is running too hot. This may be caused by an air leak, incorrect timing, a dirty air filter, the wrong spark plug, clogged sawdust guards or cooling fins, a missing air baffle, a dirty exhaust system, or a broken flywheel—and you ought to find out which.

Parp says that if you're fifty miles west of Nowhere and you have only one spark plug, you might think about moving to the city.

The spark plug wire or high-tension wire of many chain saws is a permanent part of the magneto coil. In that case, the entire unit must be replaced if a part becomes defective. You may be able temporarily to patch a high-tension wire if the only problem is frayed insulation, but this should be considered an emergency repair that won't hold up long.

If your high-tension wire throws sparks or is cracked or oil-soaked, or if it feels limp in the middle, you must replace it. If your saw is quite new and you're getting no spark, always suspect the high-tension wire first. If you check everything else in the ignition system and can't find your problem, replace the wire.

In the case of our example, the Stihl 031, the high-tension wire is not a part of the magneto coil and may be removed by disconnecting it at the spark plug and unscrewing the wood screw that holds the other end to the armature. First, we have to get in there.

Reaching the Ignition Parts

The ignition parts of a chain saw are located near the flywheel, as we've seen. The flywheel is always under the starter housing on the side of the saw opposite from the chain. The parts you have to remove to reach the flywheel and other ignition parts vary from saw to saw. In all cases, however, you have to remove the starter housing and starter. You do not have to disassemble the starter, and never should except when it needs repair. You should also always disconnect the high-tension wire at the spark plug before working inside the ignition system.

Reaching the ignition system of the 031 is a typical example. Remove the two screws that hold the front handle to the handle frame. Remove the air box cover and the air filter. Pry the retaining washer from the throttle shaft and unhook the throttle rod. Unscrew the handle frame and the three screws that hold the carburetor box to the handle frame. When you fold back the handle frame, you'll see the fuel line and its fitting to the fuel tank. Disconnect the fuel line. Then remove the four screws that hold the fan housing and tank housing to the rest of the saw. On our example, one of these screws is beneath the chain sprocket cover on the other side of the saw. Now pull back on the entire assembly (including starter housing, tank housing, and handle frame) until you can reach the ignition switch wire. This wire is actually a ground lead to the ignition switch. When the switch is OFF it is actually grounding out the primary windings of the ignition coil.

All of the above details vary greatly from saw to saw, as Parp just said. It is easier to reach the ignition systems of some saws and harder with others. With many, you simply remove the starter housing. Always watch for fuel line connections and ignition connections when going into an ignition system. If you realize that the above disassembly procedure allows you to reach almost all parts of the engine, it will seem more worthwhile.

Our example has a Bosch ignition system with the armature core and ignition coil positioned outside the flywheel. If you only have to replace the high-tension lead, you've gone far enough. Simply unscrew the wire at the coil, remove it, and install the new one.

Your new high-tension wire must be exactly the same length as the old one. In this case, it's 4.6 inches long, not including the boot. To attach the boot, use a small amount of Vaseline (or oil) to lubricate the end of the wire. Insert the wire into the boot and pull it through with pliers. Use a new spring connector if possible, but you can probably reuse the old one. Press the hook of the spring connector all the way into the exact center of the end of the wire. Then push the wire with the spring connector into the position in the boot. Position the wire away from any sharp edges and reassemble the saw.

Magneto Edge Gap

To check the ignition system further, turn the flywheel (which is still mounted on the crankshaft) past the magneto coil. The coil and the flywheel must not touch at anytime. Turn the flywheel enough to be sure. If they touch at all the magneto is damaged and must be replaced. If they don't touch and the magneto looks good and seems tight and has an obvious gap, it's probably good. If it's loose, tighten it down and check again for contact with the flywheel. Note that the gap between the flywheel and the magneto does not have to be very precise as long as it is within recommended specifications. In the case of our example it can be anywhere between .14 inch and .3 inch. That's a lot of room for aging. This gap is measured (with your feeler gauge) between the trailing edge of the north pole of the magnet and the inner edge of the left-hand leg of the armature when they are at their closest point. Do not change this setting if it is within the specifications since any change will affect the ignition timing.

If you find cracks or damage in your magneto coil and you don't have a replacement, you *may* be able to patch it with vinyl electrical tape. No other kind of tape will do. This goes, in an emergency, for any frayed insulation or stripped wires. Broken wires can be spliced in an emergency and covered with tape. Don't be surprised if it doesn't work since the damage is likely to be more extreme than it appears.

Armature Air Gap

To check the armature air gap, measure the distance between the pole shoes of the armature and the flywheel. The 031 calls for a gap between .012 inch and .2 inch. This gap is somewhat more critical than the magneto edge gap since it determines how close the magnets pass to the armature itself. To adjust it, loosen the armature screws in the slotted poles and carefully and gradually move the armature to the correct gap. Be sure the armature ground lead is connected.

Removing the Flywheel

Now we're up against that flywheel that causes so much trouble and concern. And it certainly can be a hassle. If you don't have to remove it, by all means leave it be. But a lot of the worry about pulling a flywheel is needless. All you need is the tool, or a good substitute.

Removing the flywheel is an easier job on most chain saws than it is on most other engines. Most chain saw crankshafts are not as tapered as the crankshafts of other machines. This means that when you remove the flywheel nut, the flywheel will be relatively easy to remove. The problem is the nut.

Once again we need some way to protect the piston and hold the entire cranking assembly, and the flywheel, while we remove the flywheel nut. In most cases, we'll need a way to deliver a considerable shock to the flywheel nut in order to loosen it. Again, we can be glad we're working on a chain saw since the flywheel nut of many chain saws is easier than the same part on other machines.

Without doubt, the best way to crack a tough flywheel nut is with an electric impact wrench. Few of us own or can borrow one of these expensive tools. If you do have access to an electric or air impact wrench, it will loosen the flywheel nut with so much

shock that you don't even have to worry about the flywheel turning. It doesn't have time to turn.

The next best choice is the hand impact tool mentioned in our basic tool list. Parp says this tool is close to essential for anyone who works on small engines. It consists of a driver that you hit with a hammer, and different bits that usually include slot-type or Phillips-type screwdriver bits. The bits fit into an adapter that you attach to the drive mechanism of the driver. These tools are available with either ¼-inch, ⅜-inch or ½-inch drive and ordinary sockets can be fitted over the drive itself without the adapter. When you hit the head of the impact tool with a hammer, the drive mechanism turns the bit or socket just a little. This small turn, combined with the shock from the hammer blow, will loosen almost any tough screw, bolt, or nut. An impact wrench is a very handy addition to any tool kit. Parp's set cost $10. Sometimes you can find them at larger auto parts stores or small engine repair shops but they are always easy to mail-order from J.C. Whitney or U.S. General Supply. Addresses are in the Appendix.

If you use a hand impact tool with a socket, or if you substitute by hitting the end of a breaker bar with a hammer, you should use a flywheel holder or flywheel wrench to hold the flywheel. Sometimes you can hold the flywheel with blocks of wood jammed between the work surface and fins on either side. Parp does not recommend using a screwdriver or bar between the flywheel fins. Flywheels are incredibly easy to break. Better than that is a flywheel holder, your socket set, and a hammer. Flywheel holders are inexpensive and can be obtained through your dealer or from any repair station or distributor. You do have to remove the flywheel to get to and replace breaker points so it's a problem you'll have to deal with eventually and the right tools make it a lot easier.

With our Stihl 031, we do have a tapered crankshaft that holds the flywheel very firmly so, even after the nut is removed, we still face a problem in removing the flywheel. You can remove most chain saw flywheels by using a pair of screwdrivers as levers. Stihl, like most other manufacturers, makes a special tool for this job, a flywheel puller. Here's the complete process for the 031.

First, remove the spark plug and screw in the crankshaft locking screw. Then remove the flywheel nut. Screw the flywheel puller onto the crankshaft by hand. Turn the flywheel clockwise until the piston bottoms against the crankshaft locking screw. Then screw in the thrust bolt of the flywheel puller and tighten it with your socket wrench until the flywheel pops loose from the taper. If it doesn't pop when you turn in the thrust bolt, whack the head of the thrust bolt with a hammer, but not too hard. You can then remove the flywheel puller and lift off the flywheel.

Before you remove the flywheel, check it for slop. Use a Vise Grip to hold the crankshaft still, being careful not to damage the crankshaft or threads. Don't tighten down hard—just enough to hold it steady.

Then try to turn the flywheel either way. If it moves at all with the crankshaft still, the flywheel half-moon key is probably damaged. A damaged half-moon key is a common ignition problem that can cause all sorts of bad chain saw behavior. You should always make this test before you remove the flywheel but after it is loose from the crankshaft taper. Damage to the key is not always obvious or visible.

If your flywheel is damaged or the magnets are dead, it must be replaced. To check the magnets of your flywheel, hold a screwdriver with the tip about an inch from the magnets. The magnets should pull the screwdriver. If they still don't pull it from a distance of ½ inch, your magnets are dead.

The flywheel and the crankshaft on the ignition side must be grease free and immaculate. If you find oil in this area, or on your breaker assembly or other ignition parts, you have a defective seal. That means an engine overhaul.

BREAKER POINT GAP

Here we run into a peculiarity of the 031 that does not apply to most chain saws but which we have already worked around. To set and check the points of the 031, you do not have to remove the flywheel. Flywheel removal was covered before this because you normally must remove the flywheel to even see the points. So, for the 031, we'll back up to before the flywheel came off.

Inside the mounted flywheel of our 031,

we find two seals, each with one counter-sunk screw. Loosen these screws just two turns and pry out the seals with a screw-driver. Underneath you'll see the breaker points. You can then check the gap with your feeler gauge. When the points are pushed all the way open by the lobe on the crankshaft, the gap should be between .014 inch and .016 inch. If the gap is incorrect, simply loosen the two screws in the breaker point assembly and move the base of the assembly until the gap is correct. Then tighten the screws and check the gap again. It may take a few tries to get it right.

With most chain saws, the flywheel is off to check the points. You'll see the points assembly and the condenser right under the flywheel. In chain saws they're often covered by a plastic case. You can easily remove the case.

As we saw in Chapter 'Nine, the points are opened by a lobe on the crankshaft and pulled closed by a spring. The gap must be checked when it is all the way open. In order to check your points, you must know what gap is specified by your manufacturer. Use your feeler gauge to check the gap. Be sure that you insert the feeler gauge straight in—if it's at an angle, you won't get an accurate reading. The gap is correct if the right feeler gauge just barely touches both points.

To adjust the gap, loosen the screw in the slotted hole of the fixed point. Loosen it just enough to enable you to move the fixed point by pushing on it with a screw-driver but not enough to allow it to move by itself. Turn the crankshaft so that the lobe is pushing the moveable point all the way open. Then move the fixed point with a screwdriver until the gap is correct. Again, this may take several tries and three hands, but you'll get it eventually. When it's right, tighten the screw in the slotted hole of the fixed point. Tighten it firmly but don't strip the threads.

If your breaker points are burned, pitted, or not aligned properly, you should replace them.

REPLACING POINTS AND CONDENSER

Parp says always to replace the condenser whenever you install new points. Since the points and condenser are usually purchased together, as a kit, it costs no more and can save another trip to the inside of your ignition system.

If you've gotten this far, you can probably see exactly what you have to do to remove and replace your breaker point assembly and condenser. Loosen the screws carefully, remove the old parts and install the new ones.

Some tips are in order. Be very careful not to drop any screws into your saw. Also, remember that that flywheel sitting there has magnets in it. If you're missing a screw, look there first. And look there last, too, to be sure you're not installing any shrapnel with your flywheel.

Be sure you disconnect all wires before you start pulling out parts. The moveable point of the breaker assembly will be connected to the magneto and the condenser with two separate wires. Sometimes you have to lift the condenser from its seat or retainer in order to reach the connections and it may fit very tightly.

Be careful to remember what goes where and what connects to what. Parp says you should draw a detailed picture for yourself. You can also use different colors of finger-nail polish to mark connections.

Be sure the new points are properly aligned and will make good contact. If necessary, bend the fixed point until the points face each other squarely.

When you install the points, lightly tighten the fixed point screw so you can adjust the points as above. The correct installation of the condenser should be obvious, but do be sure to get it in exactly the way the old one came out. Sometimes you have to force a condenser to seat it in its sleeve or retainer or whatever.

IGNITION TIMING

We haven't mentioned this before, but ignition (the spark) is always timed to occur slightly before the piston reaches the top of its stroke. Ignition timing is usually stated as a certain distance before *top-dead-center*. Top-dead-center is a term that describes the piston at the top of its upward stroke. You will often see it abbreviated as TDC, and BTDC means *"before-top-dead-center."*

Many chain saw engines have timing marks that make ignition timing easy, as with the 031. You will often find one timing mark on the flywheel. If you find that,

then there is another one someplace, or there is a specified reference that serves as the other timing mark. Some companies use the leading edge of the magneto coil as one reference. Some engine manufacturers place timing marks on the coil and the breaker housing.

The correct timing of the 031 is .092 inches BTDC. That means that the spark must occur when the piston is .092 inches below the top of its upward stroke.

Hopefully we won't need that information since we have two obvious timing marks. To set timing by ignition marks, turn the crankshaft until the marks are aligned. Now find the thinnest blade in your feeler gauge. You need to determine if the points have just begun to open. When the timing marks are lined up, there should be just the slightest gap between the points. If the gap was correct when you measured it at its maximum, points all the way open, and if it now is just barely open with the timing marks aligned, your ignition is correctly timed.

If the point gap was correct when fully open but the points are not open at all when the timing marks are aligned, or are open more than just slightly, you need to adjust the breaker plate. Loosen the breaker plate bolts and turn the breaker plate until your smallest feeler gauge just barely fits between the points. Be careful not to move the points. Anytime you move, adjust, or replace breaker points, the ignition timing must be checked and set. When the gap is as small as you can set it, tighten the breaker plate bolts.

By adjusting the breaker plate so that the points are just barely open when the timing marks are aligned, you insure that the spark occurs at the right time—just when the breaker points break the primary circuit to induce the spark.

If the ignition system doesn't have timing marks, the process is different. You can get around the problems by making your own timing marks while the saw is still new, or while the timing is still correct. Use a sharp tool to scratch a line in the flywheel and another right across from it on the engine. It doesn't matter where you put the marks, as long as they're across from each other and as long as the second mark is on a permanent part of the engine. If you install a new flywheel, it will go on the same way the old one did so you can use the engine mark as a reference for putting a mark on the new flywheel.

If the timing is already disturbed and you have no timing marks, you must use a special tool called a timing dial. These tools are made only for two-stroke engines and they are used to measure the distance of the piston from top dead center. You screw the tool into the spark plug hole and set the dial to the correct BTDC setting. Then you move the piston up against the moveable part of the tool. When the piston is at the correct distance BTDC, you loosen the contact plate and move it until the points are just barely open. Then tighten the plate and the timing is set. The only other method is to use a machinist's ruler to measure the distance of the piston from the top of the cylinder. This is difficult in any case and is impossible on many chain saws.

Whenever you remove your flywheel, check the flywheel key for damage. Also check its fit in the flywheel and the crankshaft. If one slot or the other is damaged, which is not very likely, that part must be replaced. Either part is an expensive hassle but at least you can replace the flywheel yourself. Replacing a crankshaft involves overhauling the engine.

You should always end any ignition work by rechecking all gaps and connections. Watch for any loose screws you might have dropped and blow away the ashes and seeds and sticks and stuff.

PISTON RINGS, CYLINDER, AND CYLINDER GASKET

Parp isn't going to cover any repairs that require disassembling the crankcase or removing the crankshaft. Those repairs really are advanced and you should only tackle them if you're experienced at two-stroke overhaul. There are several reasons. Many of the repairs require special tools and those tools often require expert handling. You might have a problem that seems elementary at first, like defective crankshaft seals. To replace crankshaft seals you need a cylinder pin punch, a heat gun, a seal mounting sleeve that fits only your saw, and a bearing driver—not to mention a pressure-testing device, and that doesn't name them all. You also need to check the crankshaft itself and, if it's bent, you need a machine to straighten it. If you are capable of such repairs and have suitable tools, you will certainly be able to accomplish whatever you need to do by combining your experience with *The Chain Saw Service Manual* and your shop manual. If you're interested in becoming this proficient, collect the tools, and find an experienced mechanic or (even better) a good trade school or community college course on small engine mechanics. With a little learning time, some tools, and some determination, anyone can become an expert chain saw mechanic.

There are circumstances under which you may decide to replace the piston rings without overhauling your chain saw. Let's say you live fifty miles west of Nowhere and last year you bought two used chain saws of the same model and year. You got them both for twenty dollars and neither works very well. One of them has a busted crankcase from a falling tree and the other one is tired. You don't have the tools or experience to replace the busted crankcase but you hope to rejuvenate the tired saw. You've got a carburetor kit, gasket material, new ignition parts and piston rings, and your hand tools. You can use the parts from the dead saw, such as clutch parts, sprocket, rewind starter, flywheel, or what-have-you, and you can follow the procedures in this book (or the instructions with the carburetor kit) to do a pretty good job of fixing up the tired saw. You also have decided that your saw has no compression and that's why you picked up the piston rings. You're just hoping you don't find something like a terribly scored cylinder when you get inside.

In the event that your two used saws are Stihl 031s, here's how you proceed. You'll need your long allen-head wrenches, two pieces of smooth softwood measuring $1'' \times 1'' \times 6''$, and the piston ring compressor that you purchased with the new rings. We are not going to remove the piston from the crank assembly so we won't need a heat tool or any of the special piston tools.

Remove the housings and parts necessary to strip the engine, as for ignition service. Strip the cylinder of the muffler, and so on. Clean the outside of the cylinder thoroughly and look for defects. Be sure the rest of the saw and your work area are also clean. Insert the correct size long reach allen wrench down through the holes in the top of the cylinder. There are four allen-head screws and they are at the bottoms of the holes. When the screws are loose, carefully and slowly pull the entire cylinder up off of the piston. If you're going to install a new cylinder, you must also install the new piston assembly that you had to buy with it, and you'll be doing it without Parp. The cylinder is off now and the piston is resting limply on the crankcase. Put the two pieces of wood between the piston and the crankcase for a piston support. You can also make a piston support from one piece of wood with a slot cut to fit around the connecting rod.

Now examine the inside of the cylinder. If it is heavily scored, new rings probably won't improve your performance much. You might be able to replace it with the cylinder from the dead saw. If the scores (there are bound to be some) are light, try washing the inside of the cylinder with solvent and a soft cloth. Do not use your toothbrush. If the scores are moderate and you must reuse the cylinder, you can take a desperate gamble and use an automotive body cleaner. Be sure to wash the cylinder in solvent afterwards.

Now remove the old rings and clean all exposed parts with solvent, being very careful not to get dirt or dirty solvent into the crankcase. Pay special attention to the piston head and the inside top of the cylinder. Then install the new rings the same way the old ones came off.

Whenever you remove the cylinder you must replace your cylinder gasket. Often, this is the only reason for removing the cylinder in the first place. It is impossible to correctly reinstall a used gasket and you must use a new gasket of gasket material, not Form-a-Gasket. Put the new gasket on the cylinder using a very thin coat of gasket sealer. Then install the cylinder over the piston, using the ring compressor to hold the rings. Be careful not to damage the inside of the cylinder. Remove the piston support after the cylinder is past the piston rings. Apply a very light coat of gasket sealer to the crankcase gasket seat. Move the cylinder into place. Then replace the allen-head screws lightly, and turn the engine over to make sure everything is free and aligned before torquing down the cylinder mounting screws.

This process may be applied to most chain saws.

Introduction to Building with a Chain Saw • 11

By its very nature and design, a good, well-tuned, well-sharpened, and well-maintained chain saw is a very precise tool that can be used by almost anyone to make almost anything. Correctly sharpened and maintained, a good chain saw cuts a good straight line almost without guidance. In fact, a chain saw should never cut anything but a straight line.

Many noncarpenters, not especially talented at building things, have tried their hand at putting something together with wood and have given up because of one basic problem. The straight line. Even the most primitive construction demands reasonably straight lines. If you're not used to handling tools, you'll often find that last year's tree house is this year's doghouse and next year's bonfire.

PRACTICE CUTS

A good chain saw gives you a considerable advantage. The bar alone will help guide you through a cut on a straight line but it does take some practice. Before you try building anything, get in a lot of practice cutting straight lines. The best way to do this is while you're bucking logs for firewood. Instead of just cutting the sections off, make every cut a practice cut for your future role as cabin builder. Make a conscious effort to make each cut as straight as possible until it becomes a habit. When you habitually and consistently get straight cuts on your firewood logs, you're ready to begin practicing the other cuts that are used in chain saw construction. When you can expertly perform all of *these* cuts on your firewood pieces, you can begin to think about trying them on some specially selected building logs. It does definitely take practice.

A *crosscut* is called a crosscut because you're cutting across the grain from one side of the log to the other. *Ripping* refers to cutting with the grain from an end of the log and parallel with the length of the log. It has a ripping effect on the wood.

After you've mastered crosscutting in a straight line, practice each of the following cuts, in turn, until they become easy for you.

Plunge Cut (Boring)

Parp has mentioned this cut before and if you've cut down some large trees you've probably already used it. But using this cut in construction is more exacting than it is in felling and considerable practice is

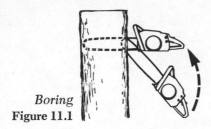

Boring
Figure 11.1

required really to get it down so that you cut where you want to cut and produce an accurately shaped cut.

The plunge cut is basic to chain saw construction. It's used to make corner joints, cross joints, mortises, and many other kinds of joints and notches. The best way to practice is on a large upright log with one end buried securely in the ground. Since all these practice cuts are made on future firewood pieces, there's little waste.

If your log is standing, begin the cut with the lower part of the nose of the guide bar. Hold the body of the saw considerably lower than the nose of the bar. This helps prevent kickback and the tendency of the chain to crawl up the log. When the chain has cut about two inches into the log, steadily move the body of the saw up, cutting all the while, until the bar is parallel with the ground and perpendicular to the cut. You can then plunge, or press the nose of the bar straight into the log. Don't press too hard and don't force the chain into the wood. Hold your saw firmly but let it do most of the work.

Be sure to begin any plunge cut with the saw held at an angle and straighten it after the cut is established. And remember to keep the chain speed up.

End Joint

This isn't as tricky as a plunge cut but it does take practice and it's a good introduction to ripping. The product is a flat surface created by removing one half, or so, of a portion of the end of a log. Two end joints can thus be joined to form a corner or a long section.

First, determine how long you want the joint to be. For practice, make it six inches or so. Then make a crosscut halfway through the log, straight down across the grain. Then turn the log so that the bottom of the crosscut is perpendicular with the ground. Stand on the opposite side of the log from the top of the crosscut. These maneuvers will prevent the saw from binding in the rip that you're about to make and will make the practice safer and easier. Be sure your log is supported well up off the ground, at least on this end, so the chain doesn't hit. Now, with the guide bar at an angle, start a ripping cut at about the center of the bottom of your guide bar and in the middle of the log. You're going to pull the chain saw back and gradually straighten it out so that the guide bar will become perpendicular to the ground just before it reaches the bottom of the crosscut. It may take a few tries and a little practice to get the ripping cut going without catching the chain. If the chain starts to bind inside the cut, leave your saw in the cut (if possible), turn it off, and insert a wedge in the top of the kerf where your chain first entered. Then finish the cut to meet the bottom of the crosscut. Practice until it seems natural and until you get an idea

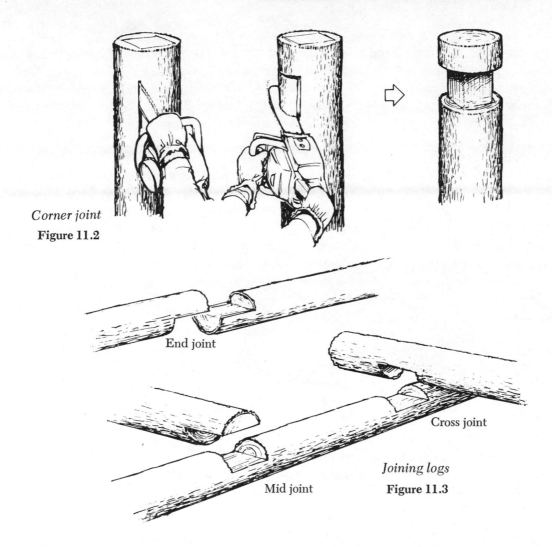

Corner joint
Figure 11.2

End joint

Cross joint

Joining logs

Mid joint

Figure 11.3

how the chain and the wood react to a ripping cut. Always try to rip logs so that the cutter is approaching the cross fiber at the same angle you would use in chopping. Avoid cutting directly across the fibers or against them.

Cross Joint

Here you combine two crosscuts with a plunge cut to produce a flat notch or joint in the body of a log.

To do it, make three crosscuts halfway through a log and about three inches apart.

Then make a plunge cut which you extend as necessary to meet the bottoms of both crosscuts. This is one of the easiest and best ways to join logs together in the body. Practice on several logs, and practice making the notch on one log fit the notch on another. When you can consistently make your logs fit together tightly, you've got it down.

Saddle Notch

A saddle notch is formed by making two shallow cross joints opposite each other. Instead of coming to the middle of the log,

each cross notch takes out about one-third of the log, leaving a center piece with two flat faces. This is the easiest and surest way of joining logs so that there is minimum space between them. Saddle notches are used in Lincoln Log sets.

Round Notch

This method of joining logs is superior to cross joining or saddle notching because the shape of the notch prevents water collection. It is also more difficult and must be fitted perfectly. The width of the notch is determined by the diameter of the log

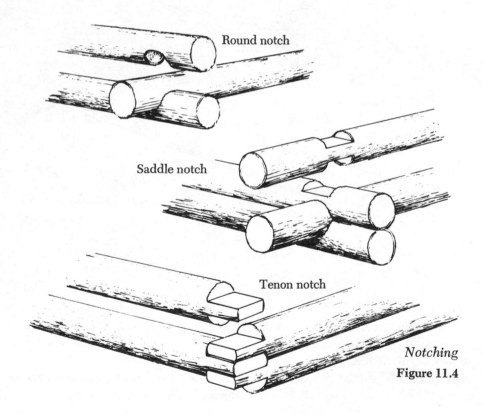

Round notch

Saddle notch

Tenon notch

Notching
Figure 11.4

that will sit in the notch. Lay the top log across the bottom log at the place they are to be joined. Use chalk to mark the diameter of the top log onto the bottom log to indicate the width of the notch. Then move the top log off and use your chain saw to cut a V between the marks.

Now you need to clean and round the notch to fit your top log. Some people do this with the chain saw too, but Parp says that an ax, a hatchet, and a wood knife are far better. It's hard on a chain saw to use it for this kind of whittling but, of course, that's what the woodcarvers do. If you do it with your saw, by all means take your time and don't ask your saw to cut any curves. It isn't meant to.

However you do it, you have to remove a little wood at a time until you've made a round notch that perfectly fits your top log. Check the fit of the notch frequently by laying the top log into it. Use chalk to mark high places when possible. A round notch is better construction than a cross joint but it's also a hell of a lot harder to do.

RIPPING

After you've practiced all of the cuts and joints described above, you should learn to rip a log freehand. This mean you're going to cut a log lengthwise to form slabs and a timber. Slabs are the rounded or bark sides of a log that have been removed with a ripping cut. A timber is what's left after four slabs have been removed. Broken slabs make great kindling or kitchen wood so you're still not going to be wasting any-thing by practicing. Whole slabs have hundreds of uses from building a doghouse and toolshed to making siding for a timber or frame cabin so when you get a solid, whole slab, you might decide not to cut it up for your fires.

To rip slabs, draw a square on the small end of a supported log. You'll want the removed slabs to leave a square timber as large as possible and you'll want the slabs to be about an inch thick in the middle, depending on the size of the log. Then start a ripping cut at one of the sides of the chalk square and cut down the full length of the log. Have the thick side of the log between you and your guide bar and turn the log for each successive slab. The chain will bind and the bar will be pinched in the cut so use plastic or home-made wooden wedges to open the kerf. Since your cutting line will be straight, each slab will be thicker on one end than on the other but the timber produced should be square and uniform for its whole length. You should practice this until you can cut perfect slabs and timbers most of the time, freehand. Be sure to start each ripping cut at the small end of the log.

BUILDING THINGS

To get a lot of really great ideas for easy things to build with a chain saw, write to Homelite for *Twenty-Two Weekend Projects* and McCulloch for *101 Reasons to Own a Chain Saw*. Both are inexpensive. And there are books available at any public library on building projects of all kinds, many of which can be adapted for chain saw users. There are many excellent standard works on the subject of cabin building. Among the best are those by Calvin Rutstrum, Bradford Angier, and Ben Hunt. Ben Hunt's *How to Build and Furnish a Cabin the Easy, Natural Way Using Only Hand Tools and the Materials Around You* (Macmillan, 1974) has a long title but is one of the classic works on this subject and everything Mr. Hunt suggests is made easier with a chain saw. Finally, *The Foxfire Book* (Anchor Press/Doubleday, 1968) will answer your remaining questions and supply considerably more technical information.

The whole problem of wood preservatives and protecting close-to-the-ground logs from decay or parasites is presently up in the air. Creosote is the traditional and safest treatment, but it's messy and difficult to use. Penta and other accepted preservatives contain dioxane, an extremely dangerous chemical that will kill wildlife, livestock, and pets. Parp says it will soon be shown that dioxane enters the food chain and, if used, becomes a threat to everything living in the area. If you must use a preservative, use creosote and follow the instructions.

One of the best things to do with some of your practice logs is to make a sandbox or other useful structure that involves making log walls that aren't too high off the ground. This will give you more practice in fitting logs together and you'll come to appreciate the difficulties of getting a tight fit.

A miniature log cabin for a doghouse or playhouse is another very rewarding project. Eight-inch logs are the easiest to manage on a small project like a playhouse, but you can do well with six-inch logs if you're careful. Make the walls in standard log cabin construction forms using saddle notches. You can make a good floor and roof by ripping a log into planks for the floor and slabs for the roof.

Which brings us to a point. Parp is especially fond of projects that use all the wood to best advantage. As nice as log cabins are, timber cabins can be better. If you're lucky enough to have a place to build such a structure, and trees to spare, you should consider ripping each log so that it supplies timbers for the walls, planks for the floor and interior, and slabs for siding. Be sure to save all the damaged or too-short pieces for building furniture.

You can elaborate the old bunk bed project into an incredibly beautiful fort for kids by ripping boards for the frame and nailing the slabs vertically all around, leaving only an entrance. You can also do the same thing for a playhouse, instead of using round logs.

When you've gained considerable proficiency and confidence through a number of small building projects, you'll be ready to build a cabin. Not a house. A cabin.

TO BUILD A CABIN

You can make any kind of lumber with a chain saw. You can make slabs, timbers, beams, posts, planks, boards, cross ties, and even laths. That's why you can build a cabin and waste no wood at all. You can also make skids so your mule can bring your stove or fireplace stones right to your brand new doorstep. And you can throw the sawdust into your compost heap. Don't even leave the chips where they fall—dry them out for kindling.

Now that you're an expert at ripping logs freehand, you're ready for the tools that make it delightfully easy. But don't get the idea you can skip Step One.

Tools

A chain saw is a portable saw mill. All it needs is a little guidance to produce accurately the most beautiful lumber in existence. You cannot buy boards at any lumber yard that look nearly as nice as those you can make yourself, with a chain saw and a lumber-making attachment or mill rig.

There are a great many mill rigs available to fit all kinds and sizes of chain saws. Some of these are expensive and elaborate, like Granberg's Alaskan Mill, and are essentially two-person tools. The Alaskan Mill is the best and most accurate mill rig available. The rig consists of braces and rollers that accurately guide the saw through the wood, and is available in either one-person or two-person models. A complete two-person Alaskan Mill with a special 32-inch bar, ripping chain, helper handle, and

Granberg Alaskan Mill in operation

Figure 11.5

auxiliary oiler runs about $375. If you're going to have help building a permanent cabin, an Alaskan Mill is a good investment. Other Alaskan Mills from Granberg cost between $95 and $435.

Other mill rigs are far less elaborate and less expensive and are made to attach very simply to your chain saw just as it is. The best and least expensive of these is the Haddon Lumber/Maker from Haddon Tool. Presently priced at less than $40, Haddon's Lumber/Maker is a one-person tool that is incredibly easy to use. Although not as much of a production aid as an Alaskan Mill, the Lumber/Maker still enables any chain saw owner to produce beautiful lumber with very little effort. It consists of a brace, a roller, and a guide, and can be helpful in many other kinds of cutting jobs.

However you make your lumber, if you start a large building project such as a garage or a cabin, you should invest in a ripping chain for producing lumber. Most chain dealers carry ripping chain, or you can mail-order it from Zip Penn. Granberg, Carleton, and Oregon make the highest-quality ripping chain and this is one of Granberg's specialities.

If you handle large logs or do a lot of ripping, you'll find that log dogs are like having another pair of arms. They are iron braces with hooked ends and can be used any time you need extra support. They are especially useful in long ripping projects and can be used with wedges or instead of them to keep the wood from binding your chain.

If you're building a cabin with a chain saw, the best tool to have is another chain saw. A heavy, older chain saw makes a good backup to your lighter, smaller modern saw. Heavy old saws are often gear-driven, which gives them a great deal of lugging power. Also, the chain moves slower, which can be a real advantage during certain stages of building, although direct drive or a gear ratio of 2:1 is best for ripping. Since heavy old chain saws can often be obtained for very little money, we're not talking about a major investment. Parp has a huge old 30-pound David Bradley gear-driven (2:1) monster that he will soon fix permanently to an Alaskan Mill. These saws often have ½-inch-pitch chains. One-half-inch-pitch ripping chain and a long guide bar are ideal for making lumber with one of the larger mills. A large old saw can also be a great help when you're sawing in doors or windows, or when you're trimming two logs for a better fit.

That brings up a cut that Parp didn't mention before. (You should not try this with a mini-saw.) If you're putting round logs together, you can make them fit very well. Place the logs next to each other and block them from rolling or secure them with log dogs. Then run the bar of your large saw between the logs so that you're removing wood from both logs at once. This will shape the logs to fit perfectly when they're placed on top of each other. Please be careful, says Parp, because shaping the fit of logs or cutting between logs is the most dangerous procedure we've mentioned. And don't try to fit logs that are already in or on a log wall. That's very dangerous and will also make accurate notching impossible.

It is very possible to build a simple cabin using only a chain saw and an ax. Some kind of mill or a Lumber/Maker makes it much easier, faster, and more accurate. Other special tools, many of them very old and traditional, have particular uses in cabin building. It is not Parp's place or intention to cover the uses of these tools, but a list may be helpful. Any of the good cabin-building books provide complete information on these tools and their uses. Among them are the gimlet for boring holes in logs, the adz for notching and shaping, the gouge for trimming, the caliper for measuring, the scribe for marking, the plane for finishing, the level and the plumb line, the froe for splitting shingles, and the drawknife for peeling logs.

Many chain saws can be fitted to a debarking attachment but this is quite expensive and a drawknife is not as difficult or as slow as it's often made out to be—it's still the best and fastest method of peeling logs by hand. If your cabin plans are elaborate and if you have no place to plug in an electric drill, you may want to get a drill attachment for your chain saw. And no doubt other attachments will soon appear that will make chain saw cabin building easier and more accurate.

Again, if you must apply preservatives to some of your logs, use creosote and avoid any treatment that contains dioxane.

Finally, a hammer is a real neat thing to have when you're building things with wood. Especially if you use nails.

Let's take a closer look at producing specific pieces of lumber. We'll use the Haddon Lumber/Maker and a medium-duty chain saw since this is the least expensive approach and does not require a helper. For ripping, the Lumber/Maker works by guiding a chain saw down a board that is fastened to the top of a log. Use 2 × 4s and 2 × 6s for the guide boards.

To make a solid 4 × 4 timber and four good slabs, use a log eight inches in diameter. Center a 2 × 4 on top of the log and nail it down firmly enough to take some pressure, but not so firmly that it's difficult to remove without splitting it. Two or three nails should do it.

Following the instructions that come with the tool, attach the Lumber/Maker or similar tool to your chain saw. Be sure to read and follow the instructions for assembly. Now set the instant portable saw mill, which is what you just put together, so that the roller rides on the guide board. Start, as always, at the small end of the log. Now start your saw and pull it back, with one roller riding on the board, to cut the first slab. Then turn your rig around and go back the other way. This time, you're cutting from the large end toward the small end.

When the first two slabs are off, remove the guide board and turn the log over so that a sawed side is up. Again, center and nail down your guide board. Now rip off the other two slabs. That's it for a 4 × 4 timber and four good slabs.

To make 6 × 6 timbers, simply adjust the Lumber/Maker, or whatever, according to the instructions and use a 2 × 6 as a guide board instead of a 2 × 4. A 2 × 6 works better anyway. You can make timbers of any size from 4 × 4 to 12 × 12 by using the appropriate size guide board and adjusting the tool accordingly. You can make guide boards of any size by adding strips of straight wood to your guide board stock. A good selection of various width guide boards comes in handy.

You can also make cross jigs to any size so you can cut lumber or logs to equal lengths. To make an eight-foot-length jig, cut a 2 × 6 to 95½ inches long. This allows for the ½-inch distance between the guide board and the saw cut. Then nail 2 × 6 pieces of sufficient length at right angles across both ends. Use a square to be sure your end pieces are precise. The end pieces then form the guides that the Lumber/Maker moves on. You can, of course, make length jigs of any size as long as you allow the ½ inch.

After the slabs are removed, a timber can be ripped into any size lumber. The boards that are produced this way are somewhat rough, of course, but are as beautiful as anything could be. Parp sighs for the light of a kerosene lamp reflected by walls of handmade boards. Only the sun itself is so completely satisfying.

To turn a 6 × 6 timber into three 2 × 6 planks, use a ruler to mark both ends of the timber into three equal parts. Use a 2 × 4 guide board and attach it to the timber so your chain saw is centered to cut at the first line. Saw off the first plank. Reset your guide board and chain saw to split the remaining two planks. It really is that easy.

To learn a great deal more about making lumber with a mill or jig, write to Granberg or order *The Chain Saw and the Lumber/Maker* from Haddon Tool.

One of the most sturdy designs for log cabin construction is the cross-and-filler type suggested by Jesse Haddon. This method produces a solid timber cabin with all the advantages of squared timbers and all the beauty of round logs.

To make a cross-and-filler cabin, cut the slabs off of three sides of the logs to be used. Cut the logs to equal thickness and

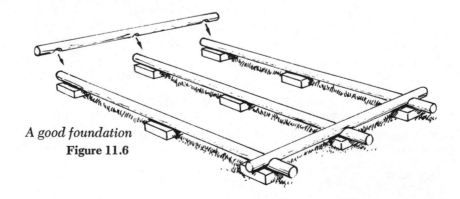

A good foundation
Figure 11.6

Cross member log

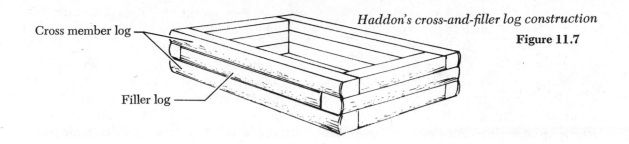

Haddon's cross-and-filler log construction

Figure 11.7

Filler log

to lengths that fit your plan. Each pair of cross logs are filled with two filler logs that fit tightly between them. Lay the logs so that the bark side is outside and you have flat sides facing up, down, and in. You alter the position of each course of logs so that filler sits on cross and cross sits on filler. Jesse say a winch helps pull the cross logs tight against the fillers. You can, of course, use any kind of hoist or hand winch, or even a Handyman Jack with chains or ropes attached. When the walls are up you can saw in the doors and windows using your Lumber/Maker and guide boards nailed to the timbers. Always make the right-hand cut first since the guide board for the right-hand cut will be nailed to the timbers you're removing. The left-hand guide board will be clear of the moving timbers, which will come out easily as the left-hand cut is made. Be careful.

MAKING PLANS

The prime purpose of this chapter is to show how the modern chain saw affects the process of building a cabin. The great Alaskan Mill and the Lumber/Maker are both inventor's dreams but they would not have appeared if the chain saw weren't around. A chain saw, a lumber-making tool, a supply of fuel, and everything else you need can be packed or pulled into even the most remote areas. Any remote area that grows trees will provide all you need to build a cabin. And it had probably better be a remote area.

When Parp was honored to serve as zoning officer for a certain county, he encouraged the use of outhouses and hand-dug wells. He made sure the outhouses were well made and well kept, but he encouraged their use. Parp was able to do this because of a liberal and sparse populace and the absence of a building code.

Most of the cabins Parp has loved would fail any inspection, though not on reasonable grounds. The point is, you can't build anything you want, any way you wish, any place you like, anymore.

If you have a piece of ground far from any zoning officer (or if you have a good security system), you can build a very serviceable cabin for hunting, fishing, hiking, or hiding out. And you can build it alone, with no waste, a minimum of effort and experience, and slight damage to the area around you. It just takes time.

Some time ago, the Oregon Saw Chain people generously distributed free copies of a fine cabin plan, loved by Parp. The cabin we're going to build here is similar to the Oregon plan, but changed somewhat and simplified a lot by Parp. Copies of the original may be obtained through your local Oregon dealer.

Now, let's be realistic. Parp has never seen anything that gives you a good idea just how long it takes to build a plain and simple cabin, step-by-step. Let's keep track of how long the average malnourished back-to-the-lander from Detroit spends on each step of building a cabin in the wilderness, all alone. We'll start out by not even counting the time it takes to find and acquire the land. The only fast way to do that is to go to Alaska or South America.

Before you build even the most informal cabin, you have to consider the possible hazards of the proposed site. It's not Parp's place to describe all of the potential hazards to dwelling but a few lesser-known although obvious ones deserve mention.

If you find a nice flat shelf in mountainous terrain where aspen grow in a clump surrounded by pines or hardwoods, don't build there. Aspen and its relatives are the first trees to grow after an area has been hit by an avalanche, a rock slide, or a flood. Also watch for avalanche paths. They look like a funnel going up between mountains, or any place on a mountain. If you see a rock slide above your proposed site, be sure you're well out of its path if it should ever move down. And any low, flat area between hills and near a body of moving water is a floodplain area. The incidence of flood is presently increasing and is likely to go on doing so. That's because many flood areas are hundred-year floodplains. They look like great building sites with their level deposits of rich earth but in any given year there is 1 percent chance of flood. We've just been lucky for a hundred years. Parp suggests you look into this in more detail at your library or through your state land control office. Plan on a week of hiking and searching for the site, at least.

So you have your land and you've chosen your building site. One year, in September, you go out and cut your building logs. Select cedar, pine, fir, or spruce, in that order. Here's what you need to build a 10 × 12-foot one-room cabin with a plain pitched roof and overhang.

1. Two solid logs 10 inches in diameter and over 12 feet long for foundation logs.
2. Three solid logs, 10 inches in diameter and over 10 feet long, for foundation cross members.
3. Six more 10-inch logs about 12 feet long to rip into floor planks.
4. Eight logs 8 inches in diameter for uprights.
5. Two 6-inch logs, 12 feet long, for top plates.
6. Four logs about 6 inches in diameter and 14 feet long for rafters and porch overhang.
7. Fifteen 3- or 4-inch poles or logs, 14 feet long for purlins.
8. Five assorted logs ranging from 6 inches

to 12 inches for miscellaneous lumber, slabs, doorstep, door planks, etc.

9. Fifteen cedar bolts or other stock for splitting shakes. You can make do with green aspen and other woods. Experiment.

What with searching for the trees, spreading the cutting, moving the logs to your building site, countless hassles and delays, it's done in a month, maybe, if you're lucky and work like a bear. Fortunately, you have a chain saw.

Now you carefully peel and stack all the logs in drying stacks with plenty of air between each log. Allow another two weeks or so. It's now late October or early November and it's time to go away until the end of next August. Spend the spring and summer of the drying year putting by a pile of firewood the size of your proposed cabin and packing in the rest of your tools, spikes and nails, a small pot belly or shepherd's stove, stove pipe, chimney jack and rain cap, hardware for your door, and a window. Also clear your building area. If you work hard, you'll get it all done in time: ten months.

CONSTRUCTION

No cabin will stand up straight for very long if it isn't set on a foundation that reaches to bedrock or below frostline, whichever comes first. Dig six deep foundation holes, each 12″ × 12″. Pack the earth down in the bottom of the holes, if earth is there. Then use a wooden form and pour concrete footings. This is the easiest and best foundation for a simple cabin. Digging, mixing, and pouring: one week.

Use the best, most solid, well-dried and peeled 10-inch logs as foundation logs. Take advantage of each log's roundness and roll it into place. Since these large logs are close to the ground, one person can do it. Use end joints to join the four outside logs and cross joints for the middle log. The joints are, of course, 10 inches wide and 5 inches deep. All log joints rest on the concrete footings. Secure the joints with 60d spikes, using two spikes at each joint. If you don't want to plunge-cut the cross joints, use your chain saw to make three cuts 5 inches apart and 5 inches deep. Then add a few more cuts between them. That makes it easy to split out the notch with your ax.

After two days to get the foundation logs notched, settled, and secured, you're ready to put in your floor.

Use your Lumber/Maker or your Alaskan Mill to rip floor planks from the chosen 10-inch logs. Or you can do it freehand, maybe. Make the planks 2 inches thick and let the slabs be good and thick. You'll be using them for siding. Spike your floor planks onto your foundation logs. Rip your planks from logs in the round, rather than from squared timbers, and alternate the beveled, outside edges of the planks so they fit tightly together. They'll take a heavy load that way. When your floor is finished, use your chain saw to trim the ends flush with the foundation logs. Be

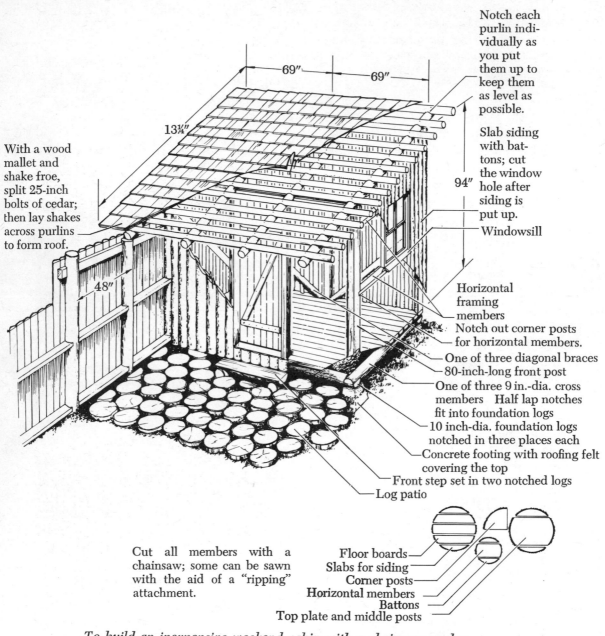

Notch each purlin individually as you put them up to keep them as level as possible.

Slab siding with battons; cut the window hole after siding is put up.

Windowsill

Horizontal framing members

Notch out corner posts for horizontal members.

One of three diagonal braces

80-inch-long front post

One of three 9 in.-dia. cross members   Half lap notches fit into foundation logs

10 inch-dia. foundation logs notched in three places each

Concrete footing with roofing felt covering the top

Front step set in two notched logs

Log patio

94"

69"   69"

13¼"

With a wood mallet and shake froe, split 25-inch bolts of cedar; then lay shakes across purlins to form roof.

48"

Cut all members with a chainsaw; some can be sawn with the aid of a "ripping" attachment.

Floor boards
Slabs for siding
Corner posts
Horizontal members
Battons
Top plate and middle posts

To build an inexpensive weekend cabin with a chain saw and a few simple tools, follow the basic techniques outlined in this illustration.

Figure 11.8

careful not to hit any spikes with your chain. Plan on a day and a half for the floor.

For corner posts and uprights, use the 8-inch logs with slabs removed from two oposite sides only. Face one bark side out. Spike each post to the floor with four 60d spikes. Brace the posts until you add the top plates. The height of your cabin and the pitch of your roof depend on the height of the uprights. The tallest go in back, of course. Three or four hours.

Top plates join the corner posts. Rip slabs from two sides of the two 6-inch logs that are 12 feet long. Lay these top plates across the upright posts with flat surfaces

Barnacle Parp's slab and log cabin in Reed Gulch, Colorado
Figure 11.9

up and down. Again, secure them with 60d spikes. One hour.

Now set four log rafters, 14 feet long and 5 inches in diameter, across the top plates with their butts toward the high side of the pitched roof. Cut and shape 1-inch notches to fit the top plates. You can now see what your cabin is going to look like. Three hours.

Now you need 15 logs, 14 feet long and 3 inches in diameter. These are purlins that go on top of the rafters at 11-inch intervals. Use a timber spiked across the purlins to align the ends. Notch the purlins individually, as you put them up, in order to get them as level as possible. This is the base for the shake roof. Four hours.

Place horizontal framing members across the window wall in 1″ × 3″ notches in the corner posts. Spike the butted ends in place with 40d nails driven through the posts from the outside. Now make permanent cross braces between the upright posts. Cut the ends of the braces at angles to fit the floor and upright. Spike the base of each cross brace to the floor planks and the tops to the upright posts. Three hours.

Before you lay your shake roof, decide where you want your stove. Center back is best, with 2 or 3 feet of air space behind the stove. Use a wooden frame of 1 × 6

boards to attach your chimney jack to the purlins. When you lay your shakes, fit them tightly to the sides of the frame. Install your chimney pipe with one length of pipe extending through the chimney jack. Then use tar to seal the shingles and the fittings of the frame and the chimney jack. Keep the tar away from the chimney itself. There should be 6 inches of clean tin jack all around the chimney. Set your stove on an asbestos pad.

Split your own roofing shakes from cedar bolts 2 feet long and finish your roof. All that and the stove comes to five days. Use slabs for siding, nailed vertically into the cross framing with 30d nails. Another day. Cut a window after the siding is on. Cut it to fit any window you're using or are going to make. Fasten your window sash with nails into the horizontal framing members. Then caulk it: one hour. Panel the interior with ripped boards: one day. Make your doorstep from a 12-inch log, 4 feet long and ripped in half. Set the doorstep in notched blocks. Make a door with 10-inch planks and use slabs for cross braces. Spend another day or two for finishing and cleaning up. Altogether, one year, one week, and twenty-seven hours or so.

A cabin, in fact.

Soft Words for Tenderfeet and Sensitive Souls • 12

It's the end of winter now, and the end of Parp's hassle with this book. We're approaching the forest where the living trees are waking in the spring and whispering of their own lives, separate and free. Somewhere in the Sierra Mountains the oldest being on earth, a bristlecone pine, knows the peace and solitude of growing where nothing else will live.

Millions of other trees have, this year, stopped the kind of growth that we call life. Mostly, that makes no immediate difference. They will stand a long time in the wind and rain. Their return to the forest floor is imperceptibly slow. Long before they are actually down, they begin relinquishing their precious elements to other beings, insects and mushrooms, birds and animals.

One of the animals, *Homo sapiens,* will greatly speed this process for a few thousand of the standing dead in an attempt to keep warm through another winter. But even in the age of the chain saw, most of the dead trees will still be left to dry and fall by themselves, and then to rot and provide homes and food for other creatures of all kinds. All of this is good and natural, including this particular human involvement, and it doesn't matter what tools the individual human uses. The individual is providing for natural needs and a natural life.

Other humans, using chain saws, work in groups to provide housing for others who are far from the forests. Even this can be done decently, and the use of forest products becomes, in one way, more efficient every year. We use more of the wood we cut for more products. Most of those products are unnecessary frills but at least we don't throw the wood away immediately.

It's not Parp's place to preach on forestry or logging methods, as many will jump to agree, but we are still clear-cutting in many forests, scalping the earth, leveling millions of acres of living, sentient creatures and we do not have to do that. There the human animal is not good or natural and it must stop. The large companies and their friends in government offer all sorts of excuses for clear-cutting, and even maintain that it is better for the forests than selective cutting. Without going into details, Parp says it's a lie. A spirit moves in the trees to which all the guilty parties, governments, and corporations, will answer. That's good enough for Parp, and he trusts to it.

We have come so far from ourselves. We accept, at conception, the elemental gift of the great trees that have gone before. But we don't return that gift to the mushrooms and insects that start the chain of giving over again. We have to learn to do intentionally all the things we no longer do naturally.

This is a book about a tool that can either take us further away from ourselves by increasing each individual's circle of destruction, or can help bring some of us back, close enough to relearn the language of the trees, by making a more natural life easier and more possible for an animal that has forgotten how to live and die. Parp offers this book and these words to those who make the second choice.

Many myths and notions surround working in the woods, especially with an ax and chain saw. Great shoulders roll and tense with the exertion of cutting trees and chopping wood. Many people, themselves dwarfed by the trees, would have us believe that you have to be big and tough and male (whatever that is) to be a woodsperson. Parp has news for those folks, yes indeed.

It is manifest that neither testicles nor large wrists contribute anything whatsoever to a person's love and understanding of the natural world. And testicles do not in any way affect one's ability to do good work with a chain saw or any other kind of tool, as we all know.

Whatever kind of human one is, we do all have to live in the same woods and we must all give up our toughness and our insistence on unimportant differences. A college education is also not conducive to a natural understanding. The fact that the University of Iowa's enormously expensive Hancher Auditorium was recently constructed plumb in the center of a serious flood plain is ample proof of that. If you're a logger living near a group of hippies, look closely at what they're really trying to do. And if you're a new homesteader living near a group of loggers, watch one of them alone in the woods sometime. You'll see a pure love of this planet, similar to your own, as that rugged face turns up toward the trees and the sky. We are all the same.

So if that logger happens by when you're out there cutting wood, stop and talk awhile. If you get unwanted or bad advice, or the silly, little boy kind of teasing that turns up now and then, remember that it's your saw and your wood and your way. Besides, you use good clean oil on your bar and chain and that logger uses old tractor drippings. You are the expert.

You should consider that working with a chain saw is very bad exercise that may add some strength to your arms but will do nothing else for your physical good. Parp suggests that you devote some time to regular meditation and good clean yoga after any chain saw session. It's the best cure, though a fine walk in the woods is just about as good.

Sleeping under the trees on a warm afternoon is another ideal way to counter the negative effects of running a gasoline-powered engine. And sitting by a river dipping your toes is good, too. Whenever you work in the woods, remember this. The natural woodsperson takes long and frequent breaks. It's the only way to remember what you are, where you fit, and why you're there. For safety's sake you should work with a partner whenever you can. For nature's sake, you should each take your breaks in solitude.

So Parp says, as we're heading out into the woods in different directions, don't forget your whistle.

Appendix

ADDRESSES OF CHAIN SAW MANUFACTURERS

ADVANCED ENGINE PRODUCTS
(*Savage and Forester Chain Saws*)
3340 Emery Street
Los Angeles, CA 90023

ALLIS CHALMERS
(*Made by Poulan*)
Box 512
Milwaukee, WI 53201

DANARM CHAIN SAWS
Yankee Clipper Trading Post
2405 Boston Post Road
Guilford, CT 06437

JOHN DEERE & COMPANY
(*Made by Echo*)
Moline, IL 61265

DOLMAR NORTH AMERICAN
947 West Foothill Blvd.
Monrovia, CA 91016

ECHO CHAIN SAWS
3240 Commercial Avenue
Northbrook, IL 60062

FRONTIER CHAIN SAWS
P. O. Box 491
Waneta Road
Trail, British Columbia
Canada

HOMELITE DIVISION OF TEXTRON, INC.
P. O. Box 7047
Charlotte, NC 28217

HUSQVARNA
151 New World Way
South Plainfield, NJ 07080

JOBU CHAIN SAWS
Elkem-Spigerverket a/s
1441 Drobak
Norway

JONSEREDS CHAIN SAWS
Tilton Equipment Company
4612 N. Chatsworth
St. Paul, MN 55112

McCULLOCH CORPORATION
5400 Alla Road
Los Angeles, CA 90066

MASSEY FERGUSON
1901 Bell Avenue
Des Moines, IA 50315

OLEO-MAC (OLYMPIC) CHAIN SAWS
Scotsco, Inc.
9180 S.E. 74th Avenue
Portland, OR 97206

PARTNER INDUSTRIES OF AMERICA,
   INC.
255 East Industry Avenue
Frankfort, IL 69423

PIONEER CHAIN SAWS
6705 Cushman Drive
P. O. Box 82409
Lincoln, NB 68501

POULAN CHAIN SAWS
Beaird-Poulan Division
Emerson Electric Company
5020 Flournoy/Lucas Road
Shreveport, LA 71109

REMINGTON CHAIN SAWS
Desa Industries
25000 South Western Avenue
Park Forest, IL 60466

SKIL CORPORATION
5033 Elston Avenue
Chicago, IL 60630

SOLO MOTORS, INC.
5100 Chestnut Avenue
Newport News, VA 23605

STIHL, INCORPORATED
P. O. Box 5514
Virginia Beach, VA 23455

OTHER ADDRESSES OF INTEREST

Alaskan Mill

See GRANBERG

ATOM INDUSTRIES
15 Reynolds Street
Balmain, N.S.W.
Australia 2041

Manufacturers of chain saw drill attachments.

BAILEY'S
P. O. Box 550
Laytonville, CA 95454

Mail order suppliers of saw chain, tools, accessories.
They also have logger's job service.

Bar Repair	See Specialty Motors.
BELL INDUSTRIES Saw and Machine Division 3390 West 11th Avenue P. O. Box 2510 Eugene, OR 97402	Formerly Nielson. Manufacturers of home and shop electric saw chain grinders, carb-cutter attachments, chain saw related machines.
BREAK-N-MEND	See GRANBERG.
CARLTON COMPANY Saw Chain Division 3901 S.E. Naef Road Portland, OR 97222	Manufacturers of saw chain.
THE CHAIN SAW MUSEUM Marshall J. Trover, Curator Box 312 Black Diamond, WA 98010	Comprehensive collection depicts the history of the chain saw.
THE DEFIANCE COMPANY Hancock, MI 48830	Manufacturers of "Little Logger" chain saw accessory.
PERRY DAVIS EQUIPMENT 21353 Endsley Avenue Rocky River, OH 44116	Manufacturers of chain saw testing equipment for mechanics.
DIDIER MANUFACTURING COMPANY 8630 Industrial Drive Franksville, WI 53126	Manufacturers of hydraulic wood splitting machines.
ENGINE SERVICE ASSOCIATION 710 North Plankinton Avenue Milwaukee, WI 53203	Association for professional air-cooled engine mechanics.
FILE-N-JOINT	See GRANBERG.
GRANBERG INDUSTRIES, INC. 200 South Garrard Blvd. Richmond, CA 94804	Manufacturers of chain saw tools, accessories, ripping chain, Alaskan Mill, BREAK-N-MEND, FILE-N-JOINT.

HADDON TOOL
4719 West Route 120
McHenry, IL 60050

Manufacturers of chain saw accessories, Lumber/
Maker attachment.

HELI-COIL PRODUCTS
Shelter Rock Lane
Danbury, CT 06810

Manufacturers of thread repair kits. A chain saw
mechanic's must.

INTERTEC PUBLISHING CORPO-
RATION
Technical Publication Division
1014 Wyandotte Street
Kansas City, MO 64105

Publishers of *Chain Saw Service Manual,* other books
for mechanics.

KWIK-WAY MANUFACTURING
COMPANY
500-57 Street
Marion, IA 52302

Manufacturers of machines and tools for small engine
mechanics.

FRED A. LEWIS COMPANY
40 Belknap Road
Medford, OR 97501

Manufacturers of chain saw winch attachments.

Little Logger

See THE DEFIANCE COMPANY.

LOCTITE CORPORATION
705 North Mountain Road
Newington, CT 06111

Manufacturers of thread-locking compounds. A mechanic's must.

Lumber/Maker

See HADDON TOOL.

MERC–O-TRONIC INSTRUMENTS
215 Branch Street
Almont, MI 48003

Manufacturers of chain saw ignition-testing equipment.

Nielson

See BELL INDUSTRIES.

OREGON SAW CHAIN DIVISION
Omark Industries
9701 S.E. McLoughlin Blvd.
Portland, OR 97222

Manufacturers of saw chain, tools, accessories.

PERMATEX COMPANY, INC.
P. O. Box 1350
West Palm Beach, FL 33402

Manufacturers of gasket sealers.

R. E. PHELON COMPANY
East Longmeadow, MA 01028

Manufacturers of ignition parts for chain saws.

PIQUA ENGINEERING, INC.
P. O. Box 605
Piqua, OH 45356

Manufacturers of hydraulic wood-splitting machines.

RAKET SAFETY CLOTHING
Oy Elfving, AB
Finland

Manufacturers of safety clothing for professional chain saw operators. No U.S. address, as yet.

SANDVIK, INCORPORATED
1702 Nevins Road
Fair Lawn, NJ 07410

Manufacturers of forestry tools, guide bars, chain saw tools and accessories. "Swedish Forestry Method."

SKIL CORPORATION
5033 Elston Avenue
Chicago, IL 60630

Manufacturers of professional air and electric impact wrenches, shop tools for chain saw mechanics.

The Stickler

See TAOS EQUIPMENT.

SPENCER PRODUCTION
    COMPANY
P. O. Box 224
Pullman, WA 99163

Manufacturers of logger's tape, falling and bucking wedges, chain saw and logger accessories.

TAOS EQUIPMENT MANU-
    FACTURERS
Box 1565
Taos, NM 87571

Manufacturers of The Stickler wood-splitting device, and hydraulic wood-splitting machines.

U.S. GENERAL SUPPLY
100 General Place
Jericho, NY 11753

Large mail-order tool supply company.

V.I.P. INDUSTRIES
300 S. Richardson Road
Ashland, VA 23005

Manufacturers of portable electric saw chain grinders.

WACO INDUSTRIES, INC.
749 Airways Blvd.
Jackson, TN 38301

Windsor Machine, in the U.S.

WALBRO CORPORATION
Cass City, MI 48726

Manufacturers of chain saw carburetors.

J. C. WHITNEY COMPANY
1917-19 Archer Avenue
P. O. Box 8410
Chicago, IL 60680

Large mail-order tool supply company.

WINDSOR MACHINE COMPANY
3147 Thunderbird Crescent
Burnaby, British Columbia
Canada

Manufacturers of saw chain, guide bars (Timber King), tools, and accessories.

ZIP PENN, INC.
2008 E. 33rd Street
P. O. Box 179
Erie, PA 16512

Mail-order suppliers of saw chain, tools, accessories.

PERIODICALS OF INTEREST

AMERICAN FORESTS
The American Forestry Association
1319-18th Street N.W.
Washington, DC 20036

Professional publication for foresters and tree farmers.

CHAIN SAW AGE
3435 N.E. Broadway
Portland, OR 97232

Trade publication. Monthly magazine.

CHAIN SAW INDUSTRY
P. O. Box 1703
Shreveport, LA 71166

Trade publication. Monthly magazine.

DIXIE LOGGER & LUMBERMAN
P. O. Box 487
Wadley, GA 30477

Regional logging magazine.

FARM EQUIPMENT
1233 Janesville Avenue
Fort Atkinson, WI 53538

Trade publication for farm equipment dealers.

FOREST FARMER
The Forest Farmer's Assn. Co-op.
Suite 380
4 Executive Park East, N.E.
Atlanta, GA 30329

Professional publication for foresters and tree farmers.

FOREST INDUSTRIES
Miller Freeman Publications
500 Howard Street
San Francisco, CA 94105

Professional publication for foresters and tree farmers.

IMPLEMENT & TRACTOR
Intertec Publishing Corporation
1014 Wyandotte Street
Kansas City, MO 64105

Trade publication for implement dealers.

JOURNAL OF FOREST HISTORY
P. O. Box 1581
Santa Cruz, CA 95061

Serious quarterly magazine devoted to the study and history of forests and forestry.

LOGGIN' TIMES
P. O. Box 2268
Montgomery, AL 36103

A magazine for loggers.

LOGGER'S WORLD
P. O. Box 1006
Chehalis, WA 98532

"The Logger's Magazine." They also sell suspenders.

THE NORTHERN LOGGER AND
    TIMBER PROCESSOR
Northeastern Logger's Association
Old Forge, NY 13402

Regional logging magazine.

PULPWOOD PRODUCTION &
    TIMBER HARVESTING
P. O. Box 2268
Montgomery, AL 36103

Professional publication.

WESTERN TIMBER INDUSTRY
500 Howard Street
San Francisco, CA 94105

Professional publication.

WOOD BURNING QUARTERLY
8009-34th Ave. South
Minneapolis, MN 55420

Quarterly magazine of general interest to chain saw users.

WORKBENCH
4251 Pennsylvania Avenue
Kansas City, MO 64111

Consumer magazine concerned with wood handcraft projects.

(Note that all the well-known consumer publications on popular science and the outdoors frequently carry articles of interest to chain saw users.)

SAW CHAIN CONVERSION CHART

Pitch	Gauge	Canad	Carlton	Homelite	Laser	McCulloch	Oregon	Pioneer
1/2	058	5, 80	D2E; D2S		5	PM 508	9AC	
1/2	063	6, 90	D3E, D3S	50-C-63	6	PM 503	10AC	
3/4	122	100			34	PM 752	11BC	
.325	050	45					20AP	
3/8	050	747				SM 370	22	
3/8	058	737				SM 378	23	
1/4	050	41		25-C-50		SM 250	25	
.404	058	767				SM 408	26	
.404	063	757				SM 403	27	
.404	050	777					28	
.354	058	354A	J2C			PM 358	45C	
.404	050	10	B1C; E; S	40-C-50	10		50C	
.404	050					SPR 400	50L	
.404	050					SPS 400	50AL	
.404	058	3, 30	B2C; E; S		3	PM 408	51AC	404R58T
.404	058					SPR 408	51L	
.404	058					SPS 408	51AL	
.404	063	4, 40	B3C; E; S	40-C-63	4	PM 403	52AC	404R63T
.404	063					SPR 403	52L	
.404	063					SPS 403	52AL	
3/8	050	9, 95	A1C; E; S	38-C-50	9	PM 370	72D	38R50T
3/8	050						72DP	
3/8	050					SPR 370G	72LP	
3/8	058	7, 75	A2C; E; S	38-C-58	7	PM 378	73D	38R58T
3/8	058						73DP	
3/8	058					SPR 378G	73LP	
3/8	063	8, 85	A3C; E; S		8	PM 373	75D	
3/8	063					SPR 373G	75LP	
3/8	050			37-N-50		MM 3 0	91	
3/8	050			37-C-50		MP 3703	91S	
3/8	050						91TS	
.315	050							
7/16	058		C-2		1		61, 68	D6EH
7/16	063		C-3		2		62, 69	D6EJ

Poulan	Remington	Sabre	Skil	Stihl	Windsor	Zip Penn
	58PF	15-150			DH58, 58D	5
P10	53PF	25-250	D58	3832	CH63,63C	6
		75			FH122, 122F	34
		325		3862	50J	11
P22		747		3857		
		737		3858		
P25		16		3856	KH50, 50K	41
		767		3822		
P27		757		3860		
		777				
		357A			GH58	
		34-340			BH50, 50B	10
	48PF	14-140		3822	BH50, 58B	3
P52	43PF	24-240	C58	3860	BH63, 63B	4
				3846		
P72	30PF	18	B58	3857	AH50, 50A	9
				3873		
	38PF	48		3881	AH58, 58A	7
						8
		28		3868	AH63, 63A	
P100						19
P101		350				
					50H	
	78PF	17			58C	1
	73PF	27			63C	2

TROUBLESHOOTING GUIDE

Trouble	Probable cause — Ignition System Possible cause											
	Defective spark plug	Spark plug gap too large	Burned breaker points	Breaker point gap incorrect	Breaker mechanism loose or other contact failure	Bad condenser	Connections loose or wire grounding	Flash-over at off/on switch	Coil failure	Incorrect ignition timing	Short-circuited spark plug	Breaker points oily
1. No spark when engine is turned over	X	X	X	X	X	X	X	X	X			X
2. Engine misfires under load, lacks power		X	X	X	X	X	X	X	X	X		X
3. Engine stalls at high speed					X	X	X	X	X	X		
4. Breaker points burned						X						
5. Engine overheats				X						X	X	
6. Excessive fuel consumption	X			X						X	X	
7. Fuel reaches carburetor, but not engine												
8. Fuel does not reach carburetor												
9. Engine lacks power, apt to race												
10. Exhaust smoke (fuel mixture too rich), engine lacks power												
11. Engine stalls when idling, operates normally at full throttle												
12. Clutch slips at operating speed												
13. Clutch engaged at idling speed												
14. Automatic oil pump does not work												
15. Oil pump delivers too much oil												
16. Poor oil pump feeding												
17. Does not respond to accelerator												
18. Oil system leaks												
19. Oil leakage at bar												
Remedy	Replace spark plug (original spare part)	Set gap to .020" (0.5 mm)	Replace breaker points	Set gap to 0.012—0.016 in (0.3—0.4 mm)	Adjust or replace	Replace condenser	Adjust or replace	Clean, adjust, or replace	Replace ignition or generator coil	See manual	Replace spark plug (original spare part)	Clean or replace breaker points

Replace plummet or plummet strainer			X								X	X					X			Fuel hose plummet clogged	**Fuel System Possible cause**
Replace fuel hose											X	X					X			Fuel hose cracked or leaking	
Fill tank with correct fuel mixture												X					X			Fuel tank empty	
Clean or replace diaphragm and filters			X						X	X	X		X	X			X			Diaphragm pump defective	
Clean or replace filter element										X				X						Air filter clogged	
See manual			X						X	X	X			X	X		X			Incorrect setting of diaphragm pump	
See manual for correct fuel mixture															X					Too little oil in fuel mixture	
Push choke control all way in										X				X						Too much choke	
Clean the valve			X							X	X	X								Fuel tank check valve clogged	
Replace gaskets and tighten loose joints														X						Gasoline leaking	
Turn back needles or blow out jets			X										X							Fuel jets closed or clogged	
Clean engine cooling fins and fan screen															X					Cylinder cooling ineffective	**Engine Possible cause**
Have the engine professionally decarbonized															X					Excessive carbon deposits on piston and cylinder	
Replace piston rings											X									Worn piston rings	
Remove clutch and clean							X													Clutch shoes jammed	
Clean and lubricate clutch bearing							X													Needle bearing jammed on crankshaft	
Replace clutch shoes								X												Worn clutch shoes	
Replace clutch spring							X		X											Damaged clutch spring	
Replace seals									X											Worn or damaged crankshaft seals	
Fill oil tank with correct grade of oil						X														Empty oil tank	**Lubrication System Possible Cause**
Clean vent hole, pump, and oil strainer				X		X														Impurities in oil tank vent hole or oil strainer	
Re-set oil pump set-screw				X	X	X														Oil pump feeding set incorrectly	
Replace gaskets and tighten loose joints		X		X		X														Defective gaskets or loose joints	
Clean oil hole	X			X		X														Sawdust in bar oil hole	
Replace O-rings		X		X		X														Damaged O-rings	
Clean before mounting	X																			Sawdust between bar, inner guard, and engine	

FUEL SYSTEM TROUBLESHOOTING

You have determined that it is likely that you have a problem in your fuel system. Eliminate these possibilities in this approximate order.

Engine Will Not Start

Probable Causes	Remedies
Fuel tank empty. Water in fuel or fuel stale.	Fill fuel tank. Empty fuel tank, dry fuel lines, refill tank.
Fuel filter clogged or water in fuel filter.	Replace fuel filter.
Air filter dirty or wet.	Clean or replace air filter.
Engine flooded.	If caused by overchoking, close choke and open throttle. Attempt to start. If that fails, remove spark plug. Pull starter rope several times. Allow air or sunlight to reach cylinder. Replace plug. If it still floods, carburetor is likely problem.
Fuel cap vent clogged.	Clean or replace fuel cap.
Fuel line clogged or plugged.	Blow out fuel line or replace.
Carburetor mixture adjustments incorrect.	Readjust carburetor.
Fuel pump diaphragm damaged.	Replace fuel pump diaphragm.
Fuel pump clogged.	Clean carburetor and integral fuel pump.
Carburetor needles, jets, gaskets, or diaphragms defective or leaking.	Clean and rebuild carburetor.

Engine Starts but Runs Poorly at All Speeds

Probable Causes	Remedies
Incorrect fuel mixture.	Empty fuel tank and refill with fresh, precisely measured fuel mixture. Clean and gap plug.
Carbon building in exhaust ports.	Scrape clean with wood or plastic scraper.

Fuel stored incorrectly, left in fuel tank. Water in fuel filter as a result.	Empty fuel tank and refill with fresh fuel. Replace fuel filter.
Carburetor incorrectly adjusted.	Adjust carburetor.
Fuel tank vent plugged.	Clean vent.
Excessive piston ring or cylinder wear.	Replace.

Engine Won't Run at Full Speed

Probable Causes	Remedies
Dirty air filter.	Replace air filter.
Fuel cap vent partially clogged.	Clean fuel cap.
Fuel filter clogged—some water in fuel filter.	Replace fuel filter.
Carburetor incorrectly adjusted.	Adjust carburetor.
Carburetor loose.	Tighten carburetor.
Choke sticking.	Adjust or replace choke linkage.
Carburetor diaphragms defective.	Replace carburetor diaphragm.
Carburetor valve dirty.	Clean and rebuild carburetor.
Fuel tank vent plugged.	Clean vent.
Pin holes in fuel line.	Replace.

Engine Overheats

Probable Causes	Remedies
Dirty air filter.	Clean or replace air filter.
Carburetor incorrectly adjusted (too lean).	Adjust carburetor.
Carburetor loose.	Tighten carburetor.
Carburetor base gasket leaking air.	Replace carburetor gasket.
Carburetor worn or defective.	Clean and rebuild carburetor.
Too little oil in fuel.	Use correct mixture.
Timing incorrectly adjusted (advanced).	Reset timing.

IGNITION SYSTEM TROUBLESHOOTING

You have determined that it is likely you have a problem in your ignition system. Eliminate these possibilities in their approximate order.

Engine Does Not Turn Over

Probable Causes	Remedies
Defective starter.	Repair or replace starter.
Engine seized.	Rebuild engine or junk saw.
Loose screws behind flywheel or caught between flywheel and coil lamination.	Replace or retighten screws.

Engine Will Not Start

Probable Causes	Remedies
Switch OFF.	Turn switch ON.
No fuel in tank.	Fill tank with correct mixture.
Switch broken or shorted.	Replace switch.
Spark plug fouled or set at incorrect gap.	Replace spark plug.
Spark plug cable loose or broken.	Tighten or replace cable.
High-tension wire shorting inside saw housing.	Replace high tension wire.
Ground connection loose.	Tighten ground connection.
Breaker points loose.	Tighten and regap points.

Condenser bad.	Replace condenser.
Points bent, burned, dirty, oily, or incorrectly set	Replace or regap points.
Timing wrong.	Set ignition timing.
Fuel pick-up plugged or split.	Replace fuel filter or line.
Armature air gap too wide.	Reset armature air gap.
Internal ignition wiring worn.	Replace ignition wiring.
Magneto bad.	Replace magneto (coil).

Engine Starts but Runs Poorly at All Speeds

Probable Causes	Remedies
Spark plug worn or wrong size.	Replace spark plug.
Timing wrong.	Set ignition timing.
Damaged magneto coil windings.	Replace magneto.
Coil assembly has loose internal connection.	Replace coil.
Condenser has poor internal connection and opens with heat or vibration.	Replace condenser.

MECHANICAL TROUBLESHOOTING

You have checked your fuel and ignition system without locating your problem. You believe that your problem is mechanical. Eliminate these possibilities in this approximate order.

Engine Will Not Start

Possible Causes	Remedies
Crankcase nuts and bolts are loose.	Tighten crankcase nuts and bolts.
Defective crankcase seals or O ring.	Replace seals and O ring.
Defective reed valve.	Replace reed valve.
Flywheel key sheared.	Replace flywheel key.
Piston rings worn or seized.	Rebuild engine.

Engine Starts But Runs Poorly At All Speeds

Possible Causes	Remedies
Muffler dirty or clogged.	Clean or replace muffler.
Exhaust ports clogged with carbon.	Clean exhaust ports.
Crankcase seals leaking.	Replace crankcase seals.
Defective cylinder gasket.	Replace cylinder gasket.
Worn piston rings.	Rebuild engine.
Piston damaged.	Replace piston.
Air leak at carburetor gasket.	Replace carburetor gasket.
Defective crankcase O ring.	Replace crankcase O ring.
Cracked casting.	If casting cannot be welded, junk it.

Engine Won't Run Full Speed

Possible Causes	Remedies
Throttle linkage bent.	Replace throttle linkage.
Muffler clogged.	Clean muffler.
Exhaust ports clogged.	Clean exhaust ports.
Reed valves leaking.	Replace reed valves.
Worn piston rings.	Rebuild engine.

Engine Overheats

Possible Causes	Remedies
Cylinder fins or exhaust system or sawdust cover dirty or clogged.	Clean entire saw. Most common cause of overheating.
Flywheel cover loose, parts of engine shrouds loose or missing.	Tighten all nuts, bolts, and screws.
Flywheel vanes broken.	Replace flywheel.
Lean carburetor mixture.	Use correct mixture.
Timing advanced.	Reset timing.
Cooling air intake plugged.	Clear cooling air intake.

EXAMPLE OF TROUBLESHOOTING PROCEDURE: IGNITION SYSTEM

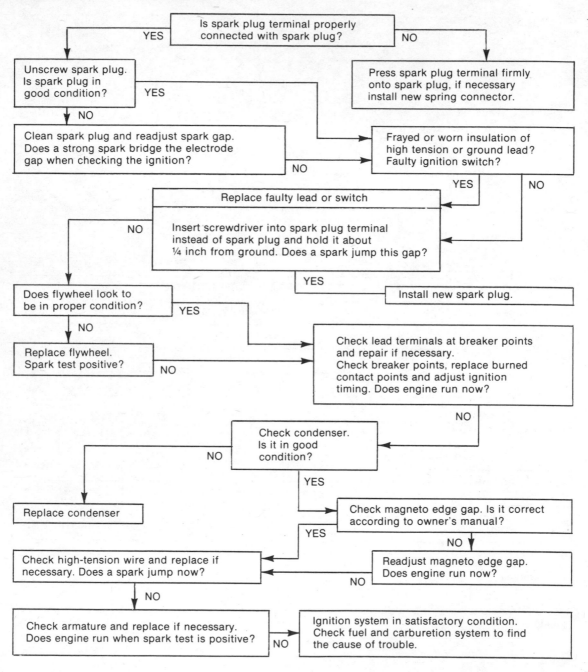

IF IT WON'T START

Troubleshooting is a process of discovering what's wrong. If your chain saw doesn't start, follow this chart first.

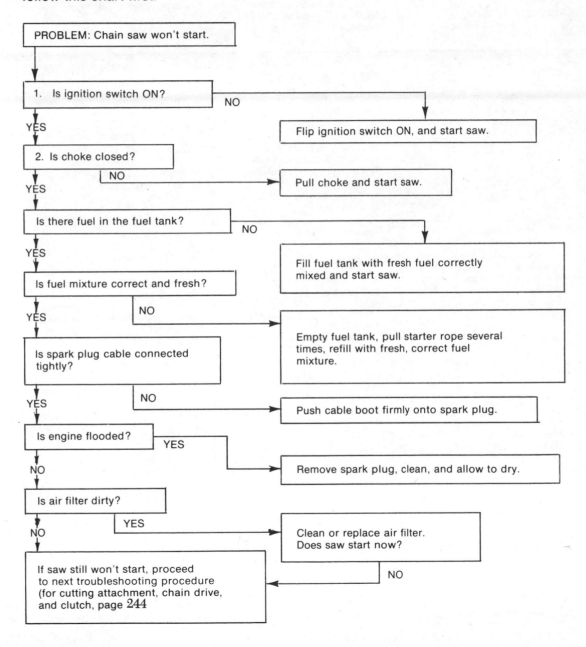

TROUBLESHOOTING: CUTTING ATTACHMENT, CHAIN DRIVE, AND CLUTCH

Trouble	Probable Causes	Remedies
Chain will not stay in adjustment, loses tension, is either too tight or too loose. (Bar and sprocket are in good condition.)	Chain adjustment screw bent or stripped or chain adjustment nut sheared.	Replace chain adjustment mechanism.
Bar wobbles, will not cut straight.	Guide bar bolts or nuts stripped.	Rethread or replace bolts, replace nuts.
Just doesn't cut right, fails to cut, cuts poorly or only with force.	1. Chain dull. 2. Improperly sharpened. 3. Chain on backwards. 4. Air filter dirty. 5. Incorrect chain tension. 6. Worn or damaged bar. 7. Carbon blocking exhaust ports. 8. Carburetor adjustment incorrect.	1. Sharpen chain. 2. See Chapter 7, owner's manual, and Saw Chain Troubleshooting Guide. 3. Reverse chain. 4. Clean or replace air filter. 5. Adjust chain tension. 6. Repair, regroove or replace bar. 7. Clean entire saw and exhaust ports. 8. Adjust carburetor.
Extreme or rapid chain wear. Chain dulls quickly.	Worn sprocket.	Replace sprocket.
1. Chain doesn't rotate properly, slips at high speeds, clutch slips. 2. Chain does not rotate.	1. Clutch linings and/or sprocket dirty or oily. 2. Clutch shoe linings worn. NOTE: EXTREMELY TIGHT CHAIN MAY CAUSE ANY OF THESE PROBLEMS.	1. Wash clutch and sprocket in clean gasoline. Dry clutch shoes and roughen linings with emery cloth. 2. Replace clutch shoes. AVOID CUTTING AT LESS THAN FULL SPEED. DOUBLE-CHECK TENSION OFTEN.
1. Saw chain rotates at idle. 2. Saw chain rotates at idle accompanied by extraneous or loud noises.	1. Engine idle speed too high. 2. Clutch springs stretched or dead. Spring hooks damaged. 3. Sprocket bearings damaged.	1. Readjust carburetor idle speed adjustment screw. 2. Replace all clutch springs and hooks. 3. Replace sprocket bearings.
No oil reaching saw chain.	1. Oil tank empty. 2. Guide bar oil inlet holes clogged. 3. Oil pick-up clogged. 4. Oil pick-up hose damaged.	1. Fill chain oil tank. 2. Clean guide bar oil holes. 3. Wash oil pick-up in gasoline, blow dry with compressed air. 4. Install new pick-up hose line.
Chain saw loses chain oil, oil leaks from saw body.	1. Gasket between oil pump and crankcase defective. 2. Gasket between handle shroud and crankcase defective.	Install new gaskets, clean oil pump.
1. Chain lubrication does not function. 2. Oil pump not operating.	1. Drive pins of cover plate broken or pump is loose. 2. Oil pick-up clogged or oil feed holes plugged. Oil vent clogged.	1. Install new pump cover plate, tighten pump. 2. Clean.

Chain Size and Type	File Size and Type	Average Depth Gauge Setting	Notes
1/4 inch chipper	1/8″ or 5/32″ round file	.020″	5/32″ best on new chain. Switch to 1/8″ as chain wears.
.354 chipper	3/16″ or 5 mm round file	.025″	
3/8″ chipper	7/32″ or 3/16″ round file	.020″	7/32″ on new chain, 3/16″ after considerable use. (Cutters shorter than .32″.)
3/8″ S70 (Oregon) chipper	7/32″ round file	.025″	
.404″ chipper	7/32″ round file	.030″	
7/16″ chipper	1/4″ round file	.030″	
1/2″ chipper	1/4″ round file	.030″ .040″	
9/16″ and 5/8″ chipper	9/32″ round file	.040″	
3/4″ chipper	5/16″ round file	.050″ .060″	
1/4″ Micro chisel	5/32″ round file	.025″	
.325 Micro chisel	3/16″ round file	.025″	
3/8″ Micro chisel	7/32″ round file	.025″	
.404 Micro chisel	7/32″ round file	.030″	
.404 Super chisel	7/32″ round file	.025″	Oregon numbers 50, 51 & 52 may be filed with round file but do not confuse with true chisel chains below.
.404 Super Chisel, Oregon types 50AL, 51AL, 52AL	beveled chisel chain file	.025″	Use 7/32″ round file to clean gullets
Super chisel Oregon types 9AL & 10AL	beveled chisel chain file	.030″	Use 7/32″ round file to clean gullets
Oregon types 4AL & 5 AL	beveled chisel chain file	.040″	Use 7/32″ round file to clean gullets
Oregon types 16AL & 17AL	beveled chisel chain file	.045″	Use 7/32″ round file to clean gullets
3/8″ chisel other than types above	beveled chisel chain file	.025″	Use 7/32″ round file to clean gullets
.404″ chisel other than types above	beveled chisel chain file	.030″	Use 7/32″ round file to clean gullets
1/2″ chisel other than types above	beveled chisel chain file	.040″	Use 1/4″ round file to clean gullets
3/4″ chisel	beveled chisel chain file	.050″	Use 5/16″ round file to clean gullets

FACTS ON LIGHTWEIGHT CHAIN SAWS

Information Taken from Manufacturers

Chain saw model	Displacement cu. in.	Power head dry weight lbs.	ozs.	Fuel cap. ozs.	Oil cap. ozs.	Chain oil system	
Echo CS 302	1.8	8	9	10.1	6.8	Auto.	Mechanical Pump
Homelite XL 2 / XL	1.6	7	15	8.5	6.1	Auto.	Pulse (Pumps at idle)
Homelite Super 2	1.9	7	5	8.5	6.1	Auto.	Pulse (Pumps at idle)
Homelite Sez Auto	2.5	9	8	14.5	4.1	Manual Auto.	Pulse (Pumps at idle)
Husqvarna 140 S	2.5	12	0	17.0	8.5	Auto.	Gear
McCulloch Mini Mac 25 / 30	1.8	7	2	11.5	3.7	Manual	
McCulloch Mini Mac 35	2.0	7	3	11.5	3.7	Manual Auto.	Pulse (Pumps at idle)
McCulloch Power Mac 6A	2.1	7	4	8.5	3.4	Auto.	Pulse (Pumps at idle)
McCulloch Super Pro 40	2.3	9	7	11.7	3.6	Auto.	Pulse (Pumps at idle)
Poulan 20 / 20D	1.8	8	2	11.0	5.5	Manual Auto.	Pressurized Tank (Pumps at idle)
Poulan S25D, DA, CVA	2.3	8lbs.9ozs. 9lbs.6ozs. (CVA).		11.0	6.0	Man. (D) Man. Auto.	Pulse (Pumps at idle)
Remington Bantam Mighty-Mite Weekender	2.1	7	1	12.7	2.4	Manual	(Throttle Trigger)
Remington Auto Mighty-Mite Delux	2.1	7	4	12.7	2.4	Auto.	Pressurized Tank (Pumps at idle)
Sears "Little Beaver"	1.9	8	6	7.0	3.3	Manual	
Sears Explorer II (25DA) / Explorer I (25D)	2.1	8	6	13.5	7.1	Manual Auto.	Pulse (Pumps at idle)
Skil 1610	2.2	6	10	10.1	3.7	Manual Auto.	Pressurized Tank (Pumps at idle)
Stihl 015L	2.0	8	2	11.2	6.1	Auto.	"Programmed" Gear
Stihl 020AV	2.0	8	6	13.5	8.5	Auto.	"Programmed" Gear
Stihl 020AV Pro	2.0	8	6	13.5	8.5	Auto.	"Programmed" Gear
Frontier Mark I Husqvarna 35— Partner Mini P Jonsereds 361— Pioneer P10	2.2	6	10	12.2	4.7	Manual Auto.	Pressurized Tank (Pumps at idle)

Published Material (Current as of 1977)

Guide bar available	Anti-vibra-tion system ?	Hand guard ?	Trigger inter-lock ?	Elec-tronic ignition ?	Comments
12" - 14"	No	No	No	No	Pro handle. Adjustable automatic oiler
10" 12"	No	No	No	No	Reed valve engine. Two throttle triggers (XL2)
14"	No	No	No	No	Reed valve engine. Two throttle triggers
12" - 20"	No	No	No	No	Reed valve engine. Pro handle
13" - 15"	Yes	Yes	Yes	No	Chain brake standard
10" 12"	No	Yes	No	No	Piston-ported engine. Slant control handle. Chain brake
14"	No	Yes	No	No	Piston-ported engine. Slant control handle. Chain brake
14" - 16"	No	Yes	No	No	Piston-ported engine. Top control handle. Chain brake
14"	Yes	Yes	Yes	No	Pro handle. Chain brake
12"	No	No	No	No	Piston-ported engine. Top handle. Many brands
14"	Yes (CVA)	No	No	No	Reed valve engine. Top handle. Many brands
10" 12"	No	No	No	No	Piston-ported engine. Pro handle
12" 14"	No	No	No	No	Piston-ported engine. Pro handle. Compression release (Delux). Elec. start available
12" - 14"	No	No	No	No	Reed valve engine. Back handle. Automatic oiler model available
14"	No	No	No	No	Reed valve engine. Top handle. Automatic chain sharpening (II)
10" - 16"	No	No	No	No	Piston-ported engine. Top handle
10" - 14"	No	Yes	Yes	Avail.	Piston-ported engine. Top handle
12" - 16"	Yes	Yes	Yes	No	Piston-ported engine. Top handle
12" - 16"	Yes	Yes	Yes	Yes	Piston-ported engine. Pro handle. Quick stop available
12" - 16"	Avail.	No	No	No	Piston-ported engine

NOTE: Many manufacturers are adding trigger interlock systems to all 1977-78 models.

Index

— T —